Sea Capabilities of the U.S. Navy SEALs

AN EXAMINATION OF AMERICA'S MARITIME COMMANDOS

By

Commander (SEAL) Tom Hawkins, USN, Retired

Sea Capabilities of the U.S. Navy SEALs
www.PhocaPress.com/sea-capabilities
Copyright © 2019 by Tom Hawkins

PHOCA
Press ❖ L L C

Published by Phoca Press
New York, NY 10025
www.PhocaPress.com

ISBN-13: 978-0-9909153-8-6

10 9 8 7 6 5 4 3 2

CONTENTS

"Most frogmen are like dogs; they live in the present and have little sense or appreciation of all that has gone before."

— *SEAL Rick Woolard*

DEDICATION

To my son Matt, a true SEAL warrior with a remarkable record of accomplishment after multiple combat and non-combat deployments.

FOREWORD

Admiral Arleigh A. Burke became the Chief of Naval Operations in 1956. He championed the cause to devote greater resources to the conduct of limited war. He argued that in an era of nuclear parity, paramount U.S. objectives should be deterrence of general war and the simultaneous maintenance of American global interests. He believed that for the Soviet Union, the fulcrum of struggle would surround the underdeveloped regions of the free world.

In early 1960, Admiral Burke directed the Navy staff to assess new or existing Navy units for smaller conflicts. He directed the staff to study the Navy's options with respect to unconventional warfare. On 13 September 1960, an Unconventional Activities Working Group was formally established to investigate "naval unconventional activity methods, techniques, and concepts, which may be employed effectively against Sino-Soviet interests under conditions of cold war." Upon study, the OPNAV staff concluded: ". . .the Underwater Demolition Teams and U.S. Marine Corps reconnaissance units are organizations capable of expansion into unconventional warfare."

Admiral Arleigh A. Burke

By 10 March 1961, the acronym SEAL had already emerged from the Strategic Plans Division of OPNAV, when recommendations were forwarded to Admiral Burke for review and concurrence. Among these was a recommendation for a wide range of "additional unconventional warfare capabilities within or as an extension of our amphibious forces." Operations conducted in restricted waters were emphasized. It was proposed that one unit each be established under Pacific and Atlantic amphibious commanders that "would represent a center or focal point through which all elements of this specialized Navy capability (naval guerrilla warfare) would be channeled." The staff concluded that "an appropriate name for such units could be SEAL units, SEAL being a contraction of SEA, AIR, LAND, and thereby, indicating an all-around, universal capability."

This book will focus on the "Sea" capabilities of U.S. Navy SEALs, and how they emerged from legacy capability units. The story begins in the early days of America's involvement in World War II. Many of the special-mission units organized during the war depended to a large measure on shipboard-based small craft for tactical mobility; using ship-to-shore tactics and techniques. Others operated with larger craft requiring tactical forward staging bases and portal-to-portal transits.

When the SEAL teams were established in January 1962, they had no boats; no form of tactical waterborne mobility. This began to occur about one year later when Boat Support Units, forerunners of today's Special Boat Teams, were organized. SEAL and Special Boat Team legacy capability units include the Amphibious Scouts and Raiders, Naval Combat Demolition Units, Office of Strategic Services Maritime Unit (OSS MU), and the Underwater Demolition Teams (UDT).

Operational and tactical transport throughout the Atlantic, Mediterranean, and Pacific Theaters of Operation required surface ships and, in the case of the UDTs, Amphibious Personnel Destroyers dedicated entirely to the UDT mission. This book will explore the past and evolutionary employment of ships, submarines, combatant submersibles, and combatant craft in the conduct of Naval Special Warfare (NSW).

Within the U.S. Navy, NSW has been designated a naval warfare area specialty (along with the Naval Air Force, Naval Surface Force, and Naval Submarine Force) for conducting operations in the coastal, riverine, and maritime environments. NSW forces today are theater based and controlled operationally as a component of the U.S. Special Operations Command, where missions are emphasized by flexible, mobile task units operating under, on, and from the sea. SEAL and Special Boat Teams operations are characterized by stealth, speed, precise, and often violent application of force. Career programs have been established for SEALs and Special Warfare Combatant-craft Crewmen (SWCC); thus, allowing the men to remain in the Teams throughout their tenure in the Navy.

NSW combatant craft and combatant submersibles have capabilities to conduct a host of special missions from the sea, in the littorals, rivers, and other inland waterways. SEAL and Special Boat capabilities involve tasks that fall into the category of maritime special operations. Such operations are more commando-like, i.e., those out of the norm and less doctrinal than conventional naval operations; those requiring voluntary service and specialized training; and those operations, actions, and activities considered extremely hazardous duty. Of course, combat swimming and diving are in a category of their own. These are foremost in the "Sea" narrative, and it is those capabilities that dramatically separate SEALs from all other special operations forces.

The conduct of special naval operations is as old as our country itself, but the definition of NSW in the U.S. Navy didn't come into being until the late 1960s, when it was defined thus:

"It is that set of naval operations, generally accepted as being unconventional in nature and, in many cases, covert or clandestine in character; including the use of specially trained forces to conduct unconventional warfare, psychological operations, beach and coastal reconnaissance, coastal and river interdiction, certain special tactical intelligence collection operations, and direct-action missions in a maritime, littoral, or riverine environment."

Since that time, the definition and operational attributes surrounding Naval Special Warfare, also called Naval Special Operations Forces or NAVSOF, have received a great deal of fine-tuning. The story presented here is not, and was not from the outset, intended to be a fully researched and footnoted analysis, or a complete historical accounting involving the "Sea" capabilities of our U.S. Navy SEAL and Special Boat Teams. It is intended to be a succinct abridgment based on a host of books, magazines, personal narratives, writings by others, and, of course, my own personal experiences.

The author in 1980 as Commanding Officer UDT-22/SDV Team TWO.

I became a SEAL operator in December 1966. It was and has been my good fortune to be involved with the development of much of the diving, demolitions, submersibles, and combatant craft capabilities employed by U.S. Navy SEAL Teams, SEAL Delivery Vehicle Teams, and Special Boat Teams. Because of where I have worked, and with respect to the exceptional people with whom I have worked, I do not delve into the business of Naval Special Warfare beyond the year 1999.

— Commander (SEAL) Thomas L. Hawkins, USN, Retired

WORLD WAR II

The state of the U.S. Navy's amphibious warfare capabilities during the period before and during the early stages of World War II was literally devoid of small craft capabilities. Moreover, most of the capabilities developed were derived from the British, who were already in a significant state of war with Germany.

To get from ship-to-shore in secrecy is a special operation with techniques akin to no others. It was during World War II and remains today very difficult to get men or supplies ashore undetected to carry out reconnaissance of beaches and shore installations, or to conduct operations, actions, and activities of maritime or coastal sabotage. Surface ships and submarines can approach an objective shoreline only to a certain point without being detected. SEALs routinely operate from nuclear submarines and surface support vessels of every kind, and they excel like no others in the conduct of clandestine maritime and other special operations.

The characteristics of special boat operations vary little from those accomplished by various maritime-focused special-mission units organized during World War II. The boats and technologies, however, are vastly different. The nature of small boat and small submersible operations involve men trained in special operations techniques; often tactically transported by a host surface ship or submarine as close to the target as possible. From the host vessel, they precede clandestinely using smaller vessels to carry out their task and then return to the host.

During World War II, the British accomplished what they called "special small boat work" that included:

1. Ferrying or delivery and recovery of agents and messaging services.

2. Laddering or delivering supplies for agents or invading troops.
3. Sabotage of maritime or coastal targets.
4. Boom destruction (blockage techniques to impede ship or submarine transits in confined waterways).
5. Reconnaissance of enemy beaches.
6. Gunnery aid to invading parties.

Special boat and host ship capabilities played significant roles in the conduct special operations throughout World War II. Generally, special units utilized host ships and small craft to perform some kind of ferrying, information gathering, demolition mission, or sabotage operation ashore. The chronology of these groups can be somewhat opaque; however, the first U.S. Navy men focused and trained to accomplish furtive maritime special operations were the Amphibious Scouts and Raiders. The first Scout and Raider boat teams were a collection of Army and Navy men trained for operations in the Atlantic, Mediterranean, and the English Channel. The Office of Strategic Services Maritime Unit (OSS MU) performed significant clandestine boat operations in the Mediterranean, European, and Southeast Asia Theaters of Operation.

CHAPTER 1

RETROSPECTIVE

European Theater

By 1940, Europe had essentially collapsed. France had fallen, and the Germans drove British Expeditionary Forces out through Dunkirk and into the sea. Norway was also gone, and the Scandinavian countries were neutralized. Thus, Britain was the only remaining buttress, and most in the U.S. didn't want to get involved. During this period, President Franklin D. Roosevelt was asked by the Secretary of the Navy, Frank Knox, to find someone to send to England to discuss with Prime Minister Winston Churchill the serious status of England, and what the risks were of its complete failure and invasion by Germany. President Roosevelt called upon a personal friend, William J. Donovan, a World War I Medal of Honor recipient and New York attorney. Mr. Donovan had traveled extensively, and President Roosevelt asked him to visit England as an unofficial envoy to consult with British officials, and to determine if they could withstand Nazi Germany. This was in November 1940.

After meetings with the British government and military leaders, Donovan reported back to President Roosevelt that there was really nothing left but Britain as a force. He also said that the existing situation where large masses of land were already occupied by the Axis Powers depended not only on invasion of occupied territories, but also on supporting insurgencies and resistance groups within those land masses. Also, that this would require methods not customarily found in the U.S. military. Although the Army and Navy had their own intelligence services, the need was for broad unconventional intelligence activities that included propaganda and sabotage, where maritime and air-drop routes would be involved. Before World War II, intelligence activities in the U.S. were mostly carried out by the Department of State, the Office of Naval Intelligence, and the War Department's Military Intelligence Division.

We know now, of course, that the United States became fully engaged with the Allies against the Axis powers under the leadership of General Dwight D. Eisenhower, and that Donovan's visit ultimately led to the establishment of the Office of the Coordinator of Information, which later became the Office of Strategic Services.

Pacific Theater

Imperial Japan, which had occupied Manchuria in northeast China since 1931, engaged Chinese troops near Beijing on 7 July 1937, thus, launching full-scale warfare there. This war, however, pushed the Japanese economy and military to the limit. Japan's supplies of rubber, iron, and oil were near the breaking point; and, they didn't have any allies in the region. Increasingly, the view within the international community was that Japan was a rogue state, with no one to assist them in procuring the materials needed to keep prosecuting the war in China. An attack on a U.S. gunboat on the Yangtze River alienated the U.S., as did widespread Japanese atrocities against the Chinese civilian population. Eventually, this led to embargoes on trade with Japan.

Japan had assembled a colonial empire to enable Western-style industrialization and to establish credibility as a great power. Because World War I hadn't affected Japan in any way approximating the same way it had Europe, its continued actions started making the country lose further respect internationally. Japan badly needed resources, and there were only two places to get them: Siberia and the South Pacific. The Imperial Japanese Army favored going after Siberia, but were forced to abandon that strategy after a disastrous 1939 Battle at Khalkhin Gol, which involved decisive engagements along the undeclared Soviet–Japanese border. The Imperial Japanese Navy prevailed, but had to deal with the fact that the South Pacific had already been colonized. On 7 December 1941, this resulted in simultaneous attacks on Pearl Harbor, Singapore, Hong Kong, the Philippines, Malaya, Thailand, and seizure of Shanghai. Later in December Japanese troops invaded Burma and Hong Kong. The Japanese didn't want the Americans or the British to resist their rush for rubber and oil. Of course, this turned out to be suicidal, and a complete misreading of how the Americans would react to Pearl Harbor.

On 8 December 1941, President Franklin D. Roosevelt delivered his "Day of Infamy" speech to American citizens. In his speech, Roosevelt asked Congress to declare war on Japan; which it did. Three days later on 11 December 1942, Congress also declared war on dictators Adolf Hitler of Germany and Benito Mussolini of Italy. On the same day, both dictators likewise declared war on the United States. Although the war began with Nazi Germany's attack on Poland in September 1939, the United States did not enter the war until after the Japanese bombed the American fleet in Pearl Harbor.

Events throughout Europe and the Pacific led to wide-spread devastation and prolonged global conflict. It was during World War II that various maritime focused special-mission units were born out of need, including the Underwater Demolition Teams—forerunners of the elite U.S. Navy SEALs.

ATTACK ON THE *USS PANAY*

On the morning of 12 December 1937, the U.S. river patrol gunboat *USS Panay* (PR-5) was anchored in the middle of the Yangtze River 27 miles upriver from Nanking. On board was a crew of four officers, 49 enlisted men, and assorted Chinese natives. Also, aboard were a number of foreign nationals escaping the looming Japanese assault on Nanking.

The *Panay* had been patrolling the waters of the Yangtze for nine years, showing the flag and protecting American interests from numerous Chinese bandits. Trouble was always a threat in China, but the situation was becoming increasingly dangerous. The Japanese army was encircling the Chinese capital of Nanking; forcing the Chinese government to flee. The *Panay*, in convoy with three American oil tankers, headed up river to withdraw from the potential danger zone.

Suddenly, Japanese planes appeared overhead. Despite the American flag draped on top of the afterdeck and the ship's obvious markings, three waves of Japanese planes bombed and strafed the ship until it sank. The three oil tankers were also destroyed. Two American Sailors and an American captain of one the oil tankers were killed.

The Japanese government apologized, called the incident a case of mistaken identity and made reparations of over $2,000,000. The apology didn't alleviate the suspicion that the act was deliberate, and the incident added to an already souring relationship between Japan and the U.S.

USS Panay before and after the Japanese bombed and strafed it.

CHAPTER 2

COMBAT SWIMMING AND DIVING

Combat swimming and diving are hallmark capabilities that separate U.S. Navy SEALs from all other U.S. special operations forces. SEAL combat swimming capabilities began with the famed UDTs of World War II. Their legacy combat-diving capabilities were derived from the Office of Strategic Services Maritime Unit (OSS MU), but not until the post-war period. These capabilities have persevered into the modern day. It is not simply having the equipment, training, and capability to swim and dive, since other special operations units train and equip for combat-diving capabilities. The differentiation involves the tactics, techniques, and procedures; the knowledge, skills, methods, means, and tasking to get combat swimmers and divers and their equipment to the target. In this regard, U.S. Navy SEALs have no peer.

UDT Combat Swimmers

Following victory at Guadalcanal in early 1943, Allied forces began planning a new offensive across the central Pacific to advance toward Japan by moving from island to island, using each as a base for capturing the next. The starting point was the small island of Betio within the Tarawa Atoll in the Gilbert Islands. The island was bordered by a reef extending 1,200 yards offshore. Intelligence planners believed the tide would be high enough to allow Navy landing craft to pass over the reef; however, during the assault on 20 November 1943, many of these assault craft became stranded on the reef and quickly came under attack from Japanese artillery and mortars.

The Marines were forced to enter the water and work their way towards shore under heavy machine gun fire. Encumbered with weapons and ammunition, many of the men drowned. Others were shot before they could get to the beach. By the end of the first day, 5,000 Marines had landed, but 1,500 were killed in the process. "Bloody Tarawa" reinforced the fact that the Navy couldn't depend entirely on aerial reconnaissance, and confirmed the need for pre-assault

CDR Edward Brewster (l), CO of UDT-1 and LCDR John T. Kohler (r), CO of UDT-2 (Photo: Sue Ann Dunford).

hydrographic reconnaissance to determine the prospect of natural and man-made obstacles. The need for UDTs was already being planned; however, that need was now accelerated.

After the Tarawa experience, Admiral Richmond Kelley Turner, Commander of the 5th Amphibious Force, directed that 30 officers and 150 enlisted men be collected at the Amphibious Training Base, Waimanalo in the Hawaiian Territory (now Bellows Air Force Station). They began gathering in early December 1943 to form the nucleus of a reconnaissance and demolition training program. Waimanalo was on Oahu directly across the island from Honolulu. Two UDTs were formed with volunteers from the U.S. Navy, Army, and Marine Corps. UDT-1 and UDT-2 were considered provisional UDTs with strength of 14 officers and 70 enlisted men each. They saw their first action on 31 January 1944 during the assaults on Kwajalein and Roy-Namur during Operation FLINTLOCK in the Marshall Islands. Following FLINTLOCK, the need for UDT capabilities had been formally established. A Naval Combat Demolition Training and Experimental Base was constructed adjacent to Amphibious Training Base, Kamaol on the island of Maui. UDT men trained and deployed from Maui between April 1944 and July 1945.

March 1943: The Navy men retained from provisional UDT-1 and UDT-2 after returning from the Marshall Islands. These men prepared the Naval Combat Demolition Training and Experimental Base on Maui during February and March 1944. Standing (l-r) CCM Jerome A. Schommer, SF2c J.W. Donahue, SK1c J.R. Reinhardt, LT William L. Hawks, LT William G. Carberry, LTCDR John T. Koehler (Commanded UDT-2) LT Thomas Christ, LT Lewis F. Luehrs, CCM R. B. McGinnis, SF1c W.O. Behne. Middle Row (l-r): GM2c E.W. Durden, GM3c Henry Green, F1c D.D.Fero, AOM1c C.W. Hoffman, UKN, S1c J.M. Brady, GM3c K.J. Rylands, SF1c R.L. Michaels, GM3c C.H. Brown, MM2c E. Fredericks, MM2c T.M. Lambert, GM3c B. Turner, SF1c James W. Conklin, S2c V. Gikey. Front Row (l-r): SF3c Robert E. Smith, GM3c Arthur Hall, EM3c L. Houk, CM2c Verdun Aitkenhead, RM2c Edward Bigham, SM2c William D. Haithcock, F2c Gordon Canizo, UKN, COX Burge Christensen, S1c Elmer L. Carlson, UKN, SC1 John M. Bisaillon. The photograph is from the book *More Than Scuttlebutt,* (page 98) by Sue Ann Dunford and James Douglas O'Dell. The men were identified by Edward T. Bigham, Jr., who was a member of UDT-1. The author added rank and rates, verified the spelling of names, and corrected where possible. (This is an official U.S. Navy photograph provided to Sue Ann Dunford by Virgil Stewart)

Naval Combat Demolition Training and Experimental Base, Maui, HI.

During July 1945, arrangements were being made to send all UDTs to Amphibious Training Base Oceanside, California for a month-long period of cold-water training in preparation for the Japan invasion. Training was to begin on 15 August. During this period, a new command organization was authorized, when the collection of teams at Oceanside was designated a UDT Flotilla, with two subordinate UDT Squadrons. Their commander served in the dual capacity of Commander, UDT Flotilla, which included 29 Amphibious Personal Destroyers (APDs), and Commander, UDTs, which included the two UDT Squadrons

The Japanese commander of Tokyo Bay Fort Number One is seen surrendering his sword to UDT-21's Commanding Officer, LCDR Edward P. Clayton, USN on 29 August 1945.

with 28 UDTs. Even today, this remains the largest single Naval Special Warfare task organization gathered under one commander for combat operations. Training at Oceanside was abruptly curtailed after President Harry S. Truman ordered the use of nuclear weapons at Hiroshima, Japan on 6 August 1945 and Nagasaki on 9 August. With the Japanese surrender on 14 August, 20 UDTs were immediately ordered to proceed to Japan, Korea, and China for occupation duties.

On 29 August, UDT-21 had the rare privilege of being the first U.S. Navy personnel to land on the Japanese homeland. As the team approached Fort Number One in Tokyo Bay, its commander surrendered his sword to Lieutenant Commander Edward P. Clayton, UDT-21's commanding officer—and someone there had a camera. As described by Doug Fane in his book the *The Naked Warrior*: "Word leaked out, and Clayton was later required to give up the sword. Nothing must mar the historic 'first' of the surrender ceremony to General MacArthur aboard the battleship *USS Missouri*. But...UDT was there first—Samurai surrender to naked warrior!"

Throughout the war, UDT men saw action across the Pacific in every major amphibious landing, including: Eniwetok, Saipan, Guam, Tinian, Angaur, Ulithi, Pelilui, Leyte, Lingayen Gulf, Zambales, Iwo Jima, Okinawa, Labuan, Brunei Bay, and Borneo. They became the most decorated Navy combat veterans of World War II. These men were awarded 750 Bronze Star Medals, 150 Silver Star Medals, two Navy Cross Medals, and an undetermined number of Purple Heart Medals—quite remarkable for the "Naked Warriors," who went in to combat carrying no weapon other than a KA-BAR knife.

Officers and men of UDT-21. Commanding Officer, LCDR Edward P. Clayton is in the middle of the front row in uniform.

GM1c Allan D. Hooper (l) of UDT-11 checks his fins and facemask before operations at Balikpapan on 3 July 1945. UDT-11 operator MoM2c George J. Bender (middle) resting aboard the *USS Kline* (APD-120) after operations. UDT-11 Ensign Frederick G. Deiner (r), USNR after returning from operations.

OSS Maritime Unit Combat Divers

While not under the domain of the U.S. Navy during World War II, maritime special boat and underwater swimmer operational capabilities were primary tasks of the Office of Strategic Services (OSS), which formed a special-mission group to focus on such capabilities. On 20 January 1943, a Marine Section was established within the Special Operations Branch of the OSS with responsibility for planning covert infiltration operations from the sea. The purpose of Special Operations was "to effect physical subversion of the enemy." As defined by the Joint Chiefs of Staff at the time, its functions included: sabotage operations in enemy-occupied countries and support and supply of resistance groups. On 10 June 1943, the Maritime Section was separated from Special Operations and reorganized as a Maritime Unit (MU) with branch status. Its responsibilities included planning and coordinating the clandestine infiltration of agents, supplying resistance groups, engaging in maritime sabotage, and developing special equipment for operations from the sea.

The OSS promulgated a 21-page booklet for the Maritime Unit. Although undated, it is surmised to have been published in December 1943. This SECRET document was the equivalent of a Naval Information Warfare Publication, wherein OSS missions and tasks were described thus: "OSS is an agency of the Joint Chiefs of Staff, charged with collecting and analyzing strategic information and secret intelligence required for military operations, and with planning and executing programs of physical sabotage and morale subversion against the enemy in support of military operations."

The men of the OSS MU were America's first combat divers. This is a photograph of MU combat swimmers assigned to the South-East Asia Command (SEAC), and OSS Detachment 101 in Galle, Ceylon from January 1944 to 15 April 1945. Kneeling (l-r): COX Jim Talmadge, USCGR; WO3 Robert Butts, USCG; LT Fred Wadley, AUS; CAPT Chris Lambertsen, MC, AUS; CAPT James J. Kamp, AUS (Group Commanding Officer); SP(X)2c Gerry Bennatts, USNR. Standing (l-r) WO John "Gunner: Richardson, USMCR; GM2C Gordon Soltau, USNR; CAPT Richard E. Sullivan, USMCR; CAPT Lillyman, Royal Navy Force 136 (SOE); BM1c Bob Millen, USCGR; COX Gene Ward, USCGR; BM1c Orrville Anderson, USCGR. (Photo: Dr. Lambertsen's collection)

OSS MU tasks were further outlined: "[The] Maritime Unit plans and carries out the amphibious phases of these activities (those in the above paragraph), and assists in the development of special equipment required. It penetrates enemy coastal areas, introducing operatives and their equipment for maritime sabotage and other Office of Strategic Services operations. Whenever targets for sabotage may be reached by water, whenever access to enemy land areas may be obtained by water, whenever information is required on water approaches and character of shoreline and coast, MU's special techniques in clandestine ferrying, maritime sabotage, and beach and hydrographic reconnaissance are required."

The men of OSS MU pioneered U.S. capabilities in maritime sabotage through use of tactical combat swimming and diving using flexible swim fins and facemasks, closed-circuit diving equipment, submersible vehicles, and limpet mines (a type of naval mine attached to a target with magnets). General Donovan acquired the services of Royal Navy Commander Herbert G. A. Woolley, Distinguished Service Cross, to develop the maritime unit. OSS MU men were trained in small-boat operations and experimented with the Lambertsen Amphibious Respiratory Unit (LARU); invented by Dr. Chris Lambertsen, who became MU's medical officer and primary trainer.

Like the whole of the OSS, the MU recruited potential members from all branches of the armed forces. Initial swimmer training was accomplished in pools at the Shoreham Hotel in Washington, DC and at the U.S. Naval Academy in Annapolis, Maryland. Training was subsequently moved to Catalina Island and Camp Pendleton in California, and then to Nassau in the Bahamas, where they worked closely with the British. The result was the first generation of U.S. combat swimmers—men skilled in waterborne infiltration, underwater demolitions, reconnaissance, small-boat work, navigation, small arms, hand-to-hand combat, and silent killing.

At the U.S. Naval Academy Norman Scott Natatorium Pool, circa October 1944 (l-r): 1st LT Chris Lambertsen, US Army 1st LT Fred Wadley, US Army; CAPT Al Lichtman, USMCR; and LT Dennis Roberts, USNR.

The first group to deploy operationally was the "L-Unit" (short for Lambertsen Unit, their underwater diving aparatus). It consisted of two separate detachments. L-Unit's mission was to infiltrate enemy harbors along the coast of France to destroy shipping and, in particular, U-boat berthing pens. The men were deployed to England for preparatory training, but never actually performed operationally, because of technical problems associated with working in cold water. L-Unit did, however, produce the first operational plans outlining actions and activities involving the use of U.S. combat swimmers. In the interim, other OSS men were organized into Operational Swimmer Groups consisting of 15 to 30 men each (there was no standard organization).

The men from Operational Swimmer Group I were loaned to the U.S. Navy for reconnaissance work in the South Pacific. This was part of a larger plan by General Donovan to allow OSS to get a foot in the door with General MacArthur. The MU men were deployed to Maui, H.T. (Hawaiian Territory) in June 1944, and became part of UDT-10 for the duration of the war. Operational Swimmer Group II was assigned to the Pacific South-East Asia Command. This unit was initially allocated to the Pacific to prepare for the invasion of Japan. General MacArthur, however, refused to permit the OSS, with its "unconventional and unorthodox methods," to operate under his command. As a result, MU personnel were sent to OSS Detachment 101 in Galle, Ceylon (now Sri Lanka) and attached to the British 14th Army. The men performed only a small number of tactical-field operations; all were along the Arakan coast of Burma (now Myanmar). In reality, the OSS trained combat swimmers spent most of their time conducting training and performing development or non-related operational support. Operational Swimmer Group III was

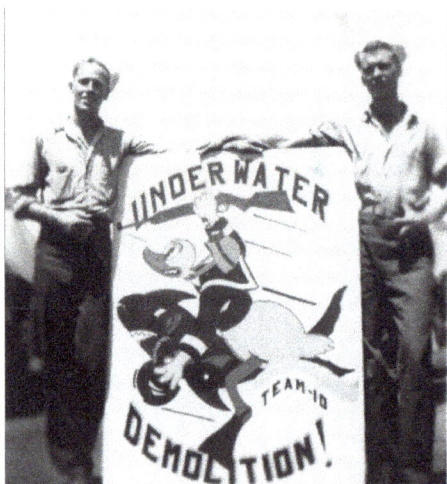
This UDT-10 logo was designed by the Walt Disney Studio.

OSS MU men that became members of UDT-10.

1st LT Chris Lambertsen, Medical Corps, U.S. Army was the medical officer and primary trainer for the OSS MU's swimmers and divers.

organized with the men from the returning L-Unit that had trained and deployed to England. After refresher training in Nassau, they, too, were deployed to Galle.

The individual largely responsible for the MU combat-swimmer program was Christian J. Lambertsen, initially as a medical student at the University of Pennsylvania, and later as a first lieutenant in the U.S. Army Medical Corps assigned to OSS MU. At the conclusion of the war, the Maritime Unit was dissolved, as was the whole of the OSS itself. Due largely to the work of Dr. Lambertsen, OSS MU's overwhelming contributions to combat swimming and their tactics, techniques, and procedures were eventually adopted by the U.S. Navy's UDTs; including use of the Lambertsen Amphibious Respiratory Unit (LARU) and the British-designed submersible *Sleeping Beauty*.

UDT Combat Divers

The UDT capability survived doctrinally after World War II, but UDT's relevance was consistently challenged. Well aware of this, Lieutenant Commander Francis Douglas "Red Dog" Fane, commander of the UDTs in the Atlantic Fleet, took action and stands out as perhaps UDT's foremost and aggressive innovator during this period. His enduring accomplishment was getting UDT's an expanded underwater capability. His successful actions resulted through collaboration with Dr. Lambertsen. Together, Fane and Lambertsen brought the full spectrum of MU diving capabilities to the UDTs. Doug Fane is remembered as one of the foremost and most eminent leaders impacting UDT during the post-war period.

The LARU diving apparatus was first introduced to the men of UDT during indoctrination and training operations at the Naval Amphibious Base, Little Creek, Virginia, followed by deployment to St. Thomas, U.S. Virgin Islands for training with a submarine.

LARU diving operations were accomplished aboard the submarine USS Grouper (SS-214) at St. Thomas, during February 1948. The following October, a UDT detachment comprised of men from Little Creek and Coronado went aboard USS Quillback (SS-424), where they conducted operations with the British submersible canoe Sleeping Beauty. This was the first time a submersible had been launched and recovered from a U.S. submarine.

OSS MU diver in an early version of the LARU. Dr. Lambertsen related that the "chain" was actually made of wood for the picture.

This was a milestone event for the UDTs, an epoch that introduced the full spectrum of clandestine maritime special operations; eventually combining the capabilities of underwater breathing apparatus, submersibles, and submarines. Also, this period introduced a first real understanding of the need for focused experimentation and research surrounding expanded UDT capabilities. Whatever the motivation, Lieutenant Commander Fane began a quest to move UDT capabilities forward. Introduction of the LARU into the UDTs led to further development or refinement of swim fins, facemasks, and compass. Introduction of the Sleeping Beauty initiated a long and sometimes challenging marriage of the UDTs and U.S. Navy submarine community, and the beginning of UDT's long and still unending pursuit of combatant submersible vehicles.

OSS MU swimmer U.S. Army SGT Larry Tweedy testing net defenses at Fort Lauderdale, FL, May 1945.

The potential scope of UDT's new capabilities included the ability to conduct undetected day or night reconnaissance of enemy beaches; underwater demolition of natural and man-made obstacles; day or night observation of enemy surface activities, and demolition attacks on enemy shipping and harbor installations. Each of the new capabilities was predicated on stealth, using the water for concealment. With the proliferation of sport diving today, it is hard to imagine that in the early 1940s it was a monumental accomplishment to allow men to breathe and move freely underwater without tether. This was likely the equivalent of early powered flight. The men of the

OSS MU diver climbing over a torpedo net during testing of harbor defenses in Guantanamo Bay.

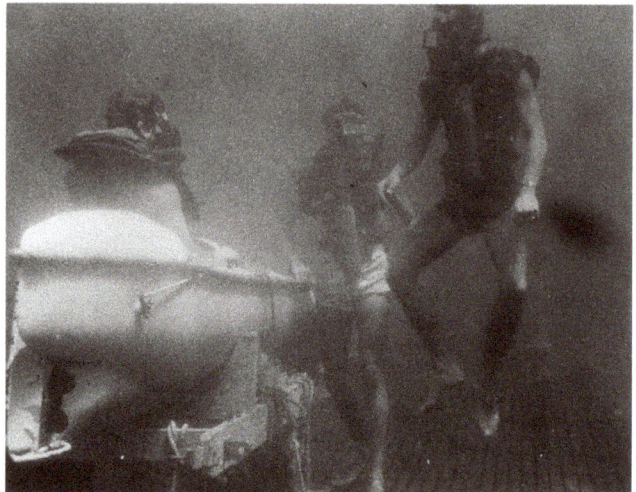

October 1948: UDT divers wearing the LARU conducting operations with *Sleeping Beauty* aboard *USS Quillback* (SS-424) at St. Thomas, USVI.

UDT operators aboard *USS Grouper* at St. Thomas, USVI in February 1948. The men wearing the LARU can be seen grouped on the after deck of the submarine's sail. Dr. Lambertsen can be seen standing on the forward deck wearing a white shirt with his back to the gun, boosting up a diver to meet with LCDR Fane. (Photo: Dr. Lambertsen's collection)

UDT and SEAL Teams progressed forward to attain the foremost combat diving capability in the world.

Men from the West Coast UDTs participated in *Quillback* operations; and also conducted LARU training in Coronado and Pearl Harbor. UDT-1 and UDT-3 men supported some operations and testing with the LARU during studies at the Scripps's Laboratory in La Jolla, California in the late 1940s and 1950s, however, I cannot find any evidence that the LARU was ever used on a large-scale basis on the West Coast. In a personal communication with SEAL and Medical Officer Captain Frank Butler, Dr. Lambertsen stated that: "The four UDTs on the East and West Coast used the LARU for submersible operations and training from 1948 into the early fifties."

The period between World War II and Korea was a phase of unrest and uncertainty about the future of UDT. There was little or no interaction between the UDTs in the Atlantic and Pacific, and small budgets constrained any major progress.

Doug Fane and Dr. Chris Lambertsen being rejoined by Tom Hawkins during the UDT-SEAL Museum's annual Muster event in 2001. This is the first time these men had met in over 40 years' time.

UDT-SEAL Association President Tom Hawkins is seen with Dr. Chris Lambertsen at the 2009 UDT-SEAL East Coast Reunion.

CHAPTER 3

EVOLUTION OF COMBAT DIVING

Combat diving involves the use of a closed-circuit underwater breathing apparatus. In a closed-circuit system, rebreathing occurs continuously. There is no loss of breathing gas to the surrounding water, unless expansion during ascent creates an excess. This is called "off-gassing," and occurs if the diver tries to ascend to quickly, or if he is in a submersible vehicle surfacing too quickly. Rebreathing necessitates provisions for two special needs: addition of oxygen and removal of exhaled carbon dioxide. Respiratory check valves maintain unidirectional flow of the breathing gas; this to ensure that rebreathing does not occur until the exhaled gas has passed through a carbon-dioxide chemical absorbent.

Jack Browne Rig

The Jack Browne Rig was a self-contained, pure oxygen rebreathing apparatus; designed by Jack Browne and manufactured by the Diving Equipment and Salvage Company (DESCO) in Milwaukee, Wisconsin under Navy contracts in the early 1940s. DESCO also developed a full-face mask. Sadly, there isn't a lot of information about this diving apparatus and its relationship to the UDTs, but it was displayed to Lieutenant Commander Draper Kauffman and others at the Naval Combat Demolition Unit (NCDU) Training School at Fort Pierce, Florida in September 1943. There was no interest at that time, since underwater diving was not viewed as needed in the NCDU training program. It was implemented into the basic training program much later on.

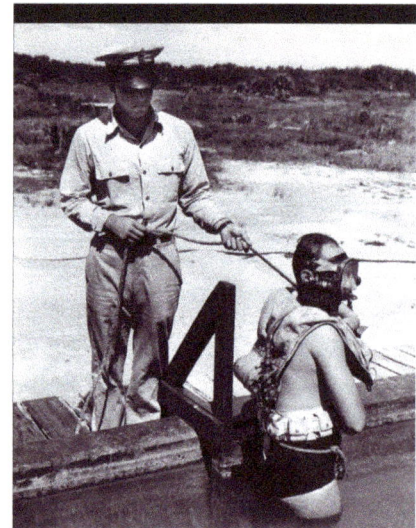

The Jack Browne rig being used in a training pool at Fort Pierce, FL, 1944.

Training and use of the Jack Browne rig by NCDU trainees and UDT personnel remain very perplexing to me. I've never seen any documentation to show that the diving apparatus was ever used operationally. I've reviewed all post-World War II histories of the UDTs, and there is only one mention of the Jack Browne. It is discussed in the Fort Pierce history of UDT-27 under a section entitled "Classes" and reads: "Another class was devoted to the art of shallow-water diving. Hardly had our diving information been given a chance to grow hazy before we visited the newly built pool on North Island. Here with 'Jack Brownes' a practical application of the lecture was made in an attempt to grope our way around the murky bottom." UDT-27 was formed at Fort Pierce in February, 1945.

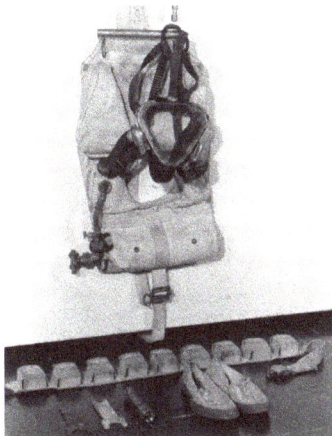

The Jack Browne oxygen rebreather and full-face mask.

Lieutenant (later Captain) Frank Kaine was in the first NCDU graduating class at Fort Pierce. He went on to command a group of six NCDUs sent to the South Pacific that remained together throughout the war. They were the only NCDUs never amalgamated into a UDT. Here is how he remembered it: "There was on the horizon a big vision of swimming with an air supply for 45 minutes or an hour or, ideally, three hours. Kauffman found the Jack Browne rebreather device, a rudimentary unit that lacked even a demand valve...So this became our unit, and we were told it was the greatest thing in the world, that it was in production, and we would have it before we went overseas and all that stuff. So, we were all excited about this and thought this was going to be great, because once you

THE TEN ESSENTIAL QUALITIES OF AN UNDERWATER DEMOLITION MAN

PRIDE — IN YOUR SELF, IN YOUR TEAM, IN THE AMPHIBIOUS FORCE AND IN THE NAVY, AND MOST IMPORTANT, PRIDE IN DEVELOPING THE SAME PRIDE IN SUBORDINATES.

LOYALTY — UP AND DOWN, IN ACTION AND WORD.

SINCERITY — IN ALL YOU DO.

RESPONSIBILITY — YOU HAVE IT—ACT ACCORDINGLY, AND LIVE UP TO IT.

LEADERSHIP — YOU ARE THE LEADER IN TITLE,—BE SURE YOU ARE IN DEED.

EXAMPLE — YOU ALWAYS SET IT—BE SURE IT'S GOOD.

FORETHOUGHT — CULTIVATE THE HABIT—AND EXERCISE IT.

FAIRNESS — BE ABSOLUTELY FAIR AND SQUARE WITH SUBORDINATES—THERE IS NO OTHER STANDARD.

SEAMANSHIP — ONLY A MAN WHO IS A COMPETENT SEAMAN CAN TRULY COMMAND RESPECT.

COMMON SENSE — USE IT—THERE IS NO SUBSTITUTE.

I EXPECT THESE QUALITIES OF EVERY UNDERWATER DEMOLITION MAN, AND I EXPECT EACH OFFICER TO PUNCTILIOUSLY REQUIRE THESE QUALITIES OF ALL SUBORDINATES.

THIS FORCE HAS NO EQUAL. I, THEREFORE, EXPECT, AND WILL ONLY ACCEPT, THE BEST OF ALL MY MEN.

F. R. KAINE
LCDR U.S.N.R.
CO. UDT – 21

get that, you don't have to keep going down and coming up to get air. Well, ultimately, we got two units (in training), so that everybody got to look at it, and a couple of us got to try it, and everybody went overseas without having it."

A *Handbook of Naval Combat Underwater Demolition Team Training* (NAVPERS 16174), dated 23 October 1944 mentions "Shallow Water Diving" in a section entitled: "The Training Program in Pictures." This section has one small paragraph that reads: "Practice in shallow water diving prepares men for underwater reconnaissance work and for placing charges on obstacles in the surf." The manual also states that 18 hours were to be devoted to diving. The shallow water diving course description was outlined as being provided during Indoctrination Week (called Hell Week by the men), and was outlined such: "Shallow water diving is taught to all hands in a pool of 8 1/2-foot depth. A lecture and a demonstration are given on the nomenclature of the gear of the Jack Browne, Victor Berg, and Navy converted gas masks...All hands are given an opportunity to use the different gear and to get acquainted with their various practical uses in the pool. Problems that involve knot tying and pipe work are used so that trainees may develop speed and ease in working with gear under water."

Undated picture captioned: "Large number of DESCO Buccaneers are made for the US Navy."

CDR Frank Kaine, Commanding Officer UDT-21, circa 1956.

An undated photograph of the DESCO Jack Browne manufacturing shop is interesting, because its caption stated that a large number of the Jack Browne rigs were being made for the U.S. Navy. Because it was a closed-circuit, pure-oxygen rebreather, it stands to reason that the diving apparatus could be employed only by selective units, and the UDTs were obviously one of those units. Yet, the Jack Browne gets sparse mention in UDT histories.

I once served as the Submersible Operations Department Head in UDT-21, and was later assigned a tour of duty at the Navy Experimental Diving Unit, Washington, DC as a test engineer. Based on my own operational experience, I find it improbable that the UDTs actually deployed with a robust underwater diving capability. If they did, it likely would have been a duty assigned to only a few selected men, and only for non-tactical administrative use. The logistics would have made it difficult. To support a diving capability: Bottled oxygen, oxygen-transfer pumps, carbon dioxide absorbent, spare parts, and perhaps a diver's recompression chamber would have been needed. The UDT men went to war on very crowded Amphibious Personnel Destroyers and it's unlikely that shipboard working and supply spaces could have been devoted to diving. The same would be less true if the UDT men deployed with a surface-supplied full-face mask. The mask, a length of hose, and an air compressor would have been simple enough; except that one air compressor would likely have been needed for each individual. Moreover, few, if any, compressors at that time existed that could provide diver-quality air uncontaminated by oil.

I've never seen a photograph of the Jack Browne rig being used operationally. My own assessment is that if the Jack Browne diving capability would have been seen as practical or essential, it surely would have been adopted during the post-war period. It was not. Commander Douglas "Red Dog" Fane sought an underwater capability for the UDTs, but not until 1947, and not with the Jack Browne rig, but rather with the LARU and OSS MU combat-diving capabilities established during World War II.

Lambertsen Amphibious Respiratory Unit

The Lambertsen Amphibious Respiratory Unit (LARU) was a revolutionary pure-oxygen, closed-circuit, underwater breathing apparatus designed and developed by Christian J. Lambertsen, a medical student at the University of Pennsylvania. In 1940, before U.S. involvement in World War II, and before establishment of the Office of Strategic Services (OSS), Chris Lambertsen had presented his concept to the U.S. Navy. Once developed, the underwater-breathing system would permit a well-trained diver the capability to swim bubble-free underwater and, thus, to operate around target areas without detection from above. With the development of this system, the U.S. Navy would be in a position to take its place in the front ranks of countries having the ability to send combat swimmers against the enemy. In those days, however, the Navy's only divers were in the salvage corps. Their officers watched his demonstration, but were uninterested, and his proposed capability was politely rebuffed.

During this same period overseas, Italian navy units were successfully utilizing underwater swimmers in their wartime endeavors against the Royal Navy. Of course, much of this was not so well known at the time. The Italian program called for swimmers equipped with a primitive underwater breathing apparatus to ride a modified torpedo into an enemy harbor to emplace explosives on the hull of a target ship. The Italians responsible for these audacious operations were from the 10th Light Flotilla, the *Decima Mas,* an elite unit specializing in operations involving the use of human

U.S. Coast Guard LT John Booth wearing a LARU in Silver Springs, FL, posing for the U.S. Navy Diving Manual, circa late 1947.

Operational LARU MK 10 with tools and equipment.

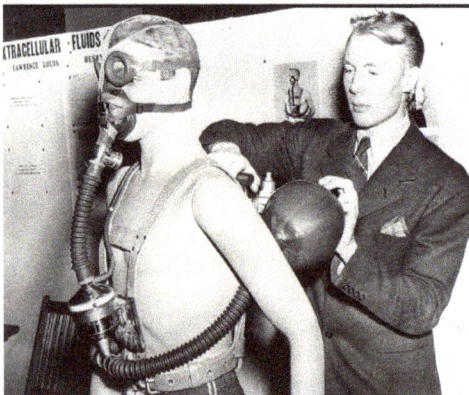

University of Pennsylvania Medical Student Chris Lambertsen displays the prototype of his underwater oxygen rebreather.

torpedoes and assault swimmers. Similar units, known as Gamma, were closely allied, used the same equipment, and participated in many operations with the *Decima Mas*. History has recorded how successful the Italians were in attacking British ships at Alexandria, Egypt and at Gibraltar. Once the British learned how they were being attacked, they became desperate to find similar capabilities and equipment for their own naval commandos.

By chance, one of Chris Lambertsen's professors was British, and had known about the Royal Navy's frantic search for something better. A meeting was arranged, and Lambertsen provided his brief. They were interested enough to order two LARUs, and went on to develop their own breathing apparatus, which was largely based on the LARU design concept. In turn, the U.S. adopted many of the tactics and techniques learned from the British and Italian experiences. Chris Lambertsen was confident that the U.S. could and should have been ahead of the British and perhaps the Italians in this stealthy form of warfare, however, the U.S. Navy Salvage Corps continued to show little interest. Lambertsen turned to the OSS Maritime Unit (OSS MU), and, unlike the U.S. Navy, OSS leadership was fascinated with the idea of employing assault swimmers to conduct clandestine missions.

Chris Lambertsen demonstrating a prototype of his pure oxygen rebreather, circa 1939.

From the prototype rebreather, he developed the Mark II and Mark III rebreathers for the OSS, and this led to the Mark 10 LARU, the production diving apparatus adopted by the OSS MU.

CAPT Chris Lambertsen instructing OSS Maritime Unit men on the use of the LARU.

After graduation from university, Dr. Lambertsen became a First Lieutenant in the U.S. Army Medical Corps, and was recruited by the OSS MU, where, in addition to becoming their medical doctor, he also became their primary trainer. He integrated a program of underwater operations, including combat swimming and diving tactics, navigation, and communications. He conceived or expanded the missions, trained the operators, and designed or coordinated the design of much of the early hardware used by this first generation of U.S. combat divers. Consequently, he has been recognized by the U.S. Navy SEALs as the "Father of U.S. Combat Diving."

Lambertsen Mixed-Gas Rebreather

In the late 1940s, Dr. Lambertsen proposed that mixtures of nitrogen or helium with elevated oxygen content could be used in Self-Contained Underwater Breathing Apparatus (SCUBA) to expand the depth range beyond that allowed by a 100-percent oxygen rebreather. Mixing nitrogen (N2) with oxygen (02) would avoid convulsions and simultaneously minimize the requirement for decompression. Mixed-gas diving in a SCUBA system was a new concept in 1940. They were called "semi-closed circuit" diving systems, because they gave off exhaled bubbles unlike a closed-circuit oxygen system.

Heretofore, mixed-gas for diving was surface supplied, and no further developments were accomplished at that time. Working with the J.H. Emerson Company in 1950, however, Dr. Lambertsen introduced the FLATUS II, a semi-closed-circuit SCUBA that continually added a small volume of mixed gas (N2-O2) to the breathing circuit to provide the necessary oxygen for metabolic consumption. Exhaled carbon dioxide was "scrubbed" in a carbon dioxide absorbent canister, and the gas mixture returned to the closed-loop of the rig. Because the inert gas was not consumed by the diver, a small amount of gas mixture was continuously exhausted when the diver exhaled. FLATUS II was tested by the Navy Experimental Diving Unit, but never brought to production. It did, however, serve as the eventual prototype for evolution of the Mark V and Mark VI underwater breathing apparatus.

Dr. Lambertsen's use of FLATUS was a play on words that he thought humorous, and he would always chuckle when he told the story. Flatus is gas produced in the digestive system by bacterial fermentation and containing high amounts of hydrogen sulfide and methane, usually expelled from the body through the anus (in other words—a fart).

Italian Pirelli

The Pirelli was manufactured by Pirelli of Milan, Italy. The military version, LS-901, was a pendulum-type system with two 1.6-liter bottles chargeable to approximately 3,000 psi. This UBA had a constant-flow regulator adjustable from .05 to two liters of oxygen per minute. Under normal working conditions, a diver could stay submerged up to four hours.

Here's how it was described by UDT-11 Master Chief Don Rose: "In the mid-'50s, we got the Pirelli 701, an oxygen rebreather

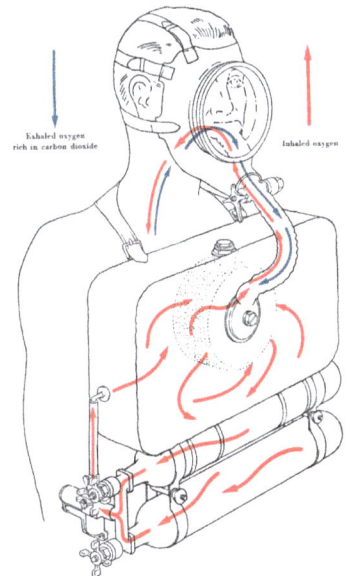

Underwater breathing apparatus
Oxygen type L.S. 901

Exhaled oxygen rich in carbon dioxide

Inhaled oxygen

UDT-21 operators Bob Shouse and George Phillips demonstrate open-circuit SCUBA and the Pirelli, circa 1955.

that came in a wicker basket and was designed for sport diving. (We never used the Lambertsen Lung. I only saw it one time on the West Coast.) The Pirelli had a full-face mask with a snorkel tube on the side and a breathing bag on the chest. You were supposed to swim on the surface using a snorkel until you spotted a fish and shifted from snorkel to bag to go after the fish. What they didn't tell you was that you needed to purge nitrogen from the bag. It was a death trap if you forgot to purge. Fortunately, we knew about that. We got rid of the snorkel and full-face mask and used a little mouthpiece. The Pirelli was really small, and you had to swim slow and easy or carbon dioxide would build up and you would get a headache." (Note: the Pirelli 701 was a single bottle unit, and intended for sport diving.)

UDT operator wearing the Italian Pirelli.

Master Chief Rose relates experiences during ship sneak-attack exercises: "With the little Pirelli, you only put gas in the bag manually—a quiet zip and that was it. The sonar operator on the destroyer used to say he

THE PURGE

A quick word about the purge. Purging is a fundamental necessity when diving a closed-circuit, pure-oxygen diving apparatus. In a closed-circuit UBA, all exhaled gas is kept within the rig. As it is exhaled, the gas is carried via the exhalation hose to an absorbent canister that chemically removes the carbon dioxide produced as the diver breathes. After the oxygen passes through the canister, the gas travels to the inhalation-breathing bag, where it is available to be used again by the diver. The pure-oxygen gas supply prevents inert gas buildup in the diving apparatus and allows all of the oxygen carried to be used for metabolic needs.

The purge is generally accomplished before entering the water. It is completed by breathing several times from the UBA, and exhaling through the nose. This procedure purges (removes) residual nitrogen from the closed-breathing loop of the UBA, creating a pure-oxygen environment.

Closed-circuit oxygen UBAs offer advantages valuable to SEALs, including stealth (no escaping bubbles), extended operating duration, and less weight than open-circuit air scuba. Disadvantages include increased hazards to the SEAL combat diver, expanded training requirements, and greater expense; however, these attributes are overtaken by tactical operational attributes.

could hear something, but he could never locate it. We tore up those destroyers with the Pirelli, but the team only had six of them, and only a few of us were qualified. I was one of those people, and every time a destroyer would get ready to go overseas, I always ended up doing the mock attack."

Pendulum rebreathers like the Pirelli, were discovered to have an inherent design flaw. The gas flow from the scrubber and breathing bag via the same hose, created a "dead space" in the loop that could result in carbon dioxide buildup. While this may not have been a problem for divers at rest, it quickly became a problem for working divers. Master Chief Petty Officer Rose recalled: "Later on we got the bigger 901 Pirelli with two oxygen tanks. It was quite a bit better than the 701, but was still a pendulum system with only one hose and dead space that gave you a headache from carbon dioxide retention. One advantage of the Pirelli was a breathing bag on the chest. All you had to do is relax to inhale. To exhale, you had to force the air out."

Navy Experimental Diving Unit Report 6-52 involved a investigation into the adequacy of the Pirelli. The "Abstract" of the report concluded this: "The evaluation places a limitation on the conditions for which the Pirelli is satisfactory: namely, for shallow-diving conditions of rest or very moderate work. The equipment is not adequate for swimming conditions in excess or one hour and 30 minutes, it is hazardous for any swimming or diving conditions involving heavy work, and it is subject to the same maximum 30-foot depth limitation as all other oxygen SCUBAs." The investigation by Navy Experimental Diving Unit resulted in a decision that no more Pirellis would be procured for the UDTs. As a result, use of the Pirelli was limited to those already in the team diving lockers. Beginning in 1957, this UBA was replaced with the German Draeger.

German Draeger — LT Lund II

The Draeger, also called the LT Lund II diving apparatus, was manufactured by Draegerwerk in Lubeck, Germany. It was a pure-oxygen rebreather, where oxygen was stored in two cylinders, each containing 0.8 liter at a pressure of 2,800 psi; giving the diver a total gas supply of 320 liters (11.2 cubic feet). The Draeger had a constant flow regulator set to provide 0.9 liter per minute into the breathing bag. Manual operation of a by-pass valve provided additional oxygen as needed. Like the Pirelli, the carbon dioxide canister was inside the breathing bag, however, only exhaled breath passed through the canister. Then men could remain submerged with the Draeger for approximately 90 minutes under UDT-like

UDT-21 combat divers training with the German Draeger in the Mediterranean, date unknown.

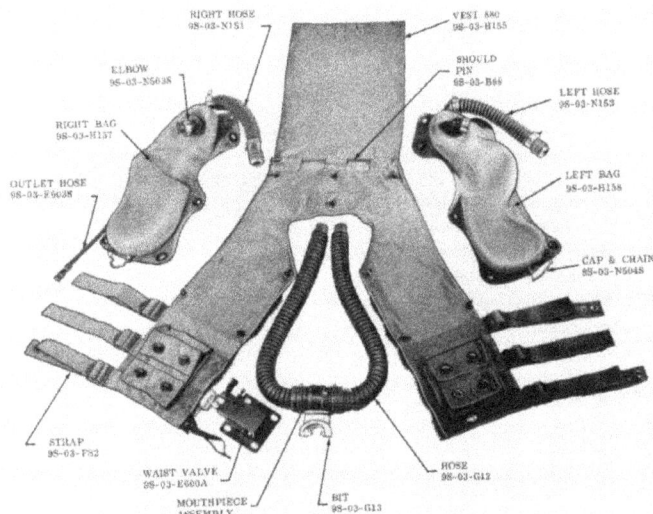

RIGHT HOSE
98-03-N151

ELBOW
98-03-35003

RIGHT BAG
98-03-H157

OUTLET HOSE
98-03-F5038

VEST 880
98-03-H155

SHOULD PIN
98-03-B66

LEFT HOSE
98-03-N153

LEFT BAG
98-03-H158

CAP & CHAIN
98-03-N5048

STRAP
98-03-F82

WAIST VALVE
98-03-E660A

MOUTHPIECE
ASSEMBLY
98-03-G700A

BIT
98-03-G13

HOSE
98-03-G12

Fig. 2-2   Breathing bag and vest assembly, model 9-SO-3

operation conditions—that is a calm, even pace so that the swimmer does not over-breathe the rig.

The Draeger LT Lund II was used for several years in the UDTs. The men liked the UBA, but spare parts and maintenance became problematic, as the U.S. Navy couldn't rely on foreign manufacturers for production or spare parts. This resulted in an attempt by the U.S. Navy to reverse engineer the Draeger for U.S. production and sparing. This task was given to the Scott Aviation Corporation. While the Draeger was visually duplicated, it never achieved the same technical quality of the German UBA, and further efforts were abandoned.

Lambertsen-Emerson

Closed-circuit oxygen SCUBA like the Pirelli, Draeger, and LARU clearly offered the advantages of being much smaller and lighter than open-circuit SCUBA. There was also no stream of tell-tale bubbles cascading to the surface to reveal the combat diver as he approached a hostile ship or pier. It was largely Doug Fane that expanded the open-circuit capability in UDT, while allowing the closed-circuit capability to slowly atrophy, even though it was a capability he had introduced to the UDTs in 1947. Dr. Lambertsen was bewildered by this, and revealed to me that he and Doug Fane had a pointed disagreement over the divesting of UDT's closed-circuit diving capability. This never did sit well with him; and, indeed, you could still see his disappointment after many years.

Limited tactical capability existed after Korea, when the UDTs began to realize that, while open-circuit diving was easy to accomplish administratively and logistically, they had strayed too far away from their tactical closed-circuit diving capability. There was some haste to reacquire the capability, but, they had few options. UDT-21's commanding officer Lieutenant Commander Frank Kaine provided the leadership to bringing closed-circuit tactical diving back to the UDTs. During the 1950s, two diving apparatus were being used in Europe: The Italian Pirelli and the German Draeger, discussed previously, were acquired by the UDTs on both coasts.

In 1952, Dr. Lambertsen began working with the J.H. Emerson Company to design a new Underwater Breathing Apparatus (UBA) that was initially called the LARU Mark 20, but later the Lambertsen-Emerson UBA. It was being conceptually designed, but hadn't completed production or testing.

In September 1966, Dr. Lambertsen responded by letter to a question from Doug Fane and Dr. Charlie Aquadro (a distinguished Navy Diving Medical Officer assigned to UDT) about when the UBA was developed. He responded by saying: "Emerson was manufacturer and contracted with the Navy off and on over 10 years of Navy modification from the original prototype to final availability to the fleet– about 1962. There is no single year, but a long delay period of 1952-1962."

UDT operator modeling the Emerson UBA.

The Lambertsen-Emerson was eventually introduced into the Navy simply as "The Emerson" UBA in 1962. It was the tactical UBA that I trained with when I became a UDT frogman in 1966. I liked the rig even though we didn't get to dive it very often. Oxygen was delivered from a single cylinder into the breathing bag by a metering valve that could be set for constant flows of .5, .9, 2.0, and 3.0 liters per minute. The cylinder could be charged to 2,000 psi, and had a capacity of 360 liters (12.7 cu/ft.). The duration of an Emerson dive was about 120 minutes for planning, but depended upon the working diver's pace, which was instructed to be methodically slow and persistent. By working too hard and fast, a diver could "over breathe" the rig, meaning a carbon dioxide build-up could result, and the diver could pass out. The Emerson UBA incorporated an over-the-shoulder dual breathing bag design.

The big difference between the Emerson and previous UBAs was that the scrubber canister was mounted on the backpack of the rig rather than inside the breathing bag. On inhalation, the diver received gas directly from the right-side bag. On exhalation the gas passed into the left bag to displace gas already there, causing it to flow through the carbon dioxide absorption canister. The purified gas then went back through the right-breathing bag to complete the cycle.

The Emerson UBAs had a T-bit mouthpiece with a "dive-surface" valve. This valve could be closed once on the surface to keep from flooding the rig. The over-the-shoulder breathing bags had the advantage of being comfortable to breathe in prone and upright positions. The four-setting oxygen supply-valve was not ideal. If oxygen consumption changed underwater, the UDT operator might find himself with insufficient oxygen to breathe, and would have to use the manual bypass valve. Conversely, if oxygen consumption was lower than the add rate, the bags would overfill and cause an undesired increase in buoyancy and also off-gas bubbles into the water. Most of these problems could be overcome with extensive training.

During much of 1968, I served as the UDT-21 Submersible Operations Department Head. Spare parts availability for the Emerson was such a problem that the men were using parts from our Mark VI diving apparatus, which was a semi-closed system. The hoses, some of the breathing bags, and a few other parts were interchangeable. The more they did this, the more the Navy Supply System went afoul, and eventually it became an untenable situation. In 1970, the Emerson was considered completely unsupportable and, therefore, unsafe to dive, and was removed from active service. A replacement, however, was on the way.

LT Chris Bent (far right) and frogmen of UDT 21 preparing to enter the water for an Emerson dive.

Semi-Closed-Circuit SCUBA

In a semi-closed-circuit system, partial rebreathing permits conservation of the gas supply; however, a certain amount of the breathing gas is intentionally discharged from the system on a continuous or intermittent low-flow basis. Open-circuit SCUBA sacrifices duration for depth, while closed-circuit SCUBA sacrifices depth for duration. Semi-closed-circuit systems combine the advantages of both. Nitrogen and helium could be used as the inert gas, but in the UDTs, we only used nitrogen. The ratio of nitrogen to oxygen was selected for various depths to provide the greatest allowable oxygen percentage. This diluted the nitrogen and reduced decompression requirements, while extending time and depth durations. To prevent oxygen toxicity, the partial pressure of oxygen could never exceed 2.0 atmospheres.

Constant flow results in a constant exhaust, causing the system to continuously purge and prevent excessive buildup of nitrogen as the mixture is rebreathed. For comparison, the efficiency of gas used in semi-closed-circuit system is approximately 10 times that of an open-circuit system at 100 feet. Closed-circuit oxygen SCUBA is theoretically 100% effective, but depth limited.

Mark V Semi-Closed-Circuit SCUBA

The Mark V SCUBA was the Navy's first a low-magnetic, semi-closed-circuit SCUBA, but it had a very short life in UDT. It was manufactured by the J.H. Emerson Company and intended for use by UDT and Explosive Ordnance Disposal (EOD) divers. The breathing loop was the same as closed-circuit UBAs, except that there was a partial and continuous exhaust of exhaled gas into the surrounding water.

With two large aluminum gas cylinders, the Mark V SCUBA weighed approximately 100 pounds. The gas cylinders could be charged to 3,000 psi, giving the diver approximately 4,800 liters (168 cu/ft) of gas. Duration of the dive was dependent on gas mixture, depth, and type of work. Depending on the gas mixture (nitrogen-oxygen), dives could be made up to 300 feet. "Due to maintenance and technical problems, the Mark V was hastily withdrawn from service use in 1962." I know that there was a technical deficiency surrounding the carbon dioxide scrubber;

President John F. Kennedy reviewing SEAL personnel at Norfolk, VA, January 1963. BM1 Lewis "Hoss" Kucinski is wearing a MK V semi-closed circuit UBA.

UDT operator entering the water with a MK V Semi-Closed-Circuit UBA.

however, having served a tour of duty at the Navy Experimental Diving Unit as a Test Engineer, and having been involved in the Navy's procurement process, I'm puzzled that the rig actually made it into the UDT and EOD diving lockers with any kind of technical problem.

For whatever reason, the rig was delivered with white breathing bags and vest. Apparently, there was an assumption that this was not a tactical diving apparatus, but rather one for dealing administratively with mines, and that might be the reason for white. When I was serving as the Submersible Operations officer at UDT-21, the Chief Petty Officers had retained a couple of Mark Vs under a bench in the diving locker. They were never used while I was there, because they had been removed from the "Approved for Navy Use" list. It was replaced by the Mark VI SCUBA.

This is a rare color photograph of President John F. Kennedy at the same presentation.

Mark VI Semi-Closed-Circuit SCUBA

The Mark VI semi-closed circuit, mixed-gas rebreather was manufactured by the Scott Aviation Corporation. It has always been my understanding that Scott bought out the J.H. Emerson UBA design and fixed all of the technical issues. The Navy adopted the Mark VI for UDT and EOD operations and activities in 1963. Except for the white breathing bags, the Mark V and Mark VI had the same outward

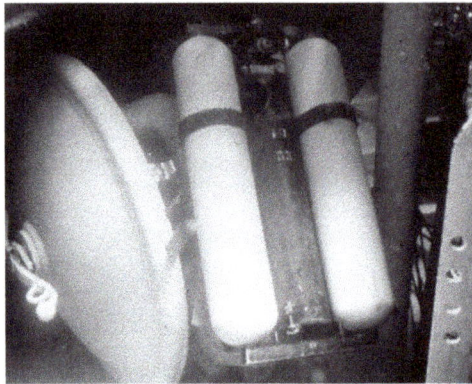
A UDT operator entering a submarine wearing the MK VI UBA.

UDT reserve operators preparing for a MK VI UBA dive.

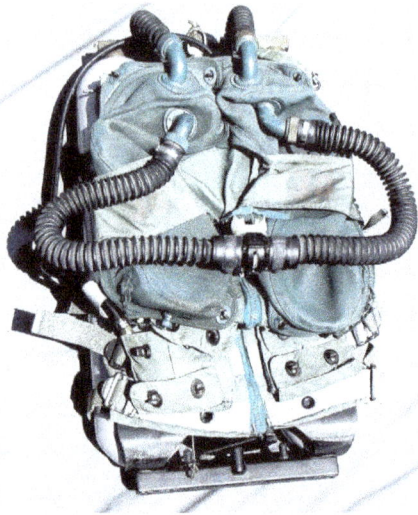
This is a bench-top view of the MK VI UBA.

appearance. The Mark VI was also a low-magnetic design intended for mine reconnaissance and clearance by UDT and render-safe tasks by Explosive Ordinance Displosal (EOD). The UDTs had no requirement to deep dive the Mark VI, but apparently EOD did. Many UDT officers and men attended the EOD School in Indian Head, Maryland, since EOD was a UDT secondary mission.

The Mark VI weighed 75 pounds, which was 25 pounds lighter than the Mark V. The gas supply was considerably less; 84 cu/ft as opposed to 168 cu/ft for the Mark V. The Mark VI had a maximum depth capability of 200 feet and a maximum endurance of three hours depending on water temperature and diver activity. Because the apparatus was based on a constant mass flow of mixed gas, the endurance was independent of the diver's depth. Decompression procedures for nitrogen and oxygen were developed at the Navy Experimental Diving Unit.

While attending the U.S. Navy Underwater Swim School in Key West, Florida, my training class had the opportunity to dive the Mark VI to a depth of 100 feet in the Gulf of Mexico. The water was beautiful and crystal clear all the way to the bottom, and after going through the first 25 feet of jelly fish, the dive was spectacular, and one that I'll never forget. We did a "bounce dive" to the bottom and back up.

My first dive with the Mark VI in UDT-21 was a night dive during a February ship sneak attack in the Chesapeake Bay. The water was cold, the tide was moving into the bay, and the current was very swift.

When my swim buddy and I came to the surface to get a visual on the ship and talk things over, I failed to fully close the valve on my mouthpiece, and let water creep inside my breathing loop. When the water hit the carbon dioxide scrubber, I knew that I'd screwed up. I got what we called a "baralyme cocktail." Baralyme was the chemical carbon dioxide absorbent. It becomes very caustic when mixed with water, and causes a choking, burning sensation. We had to abort the dive and I was, of course, embarrassed. That's another dive I'll never forget, and, as a new guy, it took me a long time to live that one down.

Open-Circuit SCUBA

Self-contained diving apparatus utilized during World War II were of the closed-circuit, pure-oxygen type. Oxygen was re-circulated through a chemical bed of soda lime to scrub out all carbon dioxide, which could be used again by the diver as pure oxygen. Oxygen restricted the divers to a depth of 30-60 feet. (It was discovered later that diving oxygen below a depth of 30 feet could result in oxygen toxicity and perhaps death without proper use.) Oxygen diving apparatus require only a small tank of compressed gas. Open-circuit air diving was a completely different concept. It used several large cylinders of compressed air, and permitted divers to descend to much deeper depths.

This diving capability was invented in Paris, France in 1943 by engineer Émile Gagnan and French Navy Lieutenant Jacques Cousteau. They obtained a patent for their work in 1944. The name adopted for the open-circuit diving capability was Aqualung®. The Aqualung let people bring compressed air with them when they went under water, thus, eliminating the need for an umbilical hose to supply air from the surface. The Aqualung today is simply known as SCUBA for Self-Contained Underwater Breathing Apparatus (a term coined by Dr. Lambertsen). The Aqualung works using a "regulator" or "demand valve." It lets a diver breathe in and out through the same mouthpiece. The regulator connects to tanks of compressed air, and these attach to a diver worn harness or vest. Time underwater is calculated by the amount of compressed air carried against the total depth of the dive. In the spring of 1949, Doug Fane arranged for Émile Gagnan to teach his UDTs in Little Creek how to dive with the Aqualung.

In 1952, a research program headed by Dr. Lambertsen conducted open-water trials in the waters off of Coronado, California with the Aqualung and the LARU to study physiological limiting factors in underwater swimming. This series of research dives was notable in that it was the first use of the newly developed wet suits by the U.S. Navy.

Later, however, and as stated by Captain Frank Butler, a former SEAL who became a Navy diving medical officer: "The Aqualung had some advantages over closed-circuit oxygen UBAs: it was less complex, easier to set up, had a greater depth range, and reduced the possibility of diving accidents. These advantages led many UDT divers to have a strong preference for the new type of SCUBA in spite of the tactical advantages of the LARU." He also related that: "In one of the least distinguished chapters of

HISTORIC OBSERVATIONS ABOUT THE AQUALUNG™

UDT MASTER CHIEF DON ROSE

Abridged from the UDT-SEAL Association's *BLAST Magazine*

The first time I saw the Aqualung was overseas and probably in 1951. We had 30 triple-bottle units with double-hose regulators and no return valves. I ended up in the diving locker, but nobody knew how to dive, nobody was qualified, and there was no school to go to. We had a lieutenant named Barker from Georgia, and I don't know where he got his knowledge about diving, but he knew diving diseases and started a class in diving. When I went to First-Class Diving School later on, I found that Barker never taught us anything wrong. (The lieutenant was Joe D. Barker of Class 001 that graduated in November 1950. He was a member of UDT-1).

I later found out that the Aqualung regulator was designed by an engineer named Gagnan. Our first 30 units were from the Spaco Corporation in Canada, and we stored them in a warehouse. We couldn't get any spare parts from Spaco, but they sold the patent rights to René Bouseau, who founded U.S. Divers in Los Angeles. We learned how to repair the Aqualung regulator from an engineer over at the Naval Electronics Laboratory (NEL) at Point Loma before René opened his repair facility in Los Angeles. We spent all day at NEL where the engineers showed us how to take down the regulators, clean them in chromic acid to remove corrosion, re-lap the seats, and set the pressures. But that didn't stop us from going to René's repair school in Los Angeles to steal everything we could get our hands on, because parts were so scarce.

René got his cylinders and regulator parts from Pressed Steel Corporation and assembled them in Los Angeles. At the same time, various companies were trying to come up with a self-contained regulator that got around the patent rights. They were all still double hose. But what really put the brakes on U.S. Divers was the Water Lung, a single-hose regulator that came out in the late '50s. The Water Lung was a giant step, because it didn't have those fragile hoses, and you could take the second stage out of your mouth to share with other divers. Of course, the Water Lung was immediately followed by single-hose regulators from Scuba Pro and a host of others.

UDT diving history, many of the remaining Office of Strategic Services World War II LARUs were consigned to a bonfire at a team beach party in 1953." This was very devastating to Dr. Lambertsen.

Open-Circuit Diving in UDT

In his book *The Naked Warriors*, Lieutenant Commander Doug Fane, talking about himself, takes credit for first U.S. military use of the Aqualung: "Its first American naval use was pioneered by Fane in the demolition of a wreck in the Norfolk (Virginia) ship channel, two years before the Korean War, although the 'lung' was still considered experimental." He stated this as a prelude to discussing the first combat use of the Aqualung in Korea: "On 12 October 1950, UDT operator William Giannotti, clad in rubber suit and mask, plus heavy steel compressed-air tanks on his back with twin air hoses running from the tanks' control valve to his mouth, plunged into the water to mark the location of the minesweepers *USS Pirate* (AM-275) and *USS Pledge* (AM-277), which sank after hitting mines." He further outlined that on the next day: "The six best qualified Aqualung divers in the team went down to survey the wreck and demolish it if necessary." Fane states several pages later: "By this time (October 1950), the Cousteau-Gagnan rig [Aqualung] was standard equipment in UDT operations."

UDT-21 operators preparing for an open-circuit SCUBA training dive in the Mediterranean, circa 1959. Note the triple-tanks and double-hose regulators.

UDT open-circuit divers wearing twin-steel tanks approaching an underwater contact mine.

UDT open-circuit diver approaching the bow of a submerged submarine.

UDT open-circuit diver transporting a demolition haversack, while wearing a three-steel tanks and a double-hose regulator

UDT men diving in the the arctic wearing three steel-bottle tanks with double-hose regulators.

CHAPTER 4

A NEW GENERATION OF UBAS

Broad attributes for advanced technology Underwater Breathing Apparatuses (UBAs) were described in the Navy's Technical Development Plan 38-02 (TDP 38-02), The Swimmer (later SEAL) Support System. Major developments involved the Class I and Class II UBAs (closed-circuit mixed gas and closed-circuit pure oxygen versions), and a host of ancillary equipment (e.g. hand-held sonar, underwater communications, a diver's decompression computer).

Detailed performance specifications for the new UBAs were completed during the 1969-70 period, and competitive contracting followed. A performance contract was eventually awarded to the Scott Aviation Corporation in Buffalo, New York for development of the Class I and Class II UBAs. The Class I mixed-gas UBA was intended to sustain a combat swimmer for six hours and operate to a depth of 66 feet or greater. This was to complement the capabilities of the new SEAL Delivery Vehicles (SDV) being contracted at the time, which included extended range, depth, and navigational capabilities. The Class II UBA would replace the aging pure-oxygen Emerson UBA.

During this period, Scott Aviation had manufactured and supported the Mark VI UBA, thus, there was great confidence that the design process would go well, but it didn't. The Scott team either had difficulty meeting or couldn't at all meet many of the performance specifications. The details don't matter now, but suffice to say, the contract was eventually canceled for cause by the Government, and the aim from that point on was to seek competitive vendors with existing or prototype UBAs. There was a lot of commercial activity, and also life-support study and technology coming from the spaceflight program, which could seemingly be transferred to diving.

Navy Experimental Diving Unit

I left SEAL Team TWO in the spring of 1972 for assignment to the Navy Experimental Diving Unit (NEDU) in Washington, DC. I relieved SEAL Lieutenant Commander Al Quist. He was greatly assisted by the only other SEAL at the NEDU, Engineman Senior Chief Tom King, whom became my assistant as well. Tom King knew diving in and out and was a great asset and stellar representative of Naval Special Warfare. He eventually was promoted to Master Chief, and I was able to get him into the Navy's Master Diver program (with great resistance from those that didn't consider SEALs worthy of becoming Master Divers). He completed the program with very high marks.

When I arrived at NEDU, the Scott Aviation Class I and Class II development program had already floundered, and commercial UBAs were being acquired for testing. I inherited all of the UDT-SEAL test programs of this major initiative. Four diving apparatus were being evaluated. The only pure oxygen rebreather being assessed was the German Draeger LAR III. The closed-circuit, mixed-gas UBAs were the Westinghouse CCM-1 and Bio Marine CCR-1000, which had been developed to target the sport diving community, and the General Electric Mark 10, MOD 5 UBA, which resulted from life-support activities in the NASA spaceflight program. General Electric also entered its Model 1500 prototype later on. All of the closed circuit, mixed-gas UBAs used nitrogen as the diluent gas, where the oxygen partial pressure was controlled at a constant value by an oxygen sensing system, which could add gas as needed. Each system had the endurance and closed-circuit characteristics of an oxygen rebreather without the concerns and limitations associated with oxygen toxicity.

The major technical testing of these diving apparatus was conducted in the "wet pot" at the Explosive Ordnance Disposal (EOD) Technology Center, Indian Head, Maryland. A wet pot is a large chamber that can be filled with water and pressurized to a depth of several hundred feet for experimental testing. Wet-pot testing was done with EOD at Indian Head, because the wet-pots at the NEDU were being used for human-based saturation-diving testing, which, at the time, had a national priority. The Indian Head wet pot could also be temperature controlled. We conducted "canister break through" tests there some time later. These tests were done in 32- degree water, with UDT and SEAL operators as test subjects, to assess when the carbon dioxide absorbent ceased to be life supporting.

LT Tom Hawkins briefing NEDU Puerto Rico test projects, circa 1973.

All open-sea tests were accomplished under supervised conditions at the U.S. Naval Station, Roosevelt Roads, Puerto Rico. UDT-SEAL divers (test subjects), including me, were required to: Swim a predetermined time or distance along a triangular jackstay course 3,000 yards in length, conduct dives to a maximum depth of 160 feet, and complete Swimmer Delivery Vehicle (SDV) mission profiles. We logged approximately 390 hours total bottom time while accomplishing these evaluations.

This is a photograph of one of the UDT-SEAL-EOD test teams in Puerto Rico. The officer in the center of the picture is CDR Pat Badger, whom at the time was commanding officer of UDT-21, and to his left LCDR Tom Hawkins, and to his left MCPO Corny Leyden.

German Draeger LAR III and LAR V

Although it had been widely used in Europe, the Draeger LAR III was only used by U.S. Navy frogmen when they participated in joint exercises in Germany and Spain. Technically, the men were not authorized by the U.S. Navy to dive the Draeger, because it was not on the Approved for Navy Use (ANU) list. They did anyway, since that is why the joint training operations were conducted. In May 1974, I spearheaded a formal evaluation of the Draeger LAR III. The Draeger UBA was designed to contemporary European standards. It didn't meet many of the stringent U.S. military specifications; particularly the standard requiring Monel (nickel-copper alloy) piping in oxygen systems. We recommended a few minor design changes, including Monel, which were later incorporated, and resulted in production and procurement of the Draeger LAR V (later designated the Mark 25 UBA). Here is the abstract from my report:

> The evaluation was conducted to determine safe operational capabilities and limitations of the LAR III with respect to instructional and training use by Naval Special Warfare divers. It was found that the LAR III is equal in many respects to the U.S. Navy Emerson UBA, although the Draeger incorporates many inherent design features that make it a somewhat more desirable apparatus. It is recommended that the Draeger LAR III be approved for limited use by U. S. Navy Underwater Demolition and SEAL Teams.

Tom Hawkins and LCDR Charles "Chuck" LeMoyne taken at the pool of the German *Kampfschwimmerkompanie*, (Combat-Swimmer Company) in Eckernförde, Germany, circa, early Fall 1973.

Navy SEAL frogmen wearing the LAR V/MK 25 UBA using an attack board to guide them to the target.

SEAL diver wearing a closed-circuit Draeger LAR V pure oxygen rebreather.

SEAL operators wearing the Draeger LAR V/MK 25 UBA exit the water in full combat mode. Such tactical dives would be routinely planned for nighttime execution. The fins are removed, when the water depth allows, permitting the men to walk or crawl out of the water.

Closed-Circuit, Mixed-Gas UBAs

Lieutenant Commander Quist and EMCS King had done much of the preliminary testing surrounding the test programs I would inherit. The Westinghouse CCM-1 and CCR-1000 were nice little diving apparatuses; compact and somewhat easily worn inside a SEAL Delivery Vehicle. In truth, there wasn't much difference between the CCM-1 and the CCR-1000 or, for that matter, the General Electric Mark 10, Mod 5 UBA – except for its large size compared to the others. Here is the abstract from NEDU Report 9-72, which I completed in August 1972:

The Bio Marine CCR-1000, General Electric Mark 10, Mod 5, and Westinghouse CCM-1 closed-circuit, mixed-gas, underwater breathing apparatus were jointly evaluated in open-sea test operations sponsored by the Navy Experimental Diving Unit during the period 9 March through 13 June 1972 at the Naval Station, Roosevelt Roads, Puerto Rico, and at the Naval Amphibious Base, Little Creek, Norfolk, Virginia. Earlier objective and subjective tests were accomplished with the individual UBAs, and are discussed in the following NAVXDIVING reports:

a. Report No. 3-72: BIO MARINE CCR-1000, Mixed-Gas, Closed-Circuit, Underwater Breathing Apparatus

b. Report No. 6-72: GENERAL ELECTRIC Mark 10, MOD 5 Mixed-Gas, Closed-Circuit, Underwater Breathing Apparatus

c. Report No. 7-72: WESTINGHOUSE CCM-1, Mixed-Gas, Closed-Circuit, Underwater Breathing Apparatus

General results of these tests concluded that each of the three UBAs were satisfactory for employment by Naval Special Warfare Forces. The series of tests discussed herein represents a culmination of comparative tests to determine and select a breathing apparatus that could subsequently replace operational UBAs now being utilized by U.S. Navy Underwater Demolition and Sea-Air-Land (SEAL) Teams. The scope of the open-sea testing included long distance, shallow water swims, deep dives to depths of 160 feet, and SEAL Delivery Vehicle (SDV) operations of six-hour durations. Tests indicated that all of the units meet or exceed a six-hour operational canister and gas-life requirement. There were, however, some limitations in areas of human engineering and incompatibility with existing equipments, which imposed some limitations on each of the units tested.

The above abstract essentially describes all or most of my work while stationed at the NEDU. While assigned to Washington, I also served as a special assistant to the SEAL officers at the Naval Sea

Systems Command: Lieutenant Commander "Irish" Flynn and Lieutenant Commander Charles Le Moyne. I worked on a Chief of Naval Operations Naval Inshore Warfare Study Group, and served as the senior officer present for the last saturation test dive series at NEDU. Upon completion of that dive, I was also responsible for shutting down NEDU North and moving the command to its new home. NEDU South, in Panama City, Florida was being established by Commander Jack Ringleburg. During this period, we labeled Washington NEDU North and Panama City NEDU South to keep things sorted out.

There was a lot going on near the end of my tour, and I also had just finished my final Naval Special Warfare project by completing 198 hours bottom-time testing with a prototype General Electric Model 1500 UBA. General Eectric knew that its Mark 10, Mod 5 was too large to be considered by Naval Special Warfare for the UDT and SEAL Teams, thus, they wanted to throw in another UBA for consideration. They provided two units, and the abstract of my report (NEDU Report No. 11-73) noted that: "General results of the tests indicate that the prototype equipment is potentially satisfactory for employment by Naval Special Warfare Forces. However, several failures were encountered with the equipment that were considered critical in nature; primarily in the electronic design, and should be corrected before further test or procurement action by the Navy."

Bio Marine CCR-1000 / Mark 15 and Mark 16 UBAs

The Bio Marine Corporation manufactured the Mark 15 UBA after development of a competitive-contract specification and bidding process. Beginning in 1979, the Mark VI semi-closed circuit underwater breathing apparatus was phased out and replaced by the Mark 15. The NEDU developed decompression procedures for the Mark 15 with nitrogen and helium tables in the early 1980s. In 1985, an improved low-magnetic signature version of the Mark 15, the Mark 16, was approved for EOD team use. The Mark 16 was also adopted by the SEALs through a

MK 15 UBA used during a training dive in Puerto Rico.

Bio Marine CCR-1000.

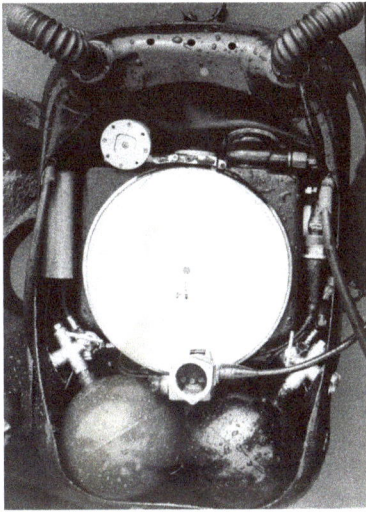

Interior of Westinghouse CCM-1.

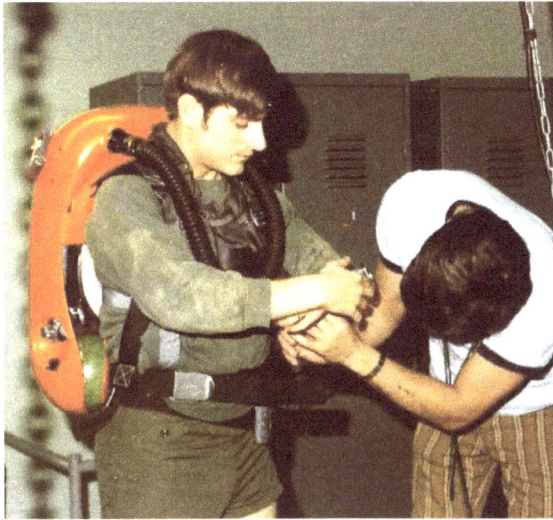

Tom Hawkins being prepared for a wet-pot test dive with the Westinghouse CCM-1 UBA at Indian Head, MD.

Tom Hawkins climbing out after a Westinghouse CCM-1UBA test dive in Puerto Rico. He is wearing the FENZY Buoyancy Compensator, which was a life preserver also being tested. Note the lead weight on top of the rig, which was used to control buoyancy.

Tom Hawkins piloting a MK VII SDV with swim buddy Jack Squires, both wearing the Westinghouse CCM-1 UBA. Note earphone headsets the men called "Mickey Mouse Ears." The SDV is sitting on the bottom in the middle of the Vieques Channel of Puerto Rico to test the underwater communications equipment, which were one-way only from the surface-support boat. They didn't work well at all.

phase-replacement process, and operationally employed largely by the SEAL Delivery Vehicle Teams for extended-duration missions.

Westinghouse CCM-1

The CCM-1 was developed by Westinghouse for the commercial marketplace. Technical testing was accomplished at the Stump Neck EOD Technology Center near Indian Head, Maryland. We used the standard UDT life preserver, and tested the FENZEY® buoyancy compensator (used by divers to establish neutral buoyancy under water and passive buoyancy on the surface when needed). Both can be seen in the photographs. Look closely, and you'll note that we also added a lead weight to the top of the CCM-1 to help compensate for sitting upright in the SDV, which made the UBA tend to float up and off gas.

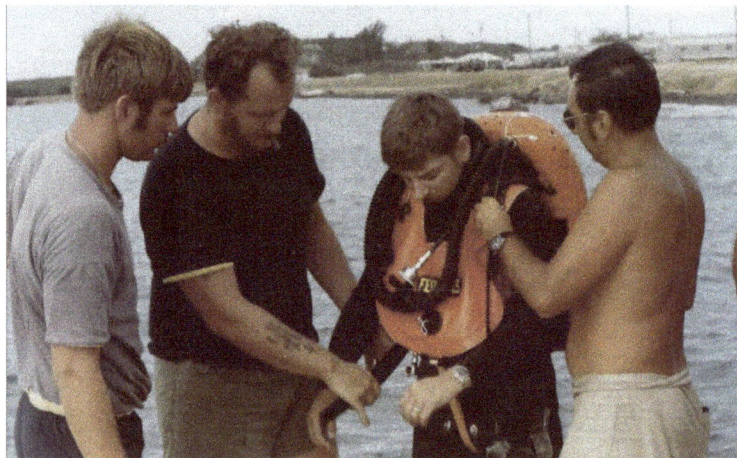

Tom Hawkins getting pre-dive checks, while testing the Westinghouse CCM-1 UBA at the U.S. Naval Station, Roosevelt Roads, Puerto Rico. In the photo (l-r) are Ken Montgomery (UDT-21), Tom Phillips (EOD-NEDU), Tom Hawkins, and Ted "Pooch" Pacuicrk (SEAL Team TWO).

We did most of the CCM testing in Puerto Rico, and it was by far the most pleasurable to use. It was designed for the sport-diving market, thus, it was small and compact. It could also fit well with two operators in the crew and passenger compartments of the SDV. For technical testing, we had to swim the rigs on an underwater jackstay (triangular line), which measured a precise length on each of the three legs. During days off, which was mostly just on Sundays, we would take the rigs out and dive for lobsters, conch shells, starfish, and other forms of sea life. Because of the extended duration of the gas supply, we could literally dive all day without coming up.

General Electric Mark 10, Mod 5

The Mark 10 design originated from the NASA spaceflight program. The Mark 10, Mod 5 UBA had a specially designed shellback in a UDT-SEAL test configuration. Because of its size, it contained other developmental designs, including under water communications, making the Mark 10 the largest UBA tested. Testing also included the FENZEY buoyancy compensator and various full-facemasks.

Testing the communications hood from the Naval Coastal Systems Center with the MK 10 UBA.

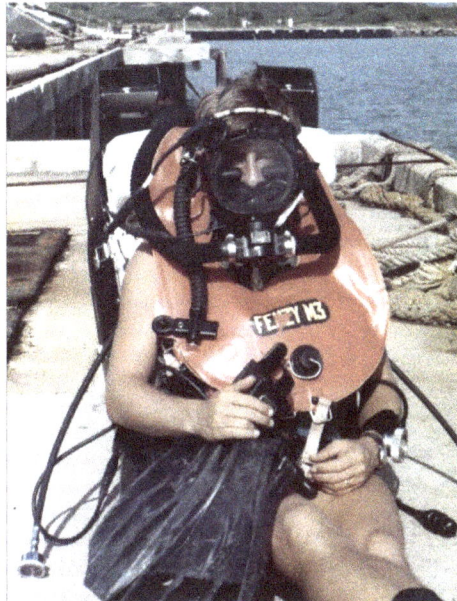

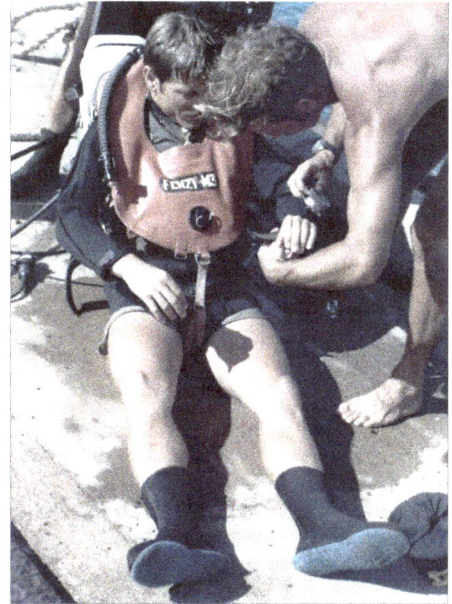

Various photographs of Tom Hawkins wearing the MK 10 UBA before and after test diving. Notice that the backpack shell is different than that of the original design model. This backpack contained other developmental designs; including underwater communications, making the MK 10 the largest UBA tested. Testing included the FENZEY buoyancy compensator and various full-facemasks.

Because of its size, the Mark 10 couldn't be used in the SDV and still conform to the requisite diver buddy system. It was fine for open-water operations, when diving on the triangular jackstay. The hardest part about swimming the jackstay was that boredom set in very quickly; especially when we had to navigate the same test area day-after-day – our underwater equivalent of "Ground Hog Day." We tested this rig using several different full facemasks and at least two underwater communications systems.

View of the interior of the MK 10, Mod 0 UBA and with the shellback attached.

Odds and Ends

A significant focus of the TDP 38-02 SEAL Support Systems program was development of a host of ancillary diving equipment; including a full facemask and underwater communications. As SDV and submarine operations became more frequent, they also became more complex, and underwater communications became essential. Heretofore, when an SDV was launched for a mission off a submarine, there was no further opportunity to communicate. It was the final time before launch that the SDV crew could be contacted until they returned to the ship. If, for example, a mission needed to be aborted, there was no way to alert the crew. During UBA testing, we had the opportunity to subjectively evaluate

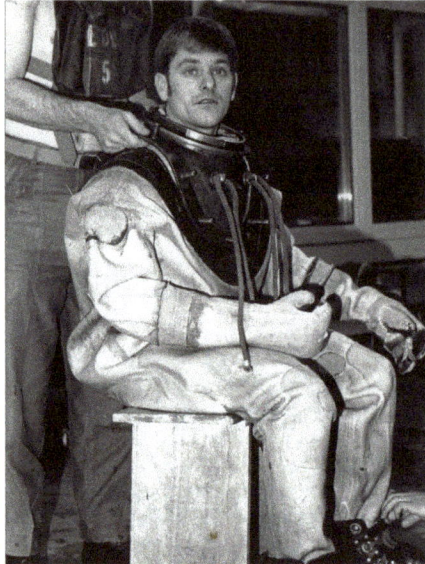

Tom Hawkins getting hard-hat diver training, while conducting NEDU testing at the EOD Technical Center, Indian Head, MD, Circa 1973.

several full facemasks with open and closed-circuit UBAs. Full facemasks were required to provide intelligible articulation of words.

Tom Hawkins test the Kirby-Morgan helmet while wearing open-circuit scuba. Nice concept, but not for SEALs. The aim during this period was to find a reliable method for SEALs to voice communicate underwater.

CHAPTER 5

NAVAL SPECIAL MISSION UNITS

Amphibious Scouts and Raiders

The Navy's Amphibious Force began early clandestine special operations efforts with a group of volunteer chief petty officers stationed in Norfolk, Virginia. As described by Chief Petty Officer Phil Bucklew: "When [the] request for volunteers occurred for a new program described only as "Amphibious Commandos," ten of my fellow shipmates were selected.... We [were] formed at Norfolk and, in May 1942, sent to Solomons, Maryland for further training in landing-craft operations under the supervision of four Coast Guard chief petty officers."

On 15 August 1942, these chief petty officers (all college graduates that had been promised reserve officer commissions), were joined with U.S. Army personnel from the 3rd and 9th Infantry Divisions at the Amphibious Training Base, Little Creek, Norfolk, Virginia. These men were organized as the Amphibious Scouts and Raiders (S&R) under the command of U.S. Army 2nd Lieutenant Lloyd Peddicord and executive officer Navy Ensign John Bell. These S&R men began intense preparation for a special-focused mission for Operation TORCH, the amphibious assault of North Africa, which would be the first allied invasion of World War II. The assault operation was conducted in November 1942.

In January 1943, S&R training was moved to Ambibious Training Base, Fort

Artwork depicting S&Rs conducting rock portage with inflatable boats during training at Ft. Pierce, FL. (Photo: Navy Art Collection)

Amphibious Force insignia worn by Scout and Raider personnel.

Amphibious S&Rs conducting infiltration training with their inflatable boat at Ft. Pierce, FL.

U.S. Army S&R men at their training base at Ft. Pierce, FL demonstrate the various uniforms and equipment, including their inflatable boat, used during tactical operations.

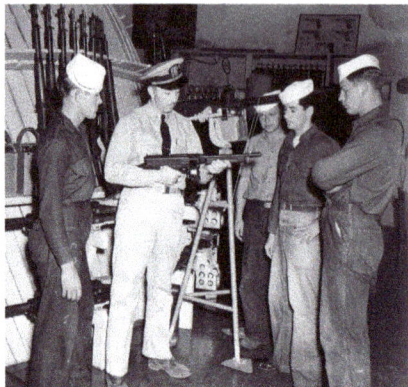

Gunnery Officer LTjg Frank teaches weapons handling and use to a crew of S&R Sailors.

Pierce, Florida. The men were trained to operate at night and tasked to identify and reconnoiter prospective landing beaches; and, using lights or other means, to accurately guide Allied assault waves to the appropriate landing beach. Army and Navy personnel were cross-trained in many areas; although the Navy men served as Scout Boat crews, while Army men were trained for operations ashore. There were seemingly no specific mission guidelines stated for S&Rs, however, a training manual was published in 1944. It describes officers and enlisted men taking a large amount of the same training.

The use of the name "Scouts and Raiders" had always caused some level of consternation regarding naval personnel; even during the period of establishment and training. The Fort Pierce Scout and Raider School mission statement included this: "The word "raider," as used in the name of the school, is of secondary importance in the training of Naval S&R units. Even though considerable training is given in raider tactics [to naval personnel], such training is retained mainly for protection of the individual and better operational performance of the unit." The training manual further outlined that S&R personnel could be used in a number of important ways:

If effectively used, Scouts can help assure that assault troops will land on the right beach at the right time. They can gather needed advanced intelligence data regarding a particular landing area. They can undertake small inland reconnaissance missions.

Through hydrographic reconnaissance, Scouts can provide required information regarding seaward approaches to beaches. In addition to these major functions, Scouts are prepared to undertake small raiding missions, to transport night raiding parties, and to land special devices and equipment ashore to aid in amphibious operations.

Scouts and Raiders...have learned to paddle, to swim, and to crawl without being seen or heard. They have learned to see in the dark and to find their way into strange places. They have established strength and skill for hazardous missions. They are ready to guide stacking forces to selected landing spots. Scouts and Raiders are indispensable aids in ship-to-shore movements.

S&R used ship-to-shore small craft from the transport ship upon which they were embarked. They never had a dedicated inventory of their own boats. Regarding host ship boats, it was stated that:

It is necessary for the ship carrying the Scout unit to furnish the following services and supplies to the unit:

1.   Landing craft best suited to the unit. (In fact, host ships had a pre-designated inventory of small craft, and it was generally the Scout and Raider crews that had to adapt.)

2.   All services of repair and maintenance, including installation of motor-silencing gear, special color of camouflage paint, etc.

3.   Scout boat to be lowered into the water prior to any other landing craft, immediately upon arriving in the transport area.

Navy S&R boat crews normally employed Landing Craft Personnel, Ramped (LCPR). Their crews were comprised of a coxswain, boat handler, gunner, and engineman. A chief specialist (chief petty officer) was assigned as Scout Boat Officer. The Amphibious Force had established a well-defined training program for S&Rs; especially after they moved to Fort Pierce. However, they were never organized into defined or cohesive operational units after training. Before Operation TORCH, they were formed as a joint unit for training, where mission tasks and training were being designed and developed as they presented themselves. For operations, S&R crews were disbursed among various transport ships for assault assignments. Lieutenant Lloyd Peddicord and Ensign John Bell were the only officers in that first group.

S&R training included: recognizing landmarks and silhouettes ashore at night, judging distances, and navigating a Scout Boat

A very innovative boat fabricated by S&R men from a French seaplane pontoon; reportedly used during the invasion of Southern France in August 1944.

S&R operatives used kayaks like this in Italy, and for pre-assault reconnaissance and information gathering at Normandy, France in May 1944.

S&Rs launch from their APA (troop transport) LCPR to conduct daytime training operations. Note the inflatable boats stacked in the stern.

offshore. S&R men were provided instruction in signaling, communications, hand-to-hand combat; combat intelligence gathering, silent landing techniques, hydrographic surveying, land navigation and patrolling, and a rigorous PT program that included swimming. All S&R operations were to be performed under the cover of darkness. During tactical operations, Army personnel were transported from their host ship to the near shore in LCPRs or Landing Craft Personnel, Large (LCPL) by the Navy Scout Boat crews. These small craft carried or towed inflatable Landing Craft, Rubber (LCRs) boats or kayaks to a pre-planned distance off the target beach, where the Army men were launched and recovered.

After the Allied landing in North Africa, S&R personnel went on to support landings in Sicily, Salerno, Anzio, Normandy, and Southern France. S&R personnel employed after Operation TORCH, were trained in theater and largely in North Africa. In June 1943, the Scout and Raider Training School was moved to Amphibious Training Base, Fort Pierce, Florida, and in the following June, the S&R training program became all naval. A host of the tactics, techniques, and procedures performed by the Scouts and Raiders represent legacy capabilities that remain very much resident in the SEAL and Special Boat Teams of the modern day.

A comprehensive and perhaps the most definitive history written about the Amphibious Scouts and Raiders can be found in the book *Scouts and Raiders: The Navy's First Special Warfare Commandos* by John B. "Barry" Dwyer. This book is rich in detail, however, Mr. Dwyer concluded his book by stating that U.S. Navy SEALs were the lineal descendants of the Scouts and Raiders, which is not accurate. That honor goes to the men of the Naval Combat Demolition Units and UDTs. Barry and I had many conversations about this, and we simply agreed to disagree. Barry passed away at the age of 65 on 19 September 2010, but, his book remains a stellar work and, to my knowledge, no better resource exists regarding the Amphibious Scouts and Raiders.

Special Services Unit #1

The commander of the Pacific Fleet 7th Amphibious Force directed establishment of a school for Amphibious Scouts in the vicinity of Cairns, Australia in July 1943. Organized as Special Services Unit #1 (SSU#1), it was an international force of personnel from Australia and the U.S. Army, Navy, and Marine Corps. They trained in martial arts, hand-to-hand combat, map making, rubber craft operations, jungle survival, Pidgin English, underwater coral formations, and sea-creatures recognition. They operated at New Guinea collecting intelligence and training and operating with indigenous guerrilla forces. Similar operations were carried out at Gasmata, Arawe, Cape Gloucester, and New Britain. On 13 October 1944, they were transferred to the 7th Amphibious Force Intelligence Section. SSU #1 never had or used small-boat capabilities until they became a part of the Amphibious Force Intelligence Section. When needed, they used boats from Ships Company.

SSU #1 LT Hank Staudt, USNR and LT Bernard Wildgen, Medical Corps, USNR.

The history of SSU #1 remained somewhat obscure until their story was told by Teresa "Pat" Staudt in her stellar, self-researched, and self-published history of SSU #1 entitled *Hidden Heroes*, published in 1994 and revised in 2004. Her husband Hank Staudt was an officer in SSU#1. In the preface to her work, Pat wrote:

This SSU#1 photograph was simply entitled "AUS and USNR Scouts" (Army United States and U.S. Naval Reserves.)

SSU #1 LT Henry E. Staudt, RM1c Maurice Tichener, and BM1c Joshua Weintraub working among the indigenous population of Fergusson Island.

61

The annals of military and naval history have been enriched by the deeds of men whose actions demonstrated their courage, dedication and valor. Most have been acknowledged and appreciated. There is a group, whose heroic sacrifices and successes were performed in secrecy and hidden in obscurity by the necessity of the moment, and which have never since been presented for appraisal or accolade. Such were the men of SPECIAL SERVICES UNIT # 1 (Amphibious Scouts). Their legendary beginnings, history, formation, and action reports are humbly presented, in an unadorned factual form.

Pat is now deceased, but we became great friends, and she provided me copies of all her photographs, research material, and final publication. Her work was also provided to the National Navy UDT-SEAL Museum in Fort Pierce, Florida.

Sino-American Cooperative Organization

It is hard to appreciate today, but China was a vital ally of the United States against the Japanese throughout World War II. China was one of the most critical, yet least known, theaters of World War II. From a "special naval warfare" capability perspective, the Chinese theatre involved Guerrilla Warfare, accomplished through the Sino-American Cooperative Organization (SACO). SACO was a combined force jointly led by U.S. Navy Captain (later Vice Admiral) Milton E. Miles and China's General Tai Li (pronounced "die lee"), who was, at that time, in charge of a China organization analogous to the CIA.

This SSU #1 photograph was simply entitled "AUS and USNR Scouts" (U.S. Army and U.S. Naval Reserve).

These two men were able to establish a friendship that transcended suspicions held on both sides. SACO was a joint agreement made on 4 July 1943. For the remainder of the war, Miles and Tai Li worked and fought closely together against the Japanese. Feared, honest, brutal, and fair, Tai Li was one of the most enigmatic characters in the Chinese theatre of World War II. They remained good friends until Tai Li's death in 1946.

General Tai Li wanted the Americans to come to China and train Chinese guerrilla troops to fight the Japanese. Of course, he was also thinking about the long-term benefit of having a well-trained army of Chinese Nationalist troops to fight the Chinese Communists after World War II. The U.S. Army, however, refused to cooperate with the Chinese, as did the OSS, since both agencies wanted to do things their own way rather than the "Chinese way." Because of Commander Miles, the U.S. Navy was much more receptive to working with the Chinese as equals rather than as subordinates. Commander Miles had served in China for many years after World War I, and had a deep respect for the people and the country. He suggested the idea of SACO to his superiors and President Roosevelt, who fully supported the idea.

S&R LT Phil Bucklew during his assignment to the U.S. Naval Group China.

U.S. Navy, Marine Corps, and Coast Guard personnel began operating with Chinese forces as early as 1942. Their first activity—the forwarding of

SACO commanders General Tai Li, leader of China's intelligence bureau, and CAPT Milton Miles, commander of U.S. Naval Group China.

CAPT Miles observes a Naval Group China-SACO military "pass and review" formation to honor guest dignitaries. (photo from Naval History and Heritage Command)

weather information—was soon expanded to include intelligence gathering and the training and equipping of Chinese guerillas for missions against the Japanese. Known initially as the "Friendship Project," and later as SACO, the group operated over a vast terrain, extending from Indochina to the Gobi Desert. As stated by the Naval History and Heritage Command: "SACO made an invaluable contribution to the common victory, and furthered to a memorable degree the bonds of friendship between the U.S. and China."

Having a U.S. Naval Group operating throughout a country as large as China seemed out of place, however, there were several strategic factors. The U.S. Navy had a long-standing tradition of keeping Chinese rivers and ports open to free commerce using U.S. gunboats. Soon after World War II began, but before development of the atomic bomb, U.S. Navy leaders felt that an amphibious invasion of Japan would likely be necessary to end the war. China would provide the best springboard. Also, the Navy needed to provide accurate weather information to Allied naval forces operating throughout the Western Pacific, and they wanted to collect information on Japanese ship movements. Thus, they had a strong motivation to establish good relations with Chinese leaders, and SACO provided the means to accomplish what the Navy wanted to accomplish. SACO eventually involved dozens of Sailors acting as "coastwatcher's," secretly gathering and reporting essential intelligence information.

A less than serious part of SACO was the "What the Hell" pennant, which had been created by Captain Miles, when he was a junior officer aboard ship. It involved three individual characters: ???!!! *** in red on a white background.

As he recounted in his book, *When I Was on Duty in the Far East with SACO:* "The pennant was for monkeyshines that served a purpose that had serious attributes, despite its nonsense." History has recorded that after many attempts, the Japanese could never figure out what the symbols meant. Indeeed, they really didn't mean anything.

"What the Hell" pennant used by Naval Group SACO group men. The Japanese could never figure out what the symbols meant.

The authoritative story about SACO is told by Admiral Miles himself in his book *A Different Kind of War: The Little-Known Story of the Combined Guerrilla Forces Created in China by the U.S. Navy and the Chinese During World War II*, which was co-authored by Hawthorne Daniel.

SACO was a unique and unprecedented combined military effort that involved 2,500 Americans, mostly from the U.S. Navy and Marines, who lived, led, trained, and fought with thousands of Chinese troops. Many of these men were often stationed behind enemy lines hundreds of miles from supplies, where they were extremely bold and resourceful. They became known as the "Rice Paddy Navy." Many of the men became totally immersed in Chinese culture, living in Chinese huts, speaking Chinese, eating Chinese food, and beginning to think "the Chinese way." SACO forces effectively battled the Japanese from 1943 until 1945. This was the first and only time in U.S. history that an American military unit had been completely integrated into a foreign military force and placed under the command of a foreign leader. SACO was one of the most effective special-mission units in World War II.

NCDUs at Normandy and Southern France

Naval Combat Demolition Units (NCDUs) participated in the invasion at Normandy in July 1944. In the following August, they participated in the invasion of Southern France. Regarding the Navy's early special mission units, a great book on this topic is *Spearheading D-Day: American Special Units in Normandy* by Johathan Gawe. Another is *More Than Scuttlebutt: The U.S. Navy Demolition Men of WWII* by Sue Ann Dunford and James Douglas O'Dell, and both are good friends. Sue Ann's father, Gunnersmate First Class John Dunford, was in NCDU 127 on Utah Beach, and later in UDT-27 in the Pacific.

The NCDU men, most of whom came originally from the Navy Construction Battalions (Seabees), were known as "assault demolitioneers." They embraced this title and crafted their own ballad, which was entitled *Song of the Demolitioneers*. Along with the Pacific UDTs, they are the true lineal precursors of U.S. Navy SEALs. The NCDU men and counterpart U.S. Army engineers led the way to the defeat of Hitler by clearing beach obstacles during the invasion at Normandy and Southern France.

At Normandy's Omaha Beach, each NCDU was augmented with four Navy seaman and task-organized with five Army demolition engineers from the 146th and 299th Engineer Combat Battalions to form "Gap Assault Teams." The four seaman were from a training pool in Scotland, and given the job of handling the inflatable boats that would be filled with additional explosives, blasting caps, and fuses. The Utah Beach NCDUs were augmented with three seaman.

The NCDU men were assigned to demolish obstacles closest to the sea and work in towards the beach. Army demolition men were to clear obstacles toward the land. In fact, because of tidal flow, they ended up working closely together. There were 16 Gap Teams assigned to Omaha Beach, and each was assigned a 50-yard gap of beach for obstacle clearance. There were eleven Gap Teams on adjacent Utah Beach. They were backed by eight support teams, each covering two NCDUs.

NCDU men at Normandy wading ashore with their inflatable boats laden with demolitions. (Navy Art Collection)

NCDU men conducting rock portage training at a jetty in Fort Pierce, FL, circa 1943.

Army and Navy demolition men were transported from England to the coastline of France by Navy crews in 100-foot long small surface transports called Landing Craft, Tank (LCT). The LCTs, in turn, towed a smaller 50-foot long Landing Craft, Medium (LCM), which were laden with their demolitions. The LCMs were towed, because the Navy didn't think the flat-bottom LCMs had the power to make the Channel crossing fully loaded. On D-Day, the men were cross-decked from the LCTs to the LCMs for the final transit ashore. Inflatable boats called Landing Craft, Rubber (LCR) were used to haul demolitions from the LCMs to the beach.

During the arduous channel crossing several LCMs broke loose from their tow, and had to be recovered. Several LCTs broke down or swamped, forcing their Gap Teams to complete the trip in the fully laden LCMs. Whether in a LCT or LCM, the men became soaked, battered, and seasick. The transport vessels finally reached the staging area several miles near the French coast at about 0200. It was overcast and pitch-dark with heavy seas and wind. As a result, there were several unfortunate accidents when transferring men from the LCTs to the LCMs. Once organized for movement toward the beach, the demolition boats were spread out at least 300 yards apart, and some came under fire while still 800 yards or more from the shore.

Some demolition craft experienced delays and lost invaluable minutes, causing later confusion with follow-on infantry waves because of the fixed landing schedule. More often, however, the infantry's landing craft were late or hit the wrong beach. In a true twist of fate, this resulted in the lightly manned NCDU-Army Gap Assault Teams leading the way into the enemy's gunfire on several beaches.

The men, each loaded with several 20 two-pound Hagensen demolition packs and combat gear, jumped into the waist-deep water and made their way toward 10-foot high steel Belgian gates on the beaches. Sniper fire quickly increased after the LCM ramps were lowered, but the men wasted no time getting to their demolition tasking. The NCDU men were not swimmers, divers, or frogmen, as has been sometimes published. They wore oil-impregnated coveralls over khaki shirts and trousers and heavy underwear; field shoes, a web belt with wire cutters, banana-like crimpers for blasting caps, cartridges, gas mask, inflatable life belt, canteen, first-aid packet, gray-striped helmet, and a fur-lined M-2 coat. Some carried carbines. Some carried heavy reels on their backs wound with 800 feet of Primacord® (explosive wire). Those picked as fuse pullers carried bags of waterproofed two-minute-delay Primacord fuse assemblies, which could also be easily exploded by bullet or shrapnel.

By the evening of D-Day, 13 buoyed gaps had been blown, some 100 to 150 yards wide, to clear the way for follow-on forces. On both beaches, demolition crews had cleared one-third of all surf-zone beach obstacles

NCDU men conducting inflatable boat training at the ATB at Fort Pierce, FL.

Each NCDU had one officer and five enlisted men. The man in the middle with his hand on his hip is thought to be MM3c William Harrison Norman. (Photo Sue Ann Dunford)

This is how the NCDU men would have been outfitted during D-Day. Note the flotation devices they have around their shoulders. (Photo Sue Ann Dunford)

NCDU men at Normandy are seen placing demolitions on a German Belgian gate obstacle. (Navy Art Collection)

Aftermath at Normandy. (Navy Art Collection)

emplaced by the Nazis during the previous four months. As a result of their efforts, an armada of ships and small craft was able to move ashore, where troops and supplies poured through the breaches; allowing the U.S. Army to move further inland to secure vital objectives.

On Normandy Beach more than half of the NCDU men were casualties—31 killed, 60 wounded—resulting in a casualty rate of 52 per cent. There were 84 non-casualties among the NCDU personnel. At Utah Beach, the opposition was less intense, however, six NCDU men were killed, and 11 were wounded. D-Day, 6 June 1944, remains the bloodiest day in the history of Naval Special Warfare.

Fifteen Distinguished Service Cross medals were awarded to Army combat demolition men. Among the NCDU men, Navy Cross medals were awarded to GMG2 William Freeman, GMG2 Robert Bass, GM2 John Line, AOC Loran Barbour, CMM Jerry Markham, Ensign Lawrence Karnowski, and Lieutenant Junior Grade William Jenkins. The Omaha NCDUs received one of only three Presidential Unit Citations awarded to the Navy for the Normandy landings. It reads:

Citation: For outstanding performance in combat during the invasion of Normandy, June 6, 1944. Determined and zealous in the fulfillment of an extremely hazardous mission, the Navy Combat Demolition Unit of Force "O" landed on the "Omaha Beach" with the first wave under devastating enemy artillery, machine-gun, and sniper fire. With practically all explosives lost and with their force seriously depleted by heavy casualties, the remaining officers and men carried on gallantly, salvaging explosives as they were swept ashore and in some instances commandeering bulldozers to remove obstacles. In spite of these grave handicaps, the Demolition Crews succeeded initially in blasting five gaps through enemy obstacles for the passage of assault forces to the Normandy shore and within two days had sapped over eighty-five percent of the "Omaha Beach" area of German-placed traps. Valiant in the face of grave danger and persistently aggressive against fierce resistance, the Navy Combat Demolition

Unit rendered daring and self-sacrificing service in the performance of a vital mission, thereby sustaining the high traditions of the United States Naval Service.

The NCDUs at Utah Beach operated in a similar manner and earned the only Navy Unit Commendation awarded for Operation NEPTUNE. It reads:

Citation: For outstanding heroism in action against the enemy German forces during the landing on the coast of Normandy, June 6, 1944. Ruggedly trained and fiercely determined to affect the gap through which would flow our whole battle effort in the assigned sector, Naval Combat Demolition Units, Assault Force "U" boldly moved in toward sands raked by German mortars, machine guns, and 88-MMs. Crowded into LCM's and LCVP's, and with only minutes in which to blow the obstacles before they were obscured by racing tides, these gallant men landed, each weighted down by forty pounds of TNT, and carrying two-pound blocks around his chest, to place demolition charges on pyramids of steel, timber or concrete; on ramps, hedgehogs, and other obstructions. Constantly in peril from terrific fire of hostile pillboxes and casemates, they ignited their fuses and as the tide swept in during the critical hours of D-Day, saw the line of khaki move slowly up the eastern American beach and inland through a 300-yard gap cleared of German emplacements. Individually courageous and working as a valiant team in the face of fearful destruction wrought by enemy fire, Naval Combat Demolition Units, Assault Force "U" achieved a hazardous mission vital to the initiation of our land war against ruthless German aggression.

U.S. troops landing on D-Day. Each post was mined with explosives. Credit: Rickard, J. (8 May 2009)

The NCDU men were engaged in combat only one more time, and this was during the invasion of Southern France in August 1944. Code named Dragoon, the NCDUs from Utah Beach were given the task. They were augmented with new units from Fort Pierce to participate in the last amphibious assault of the war in Europe. Subsequently, all Fort Pierce trained men would be sent to the Pacific and organized as UDTs.

Underwater Demolition Teams - Pacific

Between April 1944 and July 1945, the Maui-based and trained UDTs participated in every major amphibious operation across the Pacific, including: Eniwetok, Saipan, Guam, Tinian, Angaur, Ulithi, Peleliu, Leyte, Lingayen Gulf, Zamblales, Iwo Jima, Okinawa, Labuan, Brunei Bay, and Borneo.

September 1945: Men of UDT-30 at Oceanside, CA. UDT-30 was the last UDT established during WWII and the only UDT to have never trained at Maui.

On 17 June 1945, in preparation for the invasion of Japan, arrangements were being made to send all 28 UDTs, each with 100 men, and their APDs to Amphibious Training Base Oceanside, California for a month of cold-water training. This training was to begin on 15 August. As the men began assembling at Oceanside, President Truman ordered the use of atomic weapons at Hiroshima and Nagasaki, Japan, bringing the war to an abrupt end on 14 August. At this juncture, UDT-18 and UDT-21 were quickly flown to Guam to join the Third Fleet for occupation assignments aboard *USS Pattison* (APD-104) and *USS Bunch* (APD-79) respectively. Ten teams were distributed between Fort Pierce, Oceanside, and Maui, where they began closing down the bases. The remaining 16 UDTs were deployed to Japan, China, and Korea for occupation duty aboard various APDs.

On 28 September 1945, all 28 UDTs were recalled from wherever they were deployed globally for return to Amphibious Training Base, Coronado, California for disestablishment and post-war reorganization. A total of 30 UDTs were organized during World War II. UDT-1 and UDT-2, the provisional UDTs, were broken up as quickly as they were formed, thus, at most there were 28 UDTs organized by August 1945.

Early 1944: UDT-3 men rehearsing with their inflatable boats at the Naval Combat Demolition and Experimental Base at Maui. (Photo: Sue Ann Dunford/John Gikey Collection)

In early January 1946, post-war UDT-1 and UDT-3 were assigned to the Pacific Amphibious Force and homeported at the Amphibious Base in Coronado, California. UDT-2 and UDT-4 were homeported at Amphibious Base, Little Creek, Virginia, and would become the first UDTs ever assigned to the Atlantic Amphibious Force.

Although they survived the war doctrinally, the post-war UDTs were reduced to a skeleton complement of seven officers and 45 men each. With this small force, they had to prepare for possible future wars, and try to maintain combat readiness. These remarkable UDTs and their Pacific forefathers are the true legacy ancestors of the men that several decades later would become U.S. Navy SEALs.

The men of UDT-7 loading demolitions aboard a LCPR at Saipan.

UDT-7 underway in their LCPR. Note the inflatable boat propped inside the boat.

An LCPR towing an inflatable boat that will transport the men and demolitions closer to the target beach.

UDT-4 at NAB, Little Creek, Norfolk, VA in 1949. During World War II, there were no UDTs assigned to the Atlantic Fleet.

CHAPTER 6

WORLD WAR II MARITIME MOBILITY

Higgins Boats

In the 1930's, Andrew Higgins created Higgins Industries in New Orleans and designed the famous "Eureka," a boat for oil drillers and trappers along the Gulf Coast. The boat had a semi-tunnel hull protecting its propeller and allowing it to operate in shallow water. It also had a "spoonbill" bow that allowed the boat to beach itself and back off with relative ease. The design features of this boat were later improved and used in the design of a family of craft manufactured for use in every theater of conflict during World War II.

Interestingly, before the World War II, Mr. Higgins contracted with the Philippines to acquire large stocks of mahogany, which was the primary material for his boats. He had the vision to realize that steel would be in short supply if war broke out; and, if that happened, his company would be far ahead in its capability to manufacture landing craft. In 1940, the Navy received funding to purchase large quantities of transport ships and landing craft; initially converting large merchant ships as transports for personnel and equipment. These ships were equipped with davits for handling 36-foot small craft, and the "Higgins Boats" became the operational and tactical standard. Higgins boats included: Landing Craft, Personnel, Large (LCPL), Landing Craft, Vehicle, Personnel (LCVP), and Landing Craft, Personnel, Ramp (LCPR), which was the variant used by the men of UDT. These boats were transported aboard the host ships used by the UDTs throughout the war.

Higgins Boat landing somewhere on Normandy Beach, 6 June 1944.

High-Speed Transports

The "island-hopping" nature of the Pacific war required control of land, sea, and air domains. Where control of the air and sea were contested, large transports and cargo ships carrying conventional Navy landing craft was not an ideal situation. More responsive ships were needed—fast, shallow draft, yet capable of embarking troops in adequate numbers and delivering them with equipment to prospective landing beaches. The answer came in the form of high-speed transports called Auxiliary Personnel Destroyers (APDs).

UDT-8's LCPR waiting at a safe distance off shore until the UDT men were ready for pickup. Demolition shots can be seen going off in the background.

The APDs were converted destroyer-class ships intended to deliver small units such as the UDTs, U.S Marines, and Army Ranger units in tactical proximity of hostile shores. They could carry an entire 100-man UDT or up to a Marine or Army company. They were also capable of standing off shore and providing limited gunfire support. Because of the kamikaze threat, APDs were relatively well armed; three 3-inch 50 caliber guns (76mm), a single 40mm gun aft along with five 20mm anti-aircraft guns.

The earliest ships servings as high-speed transports were World War I vintage flush-deck "four-stacker" destroyers. Their torpedo tubes were removed during conversion to APDs. They were replaced with four landing craft, four davits, embarked troop stowage spaces, and berthing quarters. Later APDs were newly constructed destroyer escorts; altered to provide additional troop berthing and equipment storage amidships, adding four davits, four landing craft, and a boom crane aft.

Inflatable Rubber Boats

UDT men used several kinds of small boats for accomplishing their mission, however, the smallest was an inflatable boat employed for short-range operations. They came in seven or 10-man sizes that could be fitted with an outboard engine. During World War II, they were simply called Landing Craft Rubber (LCR). Submarine warfare in the Battle of the Atlantic resulted in many casualties among merchant and warships, and

LCRs were used by NCDU men to ferry demolitions ashore.

73

UDT ABLE AND THE *USS NOA*

AN EYEWITNESS TO THE ACCIDENT

Excerpted from an account provided by Donald M. Walker to the UDT-SEAL Museum.

In January 1944, several NCDUs from the second training class at Fort Pierce were assembled at Turner City with NCDUs from the first class. (Note: Turner City is on Florida Island at Tulagi, which is part of the Solomon Island group. A naval base there during World War II repaired small landing craft.)

These early NCDUs and boat-crew recruits from personnel pools were informally assembled as UDT ABLE for the invasion of Peleliu. They were transported aboard an old-World War I "four-stacker" *USS Noa* (APD-24-formerly DD-343). There was no formal commissioning.

At 0515 on 12 September 1944, during pre-dawn maneuvers, and in total darkness and radio silence, *Noa* was rammed in the stern by the *USS Fullam* (DD-474). As a result, the *Noa* began sinking by "friendly action." The bow and superstructure were still visible during the early dawn.

There was an opportunity to lower enough of the UDT LCPRs to get survivors (no losses), and transport them to the *USS Pennsylvania* (BB-38) and *USS Maryland* (BB-46).

Mr. Walker was a member of UDT-4, UDT ABLE, and UDT-13 during World War II. Photographs compliments of Liz Logan at the Navy UDT-SEAL Museum.

UDT operator being snared into an IBS at high speed.

the U.S. Navy began using them as life rafts. U.S. Marine Raiders used large LCRs during the Makin Island raid in August 1942, launching elements of the 2nd Raider Battalion from the submarines *USS Argonaut* (SM-1) and *USS Nautilus* (SS-168). LCRs were used by the Amphibious Scouts and Raiders to conduct over the beach operations; Naval Combat Demolition Unit men used LCRs to ferry demolitions ashore during D-Day operations at Normandy and in Southern France; and, the LCR was the mainstay for UDT operations throughout World War II.

When the term Inflatable Boat, Small (IBS)

UDT men paddling an IBS to conduct demolition work.

was first used could not be determined. It was likely done at the U.S. Navy's Bureau of Ships, when military specifications were drawn up for the inflatable. The IBS is still used in the Basic Underwater Demolition/ SEAL (BUD/S) training program. It has an overall length of 16 feet, eight-foot beam, minor draft, and weighed 396 pounds (474 pounds with a 9-1/2 HP outboard). Speed with the original outboard was roughly 4.5 knots, and speed with eight experienced men paddling was estimated at 55 yards per minute, but very much depends on weather and sea conditions.

OSS Two-Man Surfboard

The accompanying photos display various views of the OSS MU's innovative two-man inflatable surfboard. It was 10 feet long, 3.7 inches wide, and weighed 310 pounds. It was inflated using a compressed-air cylinder. It had a battery-driven 3/4 horsepower drill-motor that could attain a speed of five knots, and reach 10 miles in ideal water conditions. These photos were taken at Silver Springs, Florida in September 1943. OSS MU also developed an inflatable paddleboard. It weighed 65 pounds and could be carried in a knapsack. Once inflated, it was 10 feet long and two feet wide. There is no known record of these capabilities being used operationally. The men are seen wearing an early version of the Lambertsen diving unit.

Silver Springs, FL, 1943: GM2c Norm Wicker, USNR, and GM2c John Spence, USN practicing with the OSS MU two-man inflatable surfboard powered by an electric drill. They are wearing the Lambertsen Unit MK II.

Team	Commander	APD Assigned (*)	Major Operations
UDT-1	CDR Edward D. Brewster	Various APA (Troop Transports)	Kwajalein. Operation Flintlock, invasion of the Marshall Islands.
UDT-2	LCDR J.T. Koehler	Various APA (Troop Transports)	Roi-Namur. Operation Flintlock, invasion of the Marshall Islands.
UDT-3	LT Thomas C. Crist LT Robert P. Marshall	USS Dent (APD-9) USS Talbot (APD-7) USS Jeffery (APD-44)	Guam Leyte Okinawa Japan (pre-occupation)
UDT-4	LT William G. Carrbery	USS Talbot (APD-7) USS Loy (APD-56) USS Kane (APD-18)	Guam Leyte Ia Shima Minna Shima
UDT-5	LCDR Draper D. Kauffman LT John K. Deobld	USS Gilmer (APD-11) USS Humphreys (APD-12) USS Hobby (APD-95)	Saipan Tinian Leyte Luzon Japan (pre-occupation)
UDT-6	LT DeEarle M. Logsdon	USS Schmitt (APD-76)	Saipan Guam Pelelui Leyte Japan (pre-occupation)
UDT-7	LT Richard F. Burke LT Sidney Robbins	USS Brooks (APD-10) USS Stringham (APD-6) USS Hopping (APD-51) USS Auman (APD-117)	Saipan Tinian Pelelui Okinawa Japan (pre-occupation)
UDT-8	LT Donald E. Young	USS Badger (APD-33) USS Wolf (APD-29)	Pelelui Anguar Leyte Luzon China (pre-occupation)

UDTs and APDs of World War II

Team	Commander	APD Assigned (*)	Major Operations
UDT-9	LT James B. Eaton	USS Brooks (APD-10) USS Sands (APD-13) USS Lanning (APD-55)	Leyte Luzon Korea (pre-occupation) China (pre-occupation)
UDT-10	LT Arthur O. Choate, Jr.	USS Rathburne (APD-25)	Ulithi Leyte Luzon
UDT-11	LT Louis A. States	USS Kline (APD-120)	Okinawa Borneo Japan (pre-occupation)
UDT-12	LCDR Edward S. Hochuli LT William H. Jones	USS Bates (APD-47) USS Amesbury (APD-46)	Iwo Jima Kerama Retto Okinawa Korea (pre-occupation) China (pre-occupation)
UDT-13	LCDR Vincent J. Moranz LCDR Douglas F. Fane	USS Burdo (APD-133) USS Barr (APD-39)	Iwo Jima Kerama Retto Japan (pre-occupation)
UDT-14	LT Bruce Onderdonk	USS Bull (APD-78)	Luzon Iwo Jima Okinawa
UDT-15	LCDR Huston F. Brooks	USS Blessman (APD-48) USS Gray (APD-74)	Luzon Iwo Jima
UDT-16	LT Edward A. Mitchell	USS Herndon (APD-121)	Okinawa
UDT-17	LT Arthur M. Downes, Jr.	USS Bull (APD-78) USS Blessman (APD-48) USS Crosley (APD-87)	Okinawa Japan (pre-occupation)
UDT-18	LCDR Charles E. Coombs	USS Schmitt (APD-76) USS Pattison (APD-104)	Borneo Japan (pre-occupation)
UDT-19	LCDR George C. Rowe LT George T. Marion	USS Knudson (APD-101)	Kerama Retto

Team	Commander	APD Assigned (*)	Major Operations
UDT-20	LT "Bud" Ludwig LT R. Beverly Herbert	USS Cook (APD-130)	Japan (occupation)
UDT-21	LT Edward P. Clayton	USS Bunch (APD-79)	Ia Shima Iheya Shima Japan (occupation)
UDT-22	LT J. Fletcher Chase	USS Young (APD-131)	
UDT-23	LCDR James J. Deegan	USS Balduck (APD-132)	Korea (pre-occupation) China (occupation)
UDT-24	LCDR James Gatling	USS Ganter (APD-42)	Japan (occupation)
UDT-25	LT Walter Cooper	USS Knudson (APD-101)	China (pre-occupation)
UDT-26	LCDR A.S. Boyce LCDR John B. Horrocks	USS Inghram (APD-35)	China (pre-occupation)
UDT-27	LCDR David G. Saunders	USS Cobb (APD-106)	Japan (pre-occupation)
UDT-28	LCDR J. Giles	USS Yokes (APD-60)	Returned to Maui from Oceanside, CA to close down the NCDT&E base.
UDT-29	LT Robert Rohr	NA	Returned to Maui from Oceanside, CA to close down the NCDT&E base.
UDT-30	LCDR Murray A. Fowler	NA	Did not deploy.
USS Hollis (APD-66) – Command ship for the Underwater Demolition Flotilla			
USS Blessman (APD-48) – Command ship for UDT Squadron ONE			
USS Laning (APD-55) – Command ship for UDT Squadron TWO			

More Than Scuttlebutt: The U.S. Navy Demolition Men in World War II, by Sue Ann Dunford and James Douglas O'Dell.
The Men from Fort Pierce: A Chronological Survey of the Underwater Demolition Teams of World War II, by Marvin Cooper.

CHAPTER 7

OSS MARITIME UNIT BOAT ACTIVITIES

This aspect of the Office of Strategic Services Maritime Unit (OSS MU) history relates to their "special boat" actions and activities, and provides a somewhat direct-capability linage to the modern-day NSW Special Boat Teams. One of the foremost missions involved clandestine ferrying, which was characterized in the context of operations being conducted in the "Amphibious phases of OSS intelligence and sabotage." Mission and tasks were defined as: "Men, munitions, supplies, and communications are secretly infiltrated into enemy areas over water, and communications and returning personnel being brought out. OSS intelligence or demolition operatives, liaison officers to guerrilla or resistance groups, or special missions from the Theater Commander may be transported. Airmen shot down over enemy-held territory are brought back. Specially equipped operatives may be landed to carry out beach reconnaissance on the character and gradient of beaches and depths of shallows of the off-shore coast; data of value in planning amphibious assaults. The parent craft, which may be a submarine, destroyer, or motor torpedo boat, penetrates to within landing distances of the enemy coast. The operatives transfer to small surface craft, surfboard, rubber boat, or kayak for the trip to and from the shore."

Photograph of Area D taken from the Potomac River.

The first OSS maritime training activities were accomplished at "Area D" with personnel from the Navy and Marine Corps and later Army and U.S. Coast Guard. Area D was located in a secluded region of the Potomac River south of Washington, DC near Doncaster, Maryland (somewhat across the river from the nearby Marine Corps base at Quantico, Virginia). During the Great Depression, 1939 through

Operators from "Area D" probably taken in the spring or early summer 1943. Only two men have been identified. Standing in the blue U.S. Navy uniform is GM1c John Spence, and kneeling directly in front of him (wearing tie) is U.S. Navy LT Jack Taylor. The boat in the background is the cabin-cruiser *Maribel*, one of two such craft acquired by OSS for training on the Potomac.

1941, Area D served as Civilian Conservation Corps Camp S-43. This training base presented obvious barriers, since it lacked surf and beach conditions comparable to those in the theaters of declared war. The OSS men also had to contend with the pollution of the Potomac River. The primary advantages were proximity to Washington, DC and good base security for training.

Some years ago, it took me quite a while, but I finally discovered and walked the grounds of Area D. There was nothing left to see except one small path to the Potomac River, and massive amounts of small trees and underbrush growth.

A small cabin cruiser was procured for use in nighttime exercises. The vessel, called *Maribel*, was intended to represent a submarine or surface vessel from which the maritime infiltrators would land by rubber boat or other small

OSS MU operator at Area D stands beside a wooden boat and outboard motor holding what appears to be an inflatable life preserver.

craft. Training was designed to accomplish clandestine entry by sea, to engage in sabotage, personally or through sub-agents, of cargoes, dock facilities, warehouses, and the like. Simple seamanship, elementary navigation, and small-boat handling; particularly foldboats (kayaks), inflatable rubber boats, and rafts were studied. OSS MU men also pioneered U.S. capabilities in maritime sabotage through formation of swimmer groups. These men were especially trained in the use of underwater equipment and techniques to conduct hydrographic reconnaissance and attack enemy shipping and port installations.

Maritime Unit in the Middle East

The need for theater-based Maritime Unit boat operations was first recognized at the Middle East Theater of Operations (METO), where the OSS Secret Intelligence Greek Desk was faced with the problem of ferrying agents to and from the Greek islands and mainland. The OSS had established a headquarters in Cairo, Egypt, where the majority of operations were being directed toward Greece. In late July 1943, Navy Lieutenant Jack Taylor, USNR, arrived as Chief of the Maritime Unit in the METO to establish the Maritime Unit's first overseas presence. He was able to get a clandestine caique (Greek fishing boat) ferrying service started in August, at a time when the Germans were in control of the entire Aegean Sea.

The majority of caiques subsequently employed in the METO were small wooden-hulled vessels with auxiliary sails; averaging from 10 to 40 tons and powered with gasoline engines. They were manned almost entirely by Greek crews. Because of their slow speed and lack of armament, caiques had no protection from air and surface patrols. Their primary protection involved masquerading under the Turkish flag, hugging the Turkish coast in daytime, and staying outside the gun range of the Nazis at night. Early achievements of the caique service from September to December 1943 were considerable. In addition to landing OSS Secret Intelligence (SI) agents in enemy territory, and delivering ammunition and supplies to advanced bases in the Greek islands, they also accomplished the evacuation of Samos (a Greek island in the eastern Aegean Sea), when the island was invaded by the Nazis.

From the day of his arrival, however, Lieutenant Taylor was handicapped because of his relatively low rank, and because three additional Maritime Unit officers and 13 Navy and Marine Corps enlisted personnel scheduled to leave Washington in early August didn't arrive until late October. Another difficulty involved getting caiques into and out of Alexandria harbor. Fees had to be paid to the Egyptian Government before they could load, unload, or secure berthing space. Moreover, the British controlled all sea operations out of Alexandria, thus, Lieutenant Taylor and Maritime Unit officers that followed him were forced to explain why the caiques were sailing, and this was an obvious risk to operational security.

A Greek caique like those used by OSS in the Aegean Sea.

In late November, Lieutenant Taylor, two other Maritime Unit officers, and seven of the enlisted men were transferred to Bari, Italy to establish a Maritime Unit capability there under METO cognizance. He was relieved in Cairo by Ensign Stephen Bailey early in December.

In January 1944, the Cairo Maritime Unit was comprised of seven officers and 21 enlisted men and civilians. Ensign Bailey was relieved by Lieutenant A.G. Atwater in late March. By the end of June 1944, the caique fleet totaled 24 vessels. They were organized into Northern, Central, and Southern Fleets. The Southern Fleet had the two largest caiques and sailed between Alexandria and Cyprus bases. The Central Fleet had 10 caiques and sailed between Cyprus and the Northern bases. The Northern Fleet operated from bases off the Turkish Coast with the smallest caiques, which were used almost entirely for forays into German occupied territory. A snapshot of of Maritime Unit Cairo's caiques fleet during the period January to June 1944 displayed their value. They completed more than 100 individual ferrying trips, moved approximately 1,000 tons of supplies, and transported more than 300 personnel at the request of various OSS branches. Cargoes included food, clothing, and considerable quantities of small arms and ammunition taken to designated areas. Caiques were also utilized in five special missions.

LT Jack Taylor seen with one of his Greek caique crews.

LT Jack Taylor aboard a caique, which flew the red Turkish flag.

At the Bari base, Lieutenant Taylor and his Maritime Unit men continued infiltrating agents for Secret Intelligence and Special Operations branches, and the Maritime Unit itself. The Bari mission included operations into and out of Yugoslavia, establishment of suitable pin-points in occupied territory, and carrying out special operations. (A "pin-point" was OSS jargon for an objective spot on a nautical chart.) Many Bari operations were conducted with caiques that carried agents to Evia, where they were met by Greek guerilla fighters called Andartes. (After Crete, Evia is the second-largest Greek island in area and population.) Entry points were established at Evia for agents and supplies, setting up codes and recognition signals, locating parachute drop zones, and making arrangements to bring out rescued Allied aviators. It also resulted in valuable intelligence on conditions inside occupied Greece and adjacent islands. Plans were made for Andartes to be stationed at pin-points in the sea ports of Kalamo,

Pili, and Limnoya to handle future caique cargoes and to guide and help disguise OSS agents.

By July 1944, German resistance was waning throughout the eastern Mediterranean and Aegean, and recommendations were made to divest the caique fleet once the Germans had evacuated. Navy Lieutenant Dennis J. Roberts, Chief of the Maritime Units in Washington, arrived in Cairo in August and agreed. Several caiques were returned to their owners, and a few were retained to distribute relief supplies to various Greek Islands. Some Cairo Maritime Unit personnel were transferred to the Maritime Unit in Bari, some to the United States for leave, and others directly to Ceylon, India to join the Maritime Unit working with the British South-East Asia Command (SEAC).

Maritime Unit in the European Theater

The most conspicuous role played by the Maritime Unit in the European Theater was the work of its individual officers in planning and conducting ferrying operations across the English Channel to occupied France. These were of necessity in close collaboration with the British. The Maritime Unit frequently helped prepare intelligence for joint OSS-British missions, where the British supplied Motor Torpedo Boats were used to transport OSS agents. Maritime Unit officers acted as official observers in charge of transferring landing parties from ship to shore.

LT Dennis Roberts, USNR.

In November 1943, Lieutenant Commander Raymond Guest, USNR arrived in London as head of Maritime Units in the European Theater of Operations (ETO). His first activity was to establish contact with the British Deputy Director of Operations Division (Irregular), Combined Operations. Also, with their Special Operations Executive that had for many months successfully carried out ferrying operations between England and various occupied countries. In December, Lieutenant Commander Guest endeavored to obtain two U.S. Navy Patrol, Torpedo (PT) boats for projected clandestine operations. It was intended that these craft would be under the Maritime Unit's operational control, but operated and maintained by U.S. Navy crews.

It wasn't until 23 March 1944 that the Navy provided PTs for OSS planning; however, they came under the command of U.S. Navy Commander John D. Bulkeley instead of the Maritime Unit. In March 1942 Bulkeley had aided General MacArthur's escape from Corregidor (for which he was later awarded the Medal of Honor). The Navy commissioned PT Boat Squadron 2(2), which had three boats, PT-71, PT-72, and PT-199, and it was the smallest U.S. Navy boat squadron ever commissioned. (Note: With thanks to retired Navy Master Chief Jim Gray, the (2) indicates that it was the second PT boat Squadron 2 established). It was based in Dartmouth, England and specifically organized for duty with OSS in the English Channel area. The squadron engaged in 20 special missions; landing personnel and supplies in enemy occupied territory, primarily along the Brittany coast of France. For D-Day operations at Normandy, France, the squadron was relocated to Portland, England,

OSS MU LCDR Raymond Guest, USNR.

PT-72, a 78-foot Higgins Motor Torpedo Boat, was assigned for special duty with the OSS in the English Channel area from May to October 1944.

and departed on 5 June 1944 for the invasion the following day. Each boat was armed with a 37mm cannon on the bow, twin .50-caliber machine guns port and starboard, and a 20mm cannon mounted aft. Torpedo tubes were removed for greater speed and range. The PT boats were painted a shade called "Mountbatten Pink" that made them almost invisible during dawn and dusk.

This from Jim Gray, Combatant Craft Association Historian:

On May 19, 1944, PT 71 got the squadron's first mission. Furious mission planning and coordination between the OSS and the British had to be accomplished; boat preparations and last-minute details had to be resolved. The mission: Delivery of an agent working for the SOE.

The agent showed up on the pier dressed as a French peasant and accompanied by a British naval officer, who would act as liaison between the boat crew and agent. After dusk, the PT quietly slipped out of Dartmouth and transited to the area of operations.

Later in the evening, the blacked-out PT idled into the insertion point off the coast of Normandy. The correct light signals were exchanged with the French Resistance forces ashore. The assigned crewmen and agent silently lowered the dory into the sea and rowed ashore. After a brief challenge and correct reply, the agent was with the resistance forces and the resistance forces also passed some 'mail' in a canvas sack to be taken back. The mail was intelligence gathered; including notes recording obstacles the Germans had planted along the shoreline.

Extraction was accomplished by dory to PT. At Dartmouth, PT-71 received a hero's welcome from the rest of the squadron. The first mission was a success and set the pace for future operations.

PT-199, a 78-foot Higgins boot operated by Boat Squadron 2(2). (Photo compliments of Jim Gray.)

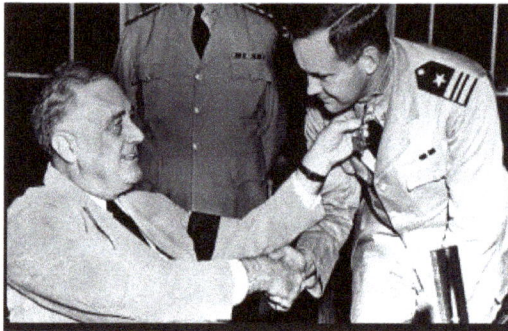
LT John D. Bulkeley, commander of PT Squadron 3 in the Pacific receiving the Medal of Honor.

Crew of PT-72 before departing England for the D-Day assault at Normandy.

A spectacular tactical mission projected for PT-72 was a plan to run the German North Sea blockade with arms and ammunition for the resistance movement in Denmark. It was expected that even if the boat succeeded in running the gauntlet of German ships, planes, mines, and shore batteries, the crew would be detained in Sweden for the duration of the war. The boat couldn't carry enough fuel for a round trip. PT-72 was to be crewed only with volunteers, outfitted with extra-large gas tanks, and loaded with seven tons of arms and ammunition. The objective was Skagen, Denmark, where they would unload to a waiting lugger (a small sailing vessel). The OSS was forced to cancel the mission, because the British were planning other operations in the area.

On another occasion, PT-72 was ordered to take five French partisans and several hundred pounds of explosives to France by transiting behind Jersey Island (a British island in the English Channel), to drop the men in the vicinity of Avranches, France. Their mission was to blow up a bridge, so the Germans couldn't escape the advancing American Army. PT-72 departed Dartmouth in the early afternoon, and was ordered to maintain radio silence. While approaching the French coast, a signal came from ashore telling them to abort. As it turned out, they would have had extreme difficulty infiltrating the French operatives through heavy German patrols.

In the European Theater, a conflict persisted between the Maritime Unit and other branches of OSS regarding the best means of infiltrating agents into enemy territory. The British and Maritime Unit believed that the best means to land agents was by sea, while others preferred infiltrating by parachute. This was a matter of high-command strategy, and out of the Maritime Unit's control. Thus, in the absence of requests from other OSS branches, the Maritime Unit tended to work more closely with British, and frequently provided its PT's for the infiltration of

British-trained agents. While operating in the ETO, the Maritime Unit PTs suffered no casualties, nor were any boats or crew members lost.

Maritime Unit in the South East Asian Command

In August 1943, the Allies created the combined South East Asian Command. The following December, British Admiral Lord Louis Mountbatten was appointed Supreme Allied Commander. Detachment 404 was formed to help coordinate OSS and British Special Operations Executive intelligence collection and operations. The Arakan Field Unit of Detachment 404 was a 175-man OSS element compromised of Secret Intelligence, Operational Group, and Maritime Unit personnel. It was employed along the Burma coast to assist the XV (15th) Indian Corps of the British XIV (14th) Army. In February 1945, Detachment 101 assumed operational control of the Arkan Field Unit.

The Operational Group and Maritime Unit personnel jointly conducted reconnaissance missions along the Arakan coast and up its numerous inlets and rivers. The Maritime Unit used Patrol Torpedo boats acquired from the U.S. Army to conduct operations in Burma. With a swimmer group attached, the the Maritime Unit was organized to carry out sabotage against enemy shipping and to conduct stealthy forays into enemy-held beaches and harbors. The Maritime Unit's largest overall contribution involved the conduct of clandestine ferrying operations of men and supplies. While helping liberate Rangoon, Arkan Field Unit elements collected considerable intelligence. These accomplishments in a highly complex political environment demonstrated how the OSS persevered and adapted to accomplish all missions.

US Coast Guard LTjg John Booth, commander of Swimmer Unit #1 (with beard), and Chief Petty Officer James Eubanks, off the coast of Burma after Operation CLEVELAND 26-27 January 1945. Their mission objective was reconnaissance of two beaches at Sagu Island, Burma.

Rope nets were used by OSS swimmers to climb back aboard support boats.

SWIMMING GROUP #2. L. to R. Cox
Reeves, C.Ph/M Becker, SpX 3/c
Abbott, SpX 3/c Priano, Sgt.
Halbarrow, Lt.Booth, Lt.Babb,
MoMM 1/c MacDonald, Cox Thorigal,
Sgt.Rief, Lt.Cdr.Lee, MoMM 1/c
Carroll, Cox Fulton, Cpl.Kniest,
W/O Medlicott, Sgt.Morrissey,
Cpl. Smith, Ch B/M Eubank.

CREW P-564. L.to R. M/Sgt.Williams,
Cpl.Jones, S/Sgt.Linville, T5 Viola,
Sgt. Floyd, T/Sgt.Johnson, Lt.Swayza
Lt.Mess, C.O., WOJG. Flynn, Sgt.
Brunaugh, T/Sgt.Woodland, Cpl.
Philpott.

British LCA were used extensively in WWII to ferry troops from transport ships to attack enemy-held shores.

PT Boat 564 was used by OSS MU personnel along the Arakan coast. The boat's torpedo tubes were removed.

CHAPTER 8

KOREA TO VIETNAM

There were no significant boat developments for the UDTs during the 1950's and into the early 1960's. Korea boat operations were closely akin to those of World War II, where the UDTs would embark host ships and use Landing Craft Personnel, Large (LCPL) and inflatable boats to complete missions ashore. After Korea, the APDs were replaced by more modern amphibious ships, and there was a period of prolonged peace before Vietnam. The U.S. Navy's Mark 4 steel LCPLs were introduced into the UDTs in the mid-1950s, and later supplemented by the newer Mark 11 LCPLs, which were made out of fiberglass. The UDTs continued to operate with the Amphibious Ready Groups in the Western Pacific, Atlantic, and Mediterranean, and continued to utilize their own boats, when embarked aboard various amphibious ships.

A UDT-11 LCPL manuevering to "snare" a UDT man out of the water. The Snare Man is seen in the bow wake of the boat.

SEAL and Special Boat Operations – Vietnam

When the SEAL Teams were established in January 1962, they had no boats in their active inventory. Their first use of boats came with deployment of training and advisory teams to Vietnam as early as February 1962. During the late 1950s and early 1960s, UDT and later SEAL personnel were involved with training and advising boat operations under the auspices of the CIA at locations in Miami, the Florida Keys, and in Louisiana. These were highly classified and compartmented programs, thus, not much was written or has yet been released about UDT-SEAL operator involvement. Boats used for these activities were procured commercially by the CIA.

SEAL Team ONE's Commanding Officer Lieutenant David Del Giudice and another SEAL Team ONE officer, Jon Stockholm, were sent to South Vietnam on 10 January 1962 – only nine days after the command was established. They were tasked to survey the support that SEALs might provide to the

Vietnamese and other U.S. advisory personnel. As a direct result, future involvement for SEALs in Vietnam was anticipated.

Indeed, the first SEALs were deployed from SEAL Team ONE in late February 1962, and arrived in Vietnam on 10 March. They were Chief Petty Officer Robert "Sully" Sullivan and Hospital Corpsman Second Class Charles "Doc" Raymond. They were assigned to the CIA, but with little equipment or direction on what to do except that they would begin a six-month assignment instructing the Vietnamese in clandestine maritime operations.

In April 1962, another detachment quickly followed with men from SEAL Teams ONE and TWO. They were a nine-man detachment designated Mobile Training Team 10-62. They were sent to Da Nang to set up

MTT 10-62 was the first formalized SEAL training and advisory detachment sent to Vietnam. Standing (l-r): SF1 Robert F. Fisher, FTG2 Carl D. Marriott, SN Robert D. Paul, SK2 William E. Burbank. Kneeling: SM2 David A. Wilson, DM2 Alwyn J. Smith, Jr., DM1 Leonard A. Waugh, EN2 Theodore E. George. This photograph was taken by BM1 Jack R. Perkins. Burbank and Waugh were from SEAL Team TWO. The other seven men were from SEAL Team ONE.

MOBILE TRAINING TEAM 10-62

TRAINING FOR THE BIET HAI, JUNK FORCE COMMANDO PLATOONS

Told by MTT 10-62 member SK2 William "Billy" Burbank of SEAL Team TWO

A mission had been assigned the new [SEAL] team at a place called Vietnam, and they [SEAL Team TWO] had picked two poor souls to go, Bill Burbank, SK1, and Lenny Waugh, DM1. (SK1 is Storekeeper First Class; DM1 is Draftsman First Class.)

They told us to stand by, but tell nobody where we were going, and they would brief us on the West Coast. We left for San Diego 28 March 1962, and arrived at USNAB, Coronado and stayed there until 17 April. We were trained in language, VC cadre, political, hand-to-hand, and small boats. We arrived in Saigon 20 April 1962.

When we got to Saigon, nobody knew what we were doing there. Our orders read from Secretary of the Navy. We were in civilian clothes, so we checked into a hotel. About two days later, a guy from the plumbers [slang for Central Intelligence Agency], came and took us to a safe house (a clandestine place of work).

So, here we sat, like a bunch of dummies, with no weapons, and no idea what the hell we are supposed to do. Then, an agent met us at the compound, and informed us that we were going to fly to a place called Da Nang up north near the bad guys and train

DM1 Leonard A. Waugh (l) and SK1 William Burbank in Da Nang, 1962.

a bunch of sailors on how to be a frogman. [The CIA] issued us one carbine and eight rounds [of ammunition], to be returned if we didn't use them. No equipment, and away we go. When we arrived at what they called a navy base, it was only a small strip of land with about six buildings and a bunch of sunken ships.

We were introduced to about 50 sailors called the junk force. None could swim, and they would not even put their head underwater. So, we decided we would make them scouts. Who was to say no; we were the bosses. We didn't work for anybody but the Secretary of the Navy,

91

Bill Burbank in his "requisitioned" jeep.

Bill Burbank training Junk Force Commandos.

A Biet Hai Junk Force Commando Platoon trained by SEALs at Da Nang, Vietnam.

and he didn't tell us what to do, so we started up the program. We built an obstacle course out of bamboo, then a small firing range. But we had no weapons. We trained them for 12 weeks and lost only two—on a helo jump—just plain drowned. One got shot by mistake, but he lived. Two weeks before they graduated, we had a boat race around a point at night—all six of their boats were at the finish line.

On the second week, we ran into an Special Forces guy. He said if we trained him in SCUBA, he would let us in his weapons locker (a hut) for a half-hour. So, we really loaded up, and had plenty weapons after that. Old Fisher [Petty Officer Robert Fisher from SEAL Team ONE] took back enough weapons to train the next group coming over. Anyway, after they graduated, we took them on a few missions north. We stayed in rubber boats, and they did a great job.

The president [of South Vietnam, Ngo Dinh Diem] liked the troops so well, he took about a dozen for his personal guard, and the rest were sent North on a mission where all were killed. They were used as soldiers, not what they were trained for. Our troops tattooed the word "Sat Cong" on their chest, which means "Death to Communism." So, when they got caught, it was certain death. The program called Mobile Training Team-10 was designed to include: surface swimming, rubber boat handling, hand-to-hand combat, silent kill, map reading, compass work, reconnaissance, some firearms training, and PT. We also did a little training with the Montagnards. Good troops. (Montagnards were fierce Vietnamese tribesmen that fought alongside Americans.)

training for the Biet Hai, which were Junk Force Commando Platoons. They conducted UDT frogman-style training for the Vietnamese. Follow-on SEAL Mobile Training Teams continued with individual SEALs or SEAL detachments training and advising for the duration of the Vietnam War.

SEAL Direct Action Platoons

In February 1966 the first direct action platoon from SEAL Team ONE deployed to the delta region of South Vietnam. SEAL Team TWO deployed its first direct action platoon in January 1967; also, in the Delta or IV (4) Corps military designated area. These early platoons came with boat support from Mobile Support Team TWO, which was comprised of specially trained men from Boat Support Unit ONE in Coronado. (Mobile Support Team ONE was supporting operations in Da Nang.) For special boats, intended or unintended, Vietnam was a pivotal period, where boats became mission-essential to the waterbourne operational capability of the SEAL Teams.

In the context of today's special operations, the United States Department of Defense defines direct action as: "Short-duration strikes and other small-scale offensive actions conducted as a special operation in hostile, denied, or politically sensitive environments, and which employ specialized military capabilities to seize, destroy, capture, exploit, recover, or damage designated targets. Direct action differs from conventional offensive actions in the level of physical and political risk, operational techniques, and the degree of discriminate and precise use of force to achieve specific objectives." (Joint Chiefs of Staff PUB 1-02)

Operation Plan 37

A lesser known part of the Naval Special Warfare special boat story involves operations conducted in support of the CIA and later the Military Assistance Command, Vietnam—Studies and Observation Group (MACV-SOG). In 1958, the South Vietnamese government created a secret Coastal Security Service to carry out missions against North Vietnam. Coastal Security Service operations were supported and financed by the CIA starting in 1961 with primary objectives of information-gathering and reconnaissance on North Vietnam coastal areas. Subsequently, harassment and short-term sabotage raids were conducted from indigenous motorized junks.

OP-37's PTF "Nasty" boats were operated out of Da Nang along with the operational headquarters, boat docks, and maintenance facilities. (PTF photos compliments of Jim Gray)

In 1962, it was decided to escalate covert maritime operations and activities with assigned U.S. Naval support and equipment. High-speed, Patrol Torpedo Boats of the Norwegian Navy's Nasty Class were procured and arrived in South Vietnam the following year. To assist the CIA in training South Vietnamese Sea Commandos, SEAL training detachments were detailed to the CIA. Boat Support Unit ONE in Coronado provided personnel and logistics to support boat operations through establishment of Mobile Support Team ONE. During this period, the patrol boats were navigated north by Norwegian and German mercenaries.

When President Kennedy directed Operation SWITCHBACK, responsibilities for these covert operations were transferred from the CIA to the Pentagon. MACV-SOG was established in 1964 to assume the CIA's role of assisting, advising, and supporting the conduct of highly classified sabotage, psychological, and special operations in North and South Vietnam, Laos, and Cambodia. MACV-SOG was a joint service unconventional-warfare task force responsible for planning and executing covert, deniable, special activities and operations throughout the Southeast Asian Theater. "Studies and Observation Group" was, of course, a cover name. Special Operations Group operations were designed to: "Execute an intensified program of harassment, diversion, political pressure, capture of prisoners, physical destruction, acquisition of intelligence, generation of propaganda, and diversion of resources against...North Vietnam."

Covert Maritime Operations was a core MACV-SOG mission inherited from the CIA. Operational and planning responsibilities were assigned to the Maritime Operations Group (OP-37). In January 1964, the Naval Advisory Detachment was established in Da Nang as a cover name for OP-37. In 1965, a small group, called the Maritime Studies Branch (OP-31) was established to function as a staff element. The Maritime Operations Group was the action arm for covert operations against the north. Maritime Operations included over-the-beach operations, such as small-scale demolition operations and capture of North Vietnamese Army officials. Others included mortar bombardment of shore targets from fast boats, interdiction of North Vietnamese Army craft moving supplies south by sea, delivery of Psychological Warfare materials, capture of North Vietnam citizens—primarily fisherman (for information gathering), insertion of pseudo-agents into the north from the sea, and collection of coastal intelligence.

The chief of the Naval Advisory Detachment was always a Navy 0-5 commander. The first four commanders, to their detriment, were Navy Surface Warfare officers with little knowledge about what they were doing and with no experience at all in Unconventional Warfare or maritime special operations. This changed on 23 April 1965 when UDT Commander Robert "Bob" Fay took over. Bob Fay had commanded UDT-4 at Little Creek during the Korean War period. That experience was a key to his selection. Unfortunately, he was killed six months later on 28 October, when his jeep was hit by a Viet Cong mortar shell. He was the first Naval Special Warfare operator to be killed in action in Vietnam;

UDT CDR Robert J. Fay was Chief of the NAD of the Military Assistance Command, Vietnam—Studies and Observation Group.

although not the first to die on an actual combat mission. That occurred on 19 August 1966, when RM2 Billy Machen of SEAL Team ONE became Naval Special Warfare's first combat fatality.

Commander Fay was replaced for a brief period by his deputy, Commander William Hawkins, a reserve Surface Warfare officer, and later by Surface Warfare Commander Willard Olson. Again, both had no experience in small-boat operations or Unconventional Warfare. On the bright side was Olson's deputy, Commander Robert "Bob" Terry, who had been task to replace him. Terry had been Commander, UDT-2 in Little Creek during the establishment of SEAL Team TWO. He was later replaced by SEAL Commander Norm Olson, who was recognized as being dynamically more effective than all others in organizing the Maritime Operations operational and training programs.

The Naval Advisory Detachment's operations and training staff planned and executed all of the covert maritime operations against North Vietnam. This staff section was comprised of personnel from SEAL Team ONE, U.S. Marine Corps Force Reconnaissance, and Boat Support Unit ONE/Mobile Support Team ONE. They trained Vietnamese crews in tactics, gunnery, navigation, and operation of fast patrol boats. OP-37 boat assets included seven Nasty Class PFTs, three 50-foot Swift boats, one LCM-6 (Landing Craft, Medium or "Mike" boat), two Vietnamese wooden fishing junks, and one skimmer boat.

RM2 Billy Machen of SEAL Team ONE became the first NSW combat fatality in Augst 1966.

During most of their service in Vietnam, the PFTs operated as the primary naval weapons platform of OP-37. The "Nasties," procured from Norway by the U.S. Navy, were actually leased to the Republic of Vietnam navy and crewed "officially" by South Vietnamese sailors, when operating north of the 17th parallel— the so called demilitarized zone. The Norwegian-made vessel was 80-feet long with a 24-foot beam and a six-foot draft. It was powered by two 3,100 horse power (HP) diesel engines, and capable of doing 45 knots. An extensive and highly classified hull and Napier-Deltic diesel engine overhaul facility was funded by the U.S. Navy in Subic Bay, Philippines.

CDR (SEAL) Norman H. Olson

OP-37 operated with three Swift boats like this one.

Filipino engineers were sent to Norway for training in the maintenance and upkeep of these unique engines.

Multiple covert maritime operations were conducted weekly in the Gulf of Tonkin, reaching as far north as Hainan Island. The Patrol Torpedo Boats conducted over a thousand raids in a secret and deadly war with North Vietnamese forces in and above the demilitarized zone during the period April 1964 to January 1972. Officially, no American personnel accompanied the Patrol Torpedo Boat missions, and this has never been confirmed or denied.

These operations had the highest level of scrutiny and oversight by the U.S. Navy and the Joint Chiefs of Staff throughout the Vietnam conflict. Accordingly, this significant contribution to Naval Special Warfare's legacy should be highly regarded. The OP-37 MACV-SOG story is important, because it established a foundation for many future Naval Special Warfare operations, especially the future direction of covert actions and activities involving SEALs and special boats.

CHAPTER 9

VIETNAM FAMILY OF BOATS

Amphibious Ready Groups deployed to Vietnam usually consisted of three ship types: Landing Ship, Dock (LSD), Landing Platform, Dock (LPD), and Landing Ship, Tank (LST). The UDTs embarked with the Amphibious Ready Groups at various times during the war. They also operated aboard the submarines *USS Perch* (APSS-313), *USS Tunny* (APSS-282), and *USS Grayback* (LPSS-574). These host ships and submarines would transport the UDTs to points off prospective landing beaches. Once on station, the UDT men would use LCPLs and inflatable boats to silently approach the shore. The men would swim or row inflatable boats through the surf and carry out vital reconnaissance, raids, or other special operations and activities.

Vietnam Perspective

South Vietnam was divided into four Military Corps areas: I Corps (said as "eye" Corps) was in the north, II Corps was the central highlands, III Corps was the area around the capital city of Saigon, and IV Corps ("The Delta") was in the south. SEAL operations were largely accomplished in the Delta region, which extended from the Mekong River Delta to the tip of the Ca Mau Peninsula. The Delta was a major population and food center, but there were no large parcels of land where a big military installation could be constructed without dislocating large numbers of people. Also, numerous rivers, streams, and canals crisscrossed the Delta, which greatly restricted ground movement. American planners ruminated extensively about how they could find a way to improve mobility options.

In November 1963, less than one year after the SEAL Teams were established, Naval Operations Support Groups ATLANTIC and PACIFIC (NAVOPSUPPGRULANT and PAC) were established as components within the Navy's Amphibious Force. They became the parent staffs to the UDT and SEAL Teams, Beach Jumper Units, and Boat Support Units. NAVOPSUPPGRUPAC had administrative responsibility for all UDT, SEAL, Boat Support Unit, and Beach Jumper Unit personnel assigned to Vietnam. (In 1967 they were redesignated Naval Special Warfare Group, ATLANTIC and PACIFIC.) Naval Special Warfare Group, Vietnam

(NAVSPECWARV) was established in 1968 as a staff component of the U.S. Naval Forces, Vietnam staff in Saigon. This staff provided planning and logistic support to all Naval Special Warfare (NSW) personnel deployed to South Vietnam. NAVSPECWARV was the first and only NSW Group to be established and disestablished overseas.

The Beach Jumper Units had a classified mission involving tactical cover and deception. As a rule, they generally operated in direct support of the Fleet Commanders. Why they were assigned to NSW during the Vietnam period is not exactly clear. Likely it was because they had the potential to accomplish psychological operations, which was something the Army usually accomplished. A SEAL senior officer once observed that the biggest benefit NSW got from the Beach Jumper Units was that they taught us (SEALs) how to write good correspondence and provided us with first-hand knowledge about planning, programming, and budgeting within the Navy system. Beach Jumper Units were first established during World War II. A book entitled *Seaborne Deception: The History of the U.S. Navy Beach Jumpers* by John B. Dwyer provides a definitive accounting.

The COMNAVSPECWARGRUPAC's first commander was Navy Captain Phil Bucklew, who had been in the Amphibious Scouts and Raiders during World War II. He was chosen for this job, because there were no UDT Captains (0-6) to be assigned. In early 1964, Captain Bucklew and eight other Navy officers (including Lieutenant David Del Giudice, the first commanding officer of SEAL Team ONE.) formed the

CAPT Phil H. Bucklew, USN.

Vietnam Delta Infiltration Study Group. This group was tasked by Admiral Harry D. Felt, Commander-in-Chief, U.S. Pacific Command (CINCPAC) to conduct a comprehensive study concerning the infiltration of war supplies by North Vietnam into the south. Supplies were coming into South Vietnam from the sea at the major rivers or along smaller rivers and tributaries along the borders. The river systems in the Mekong Delta region were dominated by the North Vietnamese Army and Viet Cong troops moving men, munitions, and other war supplies freely in the region. In reflecting upon the group's tasking, Captain Bucklew recalled Admiral Felt's direction: "In a nutshell, I want to know why all I get from Vietnam are glowing reports about our accomplishments, and meanwhile we're getting the hell kicked out of us. That's your job."

SEAL LT David Del Guiduice.

The findings of the group were significant and published in what became known simply as *The Bucklew Report*. This report had 15 conclusions, comments, and recommendations, which ultimately determined that coastal and river infiltrations of supplies from the north was substantial, and that they needed to be stopped if communist forces in Vietnam were to be defeated. *The Bucklew Report* also concluded that the South Vietnamese Navy didn't possess the capability to single-handedly stop the infiltration problem. The only way to counter enemy infiltration was for the U.S. to advise and assist the Vietnamese navy by establishing a riverine warfare capability. *The Bucklew Report* provided a major blueprint for future advise and assist operations in South Vietnam.

As I do at every opportunity, I dispel any notion that Captain Bucklew is "The Father of NSW." He was not. This honor goes to a handful of UDT and SEAL officers and not any one individually. This title was inaccurately bestowed upon Captain Bucklew during a ceremony dedicating the Basic Underwater Demolition/SEAL (BUD/S) training center in his honor. Captain Bucklew himself never embraced this title, which is evident in his oral history at the U.S. Naval Institute. When Captain Bucklew left command of NAVSPECWARGRUPAC, he was transferred to the Pentagon, where he and others were largely responsible for staffing that led to establishment of the NSW UDT-SEAL officer career program and designator or Naval Officer Billet Code: 1130 for SEAL unrestricted line officers and 1135 for reserve SEAL officers. Captain Bucklew was clearly a principal in making it happen.

SEAL Direct Action Platoons

From the earliest days of their establishment, the SEAL Teams began sending personnel to advise and assist Vietnam navy personnel; first in support of the CIA at Da Nang and later at other locations. SEAL Team ONE began sending direct action platoons to Vietnam in January 1966, and two things became apparent very early on: SEAL operators needed boats with speed, shallow draft, firepower, and armor; and, their boats needed to be driven by Sailors, who were familiar with the kind of tactics that were being developed. Initially, the SEALs had to make do with a scrounged collection of small boats. This resulted in Project ZULU.

A SEAL Team ONE Direct Action Platoon.

Project ZULU

Vietnam special boat veteran Bob Stoner described Project ZULU:

Volunteers from Boat Support Unit ONE trained with members of SEAL Team ONE for six months prior to deployment to Vietnam. The experiment was the support of UDT and SEAL operators under wartime conditions. They began a six-month trial (March to August 1967) with a modified LCM-6, a modified Mark IV LCPL, a 14-foot Boston Whaler (with silenced outboard), and an Inflatable Boat, Small. The LCPL and LCM-6 (dubbed "Mighty Mo"), were modified to accommodate numerous gun positions, and had armor added to protect vulnerable spaces. The heavily modified LCPLs and LCMs were subsequently based at Can Tho, My Tho, and later Nah Be. It was in the swamps of the river deltas of Southeast Asia that the SEALs, UDTs, and Boat Support Unit ONE/Mobile Support Tean ONE Sailors learned the tradecraft of Unconventional Warfare. The success of Project ZULU saw the Mobile Support Team detachments add another Heavy SEAL Support Craft/LCM-6 and three more LCPL's to their inventory to support UDT and SEAL operations along the Bassac, Mekong, and Saigon Rivers.

When SEAL Platoons and Boat Support Unit Detachments began deploying together, Project ZULU was transitioned as Mobile Support Team TWO to provide in-country support to SEALs. From mid-1968 until the end of 1971 at least six, sometimes seven, Mobile Support Team detachments were in-country to support UDT and SEAL operations. The last Mobile Support Team detachments were withdrawn from Vietnam along with SEAL Team ONE's MIKE Platoon on 7 December 1971.

Skimmers

During 1967 and 1968 the Mobile Support Team TWO detachment at Nah Be employed modified 14-foot Boston Whalers and 17-foot Power Cat boats for both day and night operations. Mobile Support Team boat crews frequently intercepted and checked out sampans (Vietnamese watercraft) for supplies being smuggled. These boats were also called skimmers. They had good speed, but limited endurance, no armor, and virtually no armament other than that carried by the crew and passengers. The boats utilized 35-hp gasoline engines and could attain a speed of 28+ knots.

17-foot Power Cat, called a "skimmer."

Mark IV Landing Craft, Personnel, Large (LCPL)

The 36-foot Mark IV LCPL had a steel hull with a 10.7 foot beam and a draft of 3 feet. It was powered by a 225 hp diesel engine driven by one shaft. The boat had a design range of 140 nautical miles at a speed of 19 knots fully loaded. Four Mark IV LCPLs were converted for SEAL support in South Vietnam.

It was the workhorse ship-to-shore craft used by the UDTs from the post-Korean War period through the Vietnam period. The UDTs had these boats in their active inventory and operated and

SEALs aboard modified LCPL in the waters of South Vietnam. Note the gun-tub in the bow.

maintained them using frogman labor. I remember seeing boats in the back yard of the old UDT compound at Little Creek sitting in cradles, while being stripped of paint and rust accumulated while sitting on the deck of an amphibious ship during a cruise to the Mediterranean or Caribbean. Using hand-held electric grinders, the men would strip the boats down to bare metal in spots and repaint the affected areas with red lead undercoating and haze gray paint to make it look new again (except for the multiple dents). They also performed all operator-level engine maintenance.

PBR Mark 1 inserting SEALs in Vietnam.

SEAL Team Attack Boat

When the SEALs were established in January 1962, there was no experience surrounding Jungle Warfare or Riverine Warfare operations. For contingency operations in Cuba and Vietnam, SEAL Team TWO accomplished some experimentation with four boats, which they modified extensively. Part of the concept included transporting these boats by air into denied areas. The boat was called SEAL Team Attack Boat or STAB by the men. In some publications, it's also been called the SEAL Tactical Assault Boat.

The STAB capability was the brainchild of SEAL Lieutenant Jack Macione at SEAL Team TWO. When they were first established, SEALs had no dedicated boats in their inventory, thus, operational concepts forced them to rely on others. Based on Lieutenant Macione's design—and a bit of trial and error—the four STABs evolved. They were modified Power Cat® Model 23T boats, with an overall length of 21 feet and a draft of 31 inches with a full load. Armament included seven hull pintle (gun-mount) positions, which would accept .50 caliber machine guns and Mark 18 Honeywell® Grenade Launchers or M-60 machine guns. Operational experience demonstrated that only the swing mounts and center mounts were suitable for the 50 caliber machine guns. One-quarter inch armor plating was installed along each side of the cockpit area and on each side of the coxswain's seat. The STAB was adapted for use in Vietnam. During its development, several attempts were made to transport the boat by helicopter, which resulted in some painful lessons. Testing resulted in an unintended drop. The boat hit the ground in a parking lot that, according to Bob Stoner: "Killed a car when it hit." No additional air-delivery experimentation was attempted after that incident.

SEAL Team Attack Boats underway in South Vietnam. (Photo compliments of Jim Gray)

Various views of the STAB seen at SEAL Team TWO's compound at NAB, Little Creek, Virginia.

A Navy CH-46 helicopters transporting a STAB.

The STABs were deployed to Vietnam with the first SEAL Team TWO direct-action platoon in January 1967. During this period, the boats were operated and maintained by SEAL operators, however, in late March; Mobile Support Team TWO personnel (from Boat Support Unit ONE) relieved the SEALs of these duties. Thereafter, Mobile Support Team TWO crews manned all SEAL support boats in-country, leaving the SEALs to focus on information gathering and direct-action operations against Viet Cong and North Vietnamese forces. This organizational and doctrinal relationship remains steadfast between Special Boat Team and SEAL Team operators today. When the first Mobile Support Team detachments arrived from Coronado, they brought six spare 115 hp Mercury outboards and two General Electric® Mini-Guns (7.62mm electric-powered, rotary barrel, machine guns). The outboards were for the STABs and the two mini-guns were installed on an LCM-6 and an LCPL.

SEAL Support Craft

By mid-1968 it became obvious that the Boston Whalers and Power Cat STABs were becoming unsuitable owing to extreme use. The LCPLs and LCM-6/HSSCs had good firepower, but they were slow and difficult to maneuver in confined waterways. Back in Washington, budgets for the UDT and SEAL Teams had been substantially increased and, literally, for the first time, research and development dollars were being made available to solve weapons and boat problems associated with SEALs in Vietnam. The Naval Ships Systems Command developed design specifications for new, purpose-built boats for SEAL operations. These boats would become known as the Light SEAL Support Craft (LSSC) and Medium SEAL Support Craft (MSSC), and they would become the workhorses of the Mobile Support Teams and SEALs for the duration of the war effort. The LSSC and MSSC were acquired as "quick-reaction" development programs, since the Mobile Support Teams and SEALs needed replacement boats as quickly as possible.

I was the Research, Development, Test and Evaluation Officer at the Naval Operations Support Group, Atlantic staff in 1968, when these boats were being designed and built. It was my responsibility to monitor this development from a UDT-SEAL operator's perspective. The SEAL officer almost individually responsible for getting the LSSC and the MSSC through the Navy's bureaucracy was SEAL Lieutenant Commander (later Captain) Dan Hendrickson. From his desk in Washington, I and others watched as he masterly wooed the Naval Ship Systems Command program managers, and got the boats through the system in little over a year. Of course, it always helps when you come with money, and in this instance NSW got the money from the essential resource sponsors in the Pentagon.

Light SEAL Support Craft

The Light SEAL Support Craft (LSSC) was a squad-sized boat with water-jet propulsion. Grafton Boat Works in Alton, Illinois built 16 LSSC's in 1968, and 15 were deployed to Vietnam. One was retained at Coronado for training. The boat was 24 feet long, 9.5 feet wide, and had a draft of 1.5 feet. It was

powered by two Ford 427 V-8 gasoline engines; generating 350 horsepower and driving two Jacuzzi™ water pumps for propulsion. The engines were exhausted underwater to reduce

A fully loaded LSSC is seen here from a bow-on aspect. The radar dome seen behind the boat coxswain was later removed from all LSSCs for tactical and safety reasons.

A SEAL squad aboard a LSSC in Vietnam.

The LSSC starboard mounted M-60 machine gun firing positions.

noise; allowing the boats to furtively enter some very shallow-water areas. The LSSC was designed to have three crewmen and carry a squad of SEALs. The boat had mounts for two 7.62 caliber machine guns and one .50 caliber machine gun. My platoon used this boat extensively when we got to Nah Be, South Vietnam in the summer of 1970.

The LSSC suffered several persistent complaints: The Jacuzzi® pumps clogged frequently in the dirty waters of the delta. Replacement parts were difficult obtain and they were often substandard, causing additional breakdowns. By 1970, the LSSCs radars were removed to increase interior room, and to provide additional protection from shrapnel if they were hit by enemy fire.

SEAL Team TWO 7th Platoon in Da Nang, Vietnam, November 1970: Kneeling (l-r): LT Tom Hawkins, IC1 Ed McQueen, and BM1 James "Buck" Owens (MST); Standing: EM2 Guntis J. Jaunzems, ETN2 Carl T. Zellers, BM1 James F. Finley, Vietnamese SEAL, SFP2 Joseph M. Silva, GMGC Mike Spencer, LTJG Bob Reive, SFP2 Frederick J. Keener, and HM1 Charles P. O'Bryan; Top: EM3 Lester Oakman (MST), GMG2 Dennis H. Johnson, BM2 Michael L. Naus, and QM3 William K. Day.

The LSSC is seen with the bow abutting the shoreline for a SEAL insertion.

LT Tom Hawkins (far left), with his SEAL squad in Vietnam aboard an LSSC.

NAVAL SPECIAL FORCES

NAH BE, SOUTH VIETNAM
RUNG SAT SPECIAL ZONE

(June 1970 - Dec 1970)

7th Platoon, SEAL Team TWO

LT Thomas. L. Hawkins
(Commander Task Element 116.0.1.3)
LTJG Robert M. Reive, Assistant CTE
GMGC Mike Spencer, Platoon CPO
HM1 Charles P. O'Bryan, Platoon LPO
IC1 Edward J. McQueen
BM1 William A. McCarthy
BM1 James F. Finley
ETN2 Carl T. Zellers
SFP2 Joseph M. Silva
BM2 Michael L. Naus
SFP2 Frederick J. Keener
GMG2 Dennis H. Johnson
EM2 Guntis J. Jaunzems
QM3 William K. Day

Mobile Support Team TWO Detachment DELTA*

LTjg James Marsh
(Commander Task Element 116.9.6.1)
BMC Ready
BM1 James Owen, POIC
BM1 Flowers
GM Harry Reich
Chuck Bauer
ET Richard Fowler
EN2 Doug Devoss
EN2 Sherman Olsen
EM3 Terry Fletcher
IC2 Thomas Powell
RM2 Edward Kenny
GMG2 Billie Stewart
GM3 Chuck Smales
EM3 Lester Oakman

* Regret any omissions. Accuracy not determined.

The Mobile Support Team TWO officer that supported our platoon was Lieutenant Junior Grade Jim Marsh. The Sailors that primarily operated our boats were BM1 James "Buck" Owens and EM3 Lester Oakman. Enough can never be said about NSW's Mobie Support Team men—they were the best. These men never knew the word quit, and clearly set the standard for establishment of the future Special Warfare Combatant-Craft Crewman (SWCC) program in NSW.

LSSC and Tactical-Air Mobility

In 1968, a newly established Naval Special Warfare Group, Vietnam staff authorized and tasked Mobile Support Team TWO to assess the concept of a helicopter transporting the LSSC to extend its tactical range. The concept of operation was inspired by SEAL Team TWO's failed attempt to use of helicopters to lift the STAB. These tests also failed because the transport methodology used a single-point lifting sling caused the boat to swing out of control when airborne.

The LSSC being lifted by a U.S. Army CH-47 helicopter during testing in Vietnam.

In Vietnam, the LSSC was mated with a U.S. Army heavy-lift CH-47 Chinook helicopter. The first two attempts to fly the boat were successful, and lift and transport procedures were refined. The concept got the attention of Admiral Elmo Zumwalt, Commander of all Naval Forces in Vietnam. The admiral apparently referred to them as "Strike Assault Operations." Unfortunately, during a third attempt at a higher speed and altitude, the slings snapped, and the LSSC fell 3,000 thousand feet into a rice paddy, with the obvious result. Tactical aircraft were called in to destroy the remains. The operational concept was clearly validated, however, the technical issues involved at that time could not be overcome, and no further testing was attempted.

Strike Assault Boat

A boat similar to the LSSC was also built by the Grafton Boatworks in 1969 for use in Vietnam. The Navy fielded this boat as Strike Assault Boat with the acronym STAB, creating confusion with the SEAL Team Attack Boat previously developed at SEAL Team TWO. The boat is the visual identical twin of the LSSC; except that it was two-feet longer and had MerCruiser stern drives instead of water jets. The boat used two Chevrolet 427 V-8 gasoline engines, generating 325 horsepower. Grafton built 22 STABs, and 20 were deployed to

Strike Assault Boat underway.

Strike Assault Boat Squadron TWENTY (STABRON 20) in Vietnam to support river and canal operations. The boats were used as waterborne guard posts and to conduct patrol and interdiction operations. All of the Grafton STABs were returned to the U.S. after Vietnam. Because it looked almost exactly like the LSSC and had the same acronym as the SEAL Team Attack Boat (STAB) developed at SEAL Team TWO, confusion historically persisted regarding this boat and its roles and missions.

Medium SEAL Support Craft

The Medium SEAL Support Craft (MSSC) was a platoon-sized boat with water-jet propulsion and an exceedingly small draft that could get into very shallow water regions. This boat was developed in a parallel path with the LSSC. It, too, was a quick-reaction design and procurement program at the Naval Ships Systems Command to meet urgent in-country needs. Ten boats were built by Atlantic Research.

This MSSC is seen at low tide in Vietnam. The mangled ladder on the starboard bow was a bad design, since it was the first thing to hit the side of a canal during SEAL insertions and extractions.

The MSSC was 36 feet long, 13.5 feet wide, and had a draft of two feet to four feet when fully burdened with SEALs and their equipment. The boat was powered by two Ford 427 V-8 gasoline engines, generating 350 horsepower, and driving two MerCruiser stern drives. The craft had a design speed of 35 knots, and the boat's crew consisted of one officer and four enlisted men. The MSSC could transport 16 SEALs and their equipment. It had mounts for four 7.62 caliber machine guns, one 7.62 caliber mini-gun, two or three .50 caliber machine guns, and one 60mm Mark 4 mortar. The mini-gun could fire 6,000 rounds per minute. This boat had a massive amount of fire power.

All MSSCs were deployed to Vietnam, and at least one was returned aboard USS Monticello (LSD-35) by Mobile Support Team crewmen "Buck" Owens and Billie Stewart. The MSSC was one of the boats my platoon employed once

An MSSC nested to the shoreline in South Vietnam. SEALs used the rope netting on the bow to climb on the boat after a mission.

we got to Nah Be, South Vietnam in the summer of 1970. The crew compartment was well protected by an inner and outer hull, and with Styrofoam® insulation to absorb rocket shrapnel (also to act as flotation and sound deadening). It also incorporated a ceramic-backed steel-alloy armor plate and thick Kevlar® flak curtains. The boats were, for the most part, very reliable, but had a high-failure rate when operating in very-shallow water. This resulted from the cooling system being unable to handle the muddy water kicked up by its stern drives. Another problem was the .50 caliber machine-gun mounts that sometimes cracked at the gunwale (top edge of the hull) after a heavy volume of firing. This was a great boat for its time, and served the SEALs and Mobile Support Teams substantially.

Heavy SEAL Support Craft - HSSC

A modified LCM-6 was used to support SEAL operations at bases along the Bassac, Mekong, and Saigon Rivers.

Tom Hawkins (left) onboard the Nah Be HSSC shortly after his platoon arrived in Vietnam in June 1970. They were underway for non-tactical area orientation and to accomplish live-fire weapons testing.

The Navy's LCM-6 was initially modified by SEAL Team ONE and Boat Support Unit ONE during Project ZULU. It carried three .30 caliber and four .50 caliber machine guns, a 57mm recoilless rifle, a 60mm mortar, and an Mark 18 crank-operated 40mm grenade launcher. It was nicknamed "Mighty Mo" by the men after the famous World War II battleship USS Missouri (BB-63). Its first operations were accomplished as early as 1966 at Nha Be in an area called the Rung Sat Special Zone or RSSZ, which was southeast of Saigon. The boat was later called the Heavy SEAL Support craft or HSSC.

On 7 April 1967, three SEALs were killed and 14 of 20 other SEAL and Mobile Support Team operators were wounded when "Mighty Mo" took a mortar round air burst over its well deck. The Mobile Support Teams and SEALs learned that the Soviet RPG-2 rocket propelled grenade and 57mm or 75mm recoil-less rifles were some of their worst enemies. By late 1969 the HSSC had benefited from the same anti-rocket protection afforded to the craft of the U.S. Navy's Mobile Riverine Force. Bar armor made from concrete reinforcing rods was placed on hangers about 1.5 feet away from the hull and other vulnerable areas of the boat. The bar armor would detonate the warhead of the rocket or recoilless round to prevent it from penetrating into the interior.

Patrol Gunboats, Hydrofoil

In 1968, gun boats with hydrofoils were introduced to NSW. They were *USS Flagstaff* (PGH-1) and *USS Tucumcari* (PGH-2). And, for reasons obscure, they were assigned to Naval Special Warfare Group, Pacific and its component Boat Support Unit ONE. These vessels at least rate honorable mention involving NSW's "Sea" capabilities. I've always found it perplexing that these craft were assigned to NSW, because they were commissioned vessels, and not small combatant craft needed and used by SEALs and Mobile Support Teams. I've generally assumed that it is because the ship's intended mission involved coastal patrol and interdiction, which was part of the Boat Support Unit mission. These ships were also not very quiet. In fact, they were not quiet at all—but they were fast.

The two ships were built by different contractors. *Flagstaff* was built by the Grumman Aircraft Engineering Corporation, and commissioned 14 September 1968. It was a propeller-driven system with two diesel engines driving water jet pumps and one Rolls-Royce Tyne gas turbine driving a single super-cavitating propeller. Its displacement was 67 tons, 82 feet long (foils down), 21.5 feet in beam, and had a draft of 4.5 feet (foils up) and 18 feet (foils down). Armament in Vietnam was one 40mm gun, two twin .50 machine guns, and one 81mm Navy mortar.

USS Flagstaff (PGH-1) on hydrofoils (Source: Bob Stoner)

Tucumcari was built under contract to the Boeing Aerospace Group, and commissioned 7 March 1968. It incorporated a water-jet propulsion system. The ship had two diesel engines and one Rolls-Royce Proteus gas turbine driving two water jet pumps. PGH-2's displacement was 57 tons, 72 feet long, 35.3 feet in beam, and had a draft of 4.5 feet (foils up) and 13.9 feet (foils down). Armament in Vietnam was one 40mm gun, two twin .50 machine guns, and one 81mm Navy mortar. Operations were conducted day and night, in fair weather and foul. Refueling at sea and vertical replenishment operations were also demonstrated.

Apparently because of the specialized nature of the craft and their unique logistics structure, operations were less than successful. They were also mechanically complex for the repair facilities in Vietnam. This, and a lack of logistics support, saw them phased out of any combat role after only

USS Tucumcari (PGH-2) on hydrofoils. (Source: Bob Stoner.)

Aground at Vieques. Not a good day for *Tucumcari*.

a six-month trial. The boats were returned to the U.S. in early 1970. *Flagstaff* remained at Boat Support Unit ONE in Coronado, while *Tucumcari* was transferred to Boat Support Unit TWO at Little Creek, Virginia.

Flagstaff operated again along the Pacific coast, where she participated in numerous readiness trials and training exercises. In early 1975, the ship was turned over to the U.S. Coast Guard. After operating off the east coast during 1971, *Tucumcari* was deployed to northern Europe and the Mediterranean to demonstrate the capability of hydrofoil propulsion for other NATO nations. In 1972, she ran aground near Vieques Island, Puerto Rico at a speed of 40+ knots and was damaged beyond economical repair.

CHAPTER 10

AFLOAT STAGING AND OPERATING BASES

Maritime Forward Operating Base

In 1969, the SEAL officer career program was approved, and many seasoned young officers were deciding to make Naval Special Warfare a career. With already great leadership, this led to future thinking, thus, Naval Special Warfare's officers were already looking past Vietnam. The UDTs had always deployed aboard the Navy's amphibious ships, but as embarked detachments to support their doctrinal role of pre-assault hydrographic reconnaissance and demolition of natural and man-made obstacles. SEALs, on the other hand, were looking at direct-action and information gathering missions and tasks using dedicated boats and helicopters. SEALs had already been involved with world-wide target planning in the theater-based contingency plans. A dedicated sea base seemed logical; that is, to everyone except the U.S. Navy.

I first heard the term MFOB when it was uttered by then SEAL Lieutenant Tom Truxell, with whom I'd work with in Vietnam. MFOB is short for Maritime Forward Operating Base, a concept of SEALs operating from a dedicated host ship throughout the global regions. A lot of ideas were blooming during that period, and this was one of them; especially with conditions in Europe and threats from the Soviet Union and Cuba. The MFOB concept never got any traction, since the Naval Special Warfare community was still in its infancy, with little or no influence with the "Big Navy." After Vietnam, the Navy couldn't figure out what to do about or with the SEALs—whom had left Vietnam with an already-storied reputation.

In the post-Vietnam era, SEALs had no specific mission that supported the global Navy mission. Ironically, however, it was the "Brown-Water Navy" in Vietnam that fostered and established a dedicated sea-base concept. Although anchored in a Vietnam river, the capability was named Sea Float," and it may have been that which nurtured the same kind of thinking within Naval Special Warfare.

Operation SEA FLOAT

SEA FLOAT was a collection of barges in the middle of a river in South Vietnam from which UDTs, SEALs, Mobile Support Teams, and other naval forces operated. This afloat base was established on 25 June 1968. It was located at An Xuyen Province, which was roughly 175 miles southwest of Saigon. Its purpose was to gain and extend control over the strategic Nam Can region of the Ca Mau peninsula. This was a heavily forested area with seemingly endless miles of mangrove swamp. SEA FLOAT was situated on the Cau Lon River, which connected to the Bo De and Dam Doi rivers. These were salt-water rivers. Any fresh or drinking water used afloat or ashore had to be brought in by ship. The entire area had been firmly controlled by the Viet Minh against the French, and later by the Viet Cong against the Saigon government.

According to retired Master Chief Bob Stoner, when he was with Mobile Support Team, Detachment CHARLIE, which operated and maintained the HSSC, MSSC, and both LSSC's aboard SEA FLOAT: "There were roughly 700 American officers and men on the 12 barges that made up SEA FLOAT. This included a support staff, galley, intelligence section, communications section, supply department, a detachment of HA(L)-3 "Seawolf" UH-1B attack helicopters, a motley collection of Vietnamese Navy-owned and American-advised River Assault Group boats, two Mobile Support Team detachments with two light, two medium, and one heavy SEAL support craft (LSSC, MSSC, HSSC), three SEAL platoons, a UDT detachment, six to eight coastal junks, and some miscellaneous

SEA FLOAT operating base situated on the Cau Lon River in the Nam Can region of the Ca Mau peninsula in South Vietnam. Solid Anchor can be seen under construction in the background.

Vietnamese navy and U.S. Navy Fast Patrol Craft "Swift Boats." The U.S. Navy almost immediately began construction of a shore base called SOLID ANCHOR on land adjacent to SEA FLOAT. That base became operational in mid-September 1970, and performed the same mission and support functions as SEA FLOAT. Both bases are noteworthy in the history of Naval Special Warfare, because they served as tactical operational locations for several SEAL and UDT

SOLID ANCHOR base ashore on the banks of the Cau Lon River in Vietnam. The SEA FLOAT base had been removed.

platoons and supporting Mobile Support Teams. The SOLID ANCHOR base was heavily rocketed and mortared in late January 1971. It was turned over to the Vietnamese navy the following April. The last Americans departed on 1 February 1973.

Forward Unconventional Warfare Operating Base Afloat

In the post-Vietnam period, SEALs joined with the Army's Special Forces to establish Joint Unconventional Warfare staffs for planning and exercising. SEAL Team ONE was largely focused on the Pacific Command, while SEAL Team TWO was focused largely on the European Command and Atlantic Command. Other areas were always a consideration; however, these were the hot spots of their day. Pacific Command was particularly difficult, because of the tyranny of distance in getting to targets.

Unlike the UDTs, the SEAL teams and their mission and manning structures were never intended for rotational or routine shipboard deployments—unless in times of contingency of course. Then, most likely they would be operating from a submarine. A discussion however ensued about the dedicated-ship concept. It was being dubbed a Forward Unconventional Warfare Operating Base Afloat (FUWOB). This thinking may not have been in any contingency plans, but at least it was still in the discussion. It became reality in August 1987 during Operation PRIME CHANCE, when the U.S. Special Operations Command was task to protect U.S. flagged oil tankers from Iranian attack during the Iran-Iraq War. This was done in parallel path with the better-known Operation EARNEST WILL, which was a largely U.S. Navy effort to escort tankers through the Persian Gulf.

Mobile Sea Base

During the period July 1987 through September 1988, Operation EARNEST WILL was a widely reported request from Kuwait for military assistance from attacks by Iran against Kuwaiti-owned oil tankers. Operation PRIME CHANCE was a SECRET U.S. Special Operations Command operation to protect U.S. flagged oil tankers. Operations were conducted between August 1987 and June 1989. Special Operations Command forces were deployed to the U.S. Central Command theater, where operations were conducted from barges that were called Mobile Sea Bases.

Two Mobile Sea Bases were leased by the Central Command and placed in the northern Persian Gulf as afloat staging and operating bases for U.S. Navy SEALs, Special Boat Teams, Explosive Ordnance Disposal personnel, U.S. Marines, and U.S. Army Special Operations Command aviation assets. The operational concept was to employ two mutually supporting Mobile Sea Bases utilizing the unique capabilities of Special Operations Forces. The Mobile Sea Bases were positioned opposite Farsi Island to counter Iranian aggression and provide combatant craft support to ERNEST WILL convoys for flank security. Boats deployed by the Special Boat Teams included the 65-foot Mark III Patrol Boat and the 36-foot Special Warfare Craft, Light or Sea Fox. (Note: the Special Boat Teams were known as Special Boat Units during this period.)

Central Command contracted two derrick barges from a major international company in Bahrain. The barges, named *Hercules* and *Wimbrown VII,* were originally designed for constructing at-sea oil platforms and laying pipelines in the Persian Gulf. Because of the long Iran-Iraq War, the barges had been put in a lay-up maintenance status, thus, they were readily available for conversion as Mobile Sea Bases. As necessary too, the Mobile Sea Bases could be slowly moved from place to place but, they were not maneuverable like ships. A four-point mooring system was used to stabilize both. The barges were moved frequently so that they couldn't be targeted.

U.S. Special Operations Command's helicopters flew at night, launching and recovering from the barges and Navy flight decks under cover of darkness. The helicopter pilots often flew some 30 feet (9.1 m) above the water using night vision goggles and forward looking infrared devices. SEAL operations involved Visit, Board, Search, and Seize (VBSS) operations, and actions against gas and oil platforms (GOPLATs). SEALs and Special Boat Team personnel often captured ships and took prisoners.

Mobile Sea Base Hercules. (Photo from Bob Stoner)

The Mobile Sea Bases were established as NSW Task Units, both commanded by a SEAL 0-5 Commander. Mobile Support Base *Hercules* was manned by East Coast units, while Mobile Support Base *Wimbrown VII* was manned by West Coast units. Each NSW Task Unit conducted their own missions; both answering to a NSW Task Group commander—a SEAL O-6 Captain.

Mobile Sea Base *Wimbrown VII*. Note the MK 3 Patrol Boats in the foreground.

There were at least two major lessons learned: The concept of a dedicated sea base was once again validated by NSW commanders and, unless it is a highly maneuverable ship, protection of a sea base from attack is a major planning consideration.

Afloat Forward Staging Base

While the name changes, the capability need for a ship or ships to serve as dedicated staging and operating bases for SEAL and Special Boat Teams perseveres. Within the U.S. Special Operations Command, current capability needs involve operations, actions, and activities by

MK III Patrol Boats at Mobile Sea Base *Wimbrown VII*. Note the sandbagged Marine gun positions and PB skid.

Army and Navy Special Operations Forces, and are described as an Afloat Forward Staging Base (AFSB).

The Navy partially addressed this need, when an AFSB capability was requested by the U.S. Central Command and U.S. Navy's 5th Fleet commander. In March 2012, *USS Ponce* (LPD-15), an amphibious transport dock ship, was in the process of being decommissioned. The procedure was halted, and funds quickly made available to convert the ship to U.S. Military Sealift Command (MSC) standards, preparation for overseas deployment to 5th Fleet, and service as an AFSB. The ship departed Naval Station, Norfolk, Virginia in transit to Bahrain in June 2012, fulfilling a longstanding U.S. Central Command need.

The ship was considered an "interim" capability and designated *USS Ponce* AFSB(I)-15. In theater, it was a U.S. Navy warship, commanded by a U.S. Navy captain and operated by a Military Sealift Command crew. The ship had 207 crew members, including 152 civil-service mariners, and 55 Navy officers and Sailors. It was intended to be a multi-mission platform to host primarily SEALs and other Special Operations Forces and MH-53E Sea Dragon helicopters used for conducting Airborne Mine Countermeasures. The ship could not perform the Airborne Mine Countermeasures and Special Operations

USS Ponce (AFSB(I)-15) performing flight operations in the Arabian Gulf.

Forces missions simultaneously. Operational units were to be embarked only for training and contingency operations. The ship was considered an interim capability, because the Navy was making plans for conversion of new-construction ships called Mobile Landing Platforms to serve as AFSBs. *USS Ponce* was decommissioned on 14 October 2017 in Norfolk, Virginia.

Expeditionary Sea Base

The Naval Sea Systems Command describes Expeditionary Sea Base (ESB) ship classes as: "Highly flexible platforms that may be used across a broad range of military operations supporting multiple operational phases. Acting as a mobile sea base, they will be part of the critical-access infrastructure that supports the deployment of forces and supplies to provide prepositioned equipment and sustainment with flexible distribution." ESB ships were originally called Mobile Landing Platforms (MLPs), however, in September 2015 the Secretary of the Navy designated the ships as ESBs, and all are named in honor of U.S. Marines.

The *USNS Lewis B. Puller (ESB-3)* was the first ESB, and along with follow-on ships *USNS Hershel "Woody" Williams (ESB-4)*, and *USNS Miguel Keith (ESB-5)*, the ships are optimized to support a variety of maritime-based missions; including Airborne Mine Countermeasures and Special Operations Forces missions. (Note: U.S. Naval Ships (USNS) are operated by civilian mariners of the U.S. Navy's Military Sealift Command). Each ESB has a naval aviation-certified flight deck, and each are designed around four core capabilities: aviation, berthing, equipment staging support, and command and control. ESBs are configured with a 52,000 square-foot flight deck, fuel and equipment storage, repair spaces, magazines, mission planning spaces, and accommodations for up to 250 personnel. In addition to Special Operations Forces and Airborne Mine Countermeasures, the ships are capable of supporting multiple missions that include counter-piracy operations, maritime security operations, humanitarian aid and disaster relief missions, and U.S. Marine Corps crisis-response operations. The ships can support MH-53 and MH-60 helicopters, and will be upgraded to support MV-22 tilt-rotor aircraft.

The *USNS Puller* relieved *USS Ponce* on station in the Arabian Gulf in August 2017, and was immediately commissioned a USN-USS flagged vessel for operations in the 5th Fleet area of responsibility. The ship is operated by MSC crews, however, a Navy commanding officer, other officers, and small crew of Sailors are also assigned. As touted by the Navy: "The *USS Lewis B. Puller* [is] a commissioned ship [that] will provide combatant commanders greater operational flexibility on how the platform is employed following the laws of armed conflict."

USNS Lewis B. Puller (ESB-3)

CHAPTER 11

POST-VIETNAM BOAT ACTIVITIES

During Vietnam, the UDT and SEAL Teams and Boat Support Units and Mobile Support Teams were consistently praised for their operational prowess; however, it's a sad but true fact that Naval Special Warfare (NSW) could never be praised for any dedication to recording their history. SEAL and Mobile Support Team exploits in Vietnam became legendary, but what happened to them after Vietnam remains somewhat obscure. One fact was true: The Navy didn't know what to do with Navy SEALs. After 1973, the entire country and the Navy didn't care about Vietnam. The Navy badly wanted to divest its "Brown Water Navy" as fast as it could, and also its unconventional warfare SEALs, who had no "Blue Water Navy" mission. Like the aftermath of many conflicts, special mission units are forgotten, dismantled, or strangled by budget cuts. Such was true within the U.S. Navy and its desire to get back to the business of big ships, submarines, and aircraft patrolling the seaward global commons. For combatant craft, the Navy was somewhat indulgent.

Coastal River Squadrons

In 1971, Coastal River Squadrons (COSRIVRONs) were established on each coast, and the Boat Support Units were reestablished as Coastal River Divisions (COSRIVDIVs), as were other commands throughout the United States. As active-duty commands, COSRIVRON 12 and COSRIVRON 20 continued to support the UDT and SEAL Teams, but the other commands became the de facto repository of "Brown Water Navy" capabilities after Vietnam. They were organized as naval reserve component commands.

COSRIVRON ONE – Coronado, California
COSRIVDIV 11 – Mare Island, California
COSRIVDIV 12 – Coronado, California
COSRIVDIV 13 – Coronado, California
MST-3 – Subic Bay, Philippines

COSRIVRON TWO – Little Creek, Virginia
COSRIVDIV 20 – Little Creek, Virginia
COSRIVDIV 21 – Great Lakes, Illinois
COSRIVDIV 22 – New Orleans, Louisiana

These commands were manned largely with Vietnam veterans. To maximize boats and personnel, the commands in Coronado and Little Creek tended to intermix by sharing boats and maintenance facilities; creating a nice mixture of reserve and active-duty operators. During this period, these commands operated, maintained, and trained with an expanded inventory of boats. They continued to operate Landing Craft Personnel, Large (LCPL) and Patrol Boat, River (PBR) boats. Additional craft were eventually added to the NSW inventory. They included the Landing Craft, Swimmer Reconnaissance (LCSR), Mark III Patrol Boat or Sea Specter, Sea Fox also known as the Special Warfare Craft, Light (SWCL), and the Mini-Armored Troop Carrier. The LCSR and PB Mark III were new to the inventory, and represented for the first modern-day tactical combatant craft in NSW that couldn't be launched and recovered from ships. This would be accomplished by the Sea Fox, which would replace the LCPLs in the inventory. The U.S. Navy quit purchasing LCPLs, which required NSW to acquire its own ship-to-shore craft. The Mini-Armored Troop Carrier was based on an improved design with attributes taken from the MSSC, and was never intended for shipboard deployment.

Landing Craft, Personnel, Ramped

World War II Landing Craft, Personnel, Ramped (LCPRs) were still being used at the U.S. Naval School for Underwater Swimmers in Key West, Florida. They were the training-support boats used by the School for Underwater Swimmers instructors. The bow ramp on the boat made it easy to get trainees into

UDT-22 men training in cast and recovery with an LCPR.

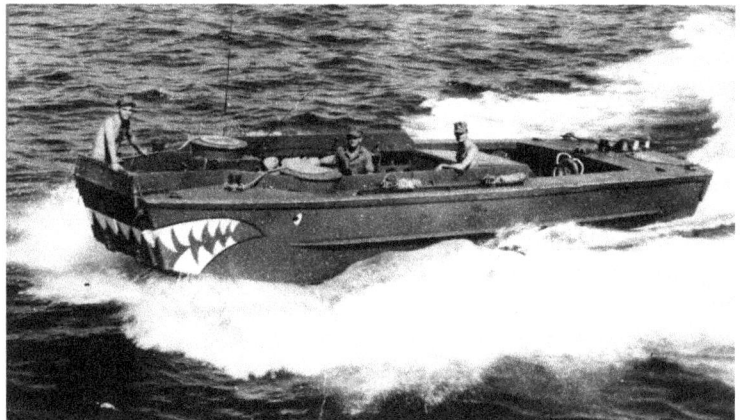

LCPR has been painted with shark's teeth and eyes by the UDT men.

and out of the water. The boat was essentially the same wooden boat from World War II and Korea. These boats were likely being used elsewhere in the Navy, but not in the UDTs.

Landing Craft, Personnel, Large

The steel-hulled Mark IV and fiberglass-hull Mark 11 Landing Craft, Personnel, Large (LCPLs) were the workhorse boats within the UDTs from the post-Korean War through the Vietnam War period. Four Mark IV LCPLs were converted for SEAL support in Viet Nam. Both boats were 36-feet long with a beam of 10.7 feet. It had a draft of three feet, and a designed speed was 19 knots. When deployed for combat, the boats utilized a four man crew with a wide variety of crew-served weapons systems (depending on how rigged) that included: the 7.62mm mini-gun, .50 caliber Browning machine Gun, 7.62mmmMachine Gun, 60mm mortar, and Mark 18 and Mark 20 grenade launchers.

Above and below: MK IV LCPL used for training with the Fulton maritime recovery system.

The Fulton Maritime Recovery System was developed and first attempted with the Mark IV LCPLs, which were common within the UDT inventory. It was also the same craft taken on deployments with the Amphibious Force, and used for the swimmer-snare-recovery method. The UDT capability included transporting up to 20 UDT men with several tons of demolitions and other equipment. It is rare that the LCPL actually achieved its design speed in any kind of sea state. In any case, tests determined that it was very under-powered in performing the Fulton recovery method reliably. The capability became much more accomplishable with the Landing Craft, Swimmer Reconnaissance (LCSR). With its gas-turbine engines, it could attain a speed of 40+ knots, providing plenty of power for the Fulton System.

To cast into the water, UDT men would simply jump off of the stern and into the boat's wake at approximately 25-yard intervals. Their subsequent recovery employed the Fulton method. The Fulton Recovery System was comprised of two small sleds that were six-feet long and manufactured with buoyant foam. Several hundred feet of polypropylene line connected the sleds, and a winch was installed on the bow to reel the men back toward the boat. To accomplish the recovery, the UDT men would cluster together as the recovery boat made a high-speed pass to drop off the sleds. The men would swim the sleds in opposite directions until the polypropylene line was taut. Simultaneously, the recovery boat proceeded in a large arc and came back around to recover the UDT men. The coxswain of the boat did this by aiming at a float in the middle of the polypropylene line until a bow rod snagged the line and guided it up from the water and into the bow winch. After the snag the men were winched to the boat. The recovery was completed when both sleds were brought to a recovery ramp on the stern of the boat, and the men simply climbed aboard.

Patrol Boat, River (PBR)

The Patrol Boat, River (PBR) Mark II was brought into service 1967. It was a redesign of the PBR MarK 1 based on lessons learned in Vietnam. The PBR Mark II was designed for high-speed patrol of rivers and other inland waterways. It had a crew of four or five enlisted operators. It was heavily armed, and vital crew areas were protected with ceramic armor.

The Mark II's fiberglass reinforced hull used waterjet propulsion so that the boat could operate in shallow water areas. Fully combat loaded with its crew on board, the PBR weighed nine tons, but drew only two-feet of water while stopped, and less when going full speed. The boat was highly maneuverable; literally having the capability to turn 180 degrees in its own wake while at full power. Engine silencing and radar systems provided capabilities to serve as

PBR MK II underway for training.

an all-weather guard post, conduct river patrol and interdiction, and to accomplish direct-action tasks. Carrying 160 gallons of fuel, the PBR had a range of about 200 miles at 25-knots speed.

Landing Craft, Swimmer Recovery

The 52-foot Landing Craft, Swimmer Recovery (LCSR) was introduced into the Boat Support Unit inventories during the mid-1960s. They were powered by very noisy gas-turbine engines that were difficult to maintain. Also, the boat was too large to be transported, launched, and recovered from host ships and would, thus, require tactical overseas basing, which was not something NSW did at that time. The East Coast Teams conducted winter training in St. Thomas, U.S. Virgin Island and later at the Naval Station Roosevelt Roads, Puerto Rico. The West Coast Teams deployed forward and staged at Subic Bay in the Philippines. Six LCSRs were built for each Boat Support Unit; although I've seen seven mentioned at BSU-1. The boats were outfitted with the Fulton maritime recovery system which, presumably, is how they got their name. The Fulton recovery capability became much more accomplishable with the LCSR. With its gas-turbine engines, it could attain a speed of 40+ knots, providing plenty of power for the Fulton System.

The LCSR was part of the Navy's first attempt to place gas-turbine engines in small craft, and it is safe to say that the effort was not very successful. When the boat was eliminated from the active inventory, and the Fulton System was also discontinued. Little information exists about the LCSR today, except in the memory of those that had the opportunity to operate with it. I actually had the opportunity to coxswain an LCSR across the channel from the island of Vieques to the mainland of Puerto Rico after completing underway submarine operations. Of course, I was under the close supervision of the boat's captain and coxswain.

Port and starboard views of the LCSR carrying the stacked sleds used for the Fulton Recovery System. The winch can clearly be seen on the bow of the boat.

Mini Armored Troup Carrier

The Mini-Armored Troop Carrier (MINI ATC), called "The Mini" by the men, was in the River Raider Class of combatant craft. It was a 36-foot all-aluminum hull craft designed for high-speed patrol, interdiction, and clandestine missions in rivers, harbors, and protected coastal areas. The Mini was almost a mirror twin of the MSSC built for SEALs in Vietnam, but had a much-improved design. The Mini and the Vietnam era Patrol Craft, Riverine (PBR) were the riverine craft of their day.

The Mini-ATC had a large ceramic-armor/nylon blanket that protected the well-deck area. The boat required a crew of two, and had the capability to carry 15 combat-equipped SEALs or up to 4,000 pounds of cargo. It had seven weapons stations that could accommodate an M60 or .50-caliber machine gun, 60mm mortar, or the Mark 19 grenade launcher. The boat had twin diesel engines that propelled two Jacuzzi water-jet pumps; making it ideal for beaching or shallow-water operations. The Mini incorporated

The Mini-Armored Troop Carrier (Mini-ATC)

a hydraulic-actuated bow ramp for ease of inserting or extracting troops. This was a major improvement incorporated from lessons learned with the MSSC in Vietnam. The boat could make a speed of 28 knots; however, the engines were up graded in the late 1980s; giving them a top speed of 40 knots.

The Mini was air transportable using a U.S. Air Force C-5 Galaxy aircraft and five-ton trucks and trailers as prime movers. This restricted their deployment capabilities to areas with landing strips available to accommodate a C-5. The Mini served NSW from the late 70s through the late 80s, but its capabilities were eventually replaced at various times by the Coastal Assault Craft, Patrol Boat, Light, and Special Operations Craft, Riverine.

Special Warfare Craft, Light - Sea Fox

The Special Warfare Craft, Light (SWCL) called the Sea Fox was designed to be a multi-mission craft. Its primary mission was over-the-horizon, ship-to-shore insertion and extraction of UDT and SEAL

SEAL operators in the swimmer compartment at the stern of the Sea Fox. The divers are purging their oxygen rebreathers to eliminate any excess CO_2 before going into the water.

Sea Fox cruising along the Corniche off the coast of Beirut 1982. (courtesy Chuck Pfarrer)

Starboard side view of Sea Fox underway. The crew compartment and swimmer compartment were separated by the engine compartment.

operators. Sea Fox incorporated many of the design features of the LCPL, including a shipboard davit-lift capability and beaching. Sea Fox was the first craft purpose-built for NSW that incorporated stealth design features. The boat was intended to be capable of surviving in high sea states. Among many design flaws, however, the boat had a tendency to bow plunge; often causing severe damage and injury to crew members. Nevertheless, prototype craft were produced in 1977 with scheduled production to begin in 1979.

I was the SEAL officer assigned to the Navy's Operational Test and Evaluation Force in the late 1970s, when the Sea Fox went through Operational Evaluation. It wasn't my test project, but I served as a subject-matter advisor to the Operational Test director, who was a Surface Warfare officer. I may be a bit off on my numbers, but as I recall, the Sea Fox had 179 deficiencies during testing, and six were considered major. A major deficiency will result in a recommendation of "Disapproval for Navy Use." Such a recommendation is a program killer. Because of the urgency to get the boat into the fleet, however, the Naval Sea Systems Command Program Manager worked out an agreement with Operational Test and Evaluation Force and the Pentagon resource sponsor to begin production and introduction of the boat into the NSW inventory. Presumably, the failures were to be addressed during production; however, the boat experienced many problems throughout its service life with the Special Boat Units.

Sea Fox could accommodate 10 combat equipped swimmers. The UDT or SEAL operators rode in a swimmer cabin at the stern of the boat, which was separated from the crew compartment by the boats engines. Sea Fox had a crew of three, was propeller driven by twin-diesel engines, and designed to operate at speeds in excess of 40 knots in Sea State 4. It incorporated a collection of advanced electronics, and could accommodate four pintle-mounted weapons. In addition to being carried in standard shipboard davits, Sea Fox could be transported in the well deck of LSDs or air transported by a C-130 or larger aircraft.

Sea Fox conducted numerous deployments with the Amphibious Ready Groups in the Atlantic, Pacific, and Mediterranean. Sea Fox was also employed extensively in a variety of roles for combat operations against Iran during Operation PRIME CHANCE; the first Persian Gulf War in 1987. The boats and their crews operated from afloat staging bases, which were barges converted for military use.

Like the MSSC and LSSC in Vietnam, Sea Fox was built exclusively to accommodate SEAL capabilities. As a result, the boat was designed with what today would be considered primitive stealth technology. Its paint was non-metallic, it incorporated infrared reduction features, the interior of the engine compartment was shielded against radar, the radar and communication mast were covered with radar absorbent material, and the exhaust was muffled and discharged under water.

Patrol Boat Mark III

In 1975, the 65-foot Patrol Boat Mark III became the newest and most advanced small boat in the Navy inventory. The boat was built by Marinette Marine and Peterson Builders following U.S. Navy specifications. The boats were designated "Sea Specter" by the Naval Systems Command, however, the name never stuck. They were simply known as the PB Mark III or simply "PB" in the Special Boat Units.

The PB was designed as a high-speed weapons platform specifically for NSW. It was capable of carrying a variety of U.S. or foreign weapons. A modular-payload concept was incorporated, allowing the PB to be adapted to a variety of missions in deep rivers, harbors, coastal, or open-sea environments. Missions included surveillance, patrol and interdiction, fire support against ashore and afloat targets, and insertion and extraction of NSW forces. The boats were extensively deployed during Operation PRIME CHANCE in the Persian Gulf from August 1987 through June 1989.

The PB was propelled by three high-power, lightweight diesel engines that provided a speed of 30 knots. Fuel and crew accommodations allowed for unsupported missions of up to five days or 500 nautical miles at maximum speed (1750 nautical miles at reduced speeds). Multi-frequency communications, high resolution surface search radar, and reasonable stability in moderately heavy seas allowed day-night, all- weather operations. The boat was made of all aluminum, and tended to get a very ugly appearance with age. The boats were never painted. The PB was designed with a low silhouette, low-radar cross section and extremely low-acoustic noise levels.

Patrol Boat, Light

The Patrol Boat, Light (PBL) concept was derived from the Skimmers used in Vietnam, and were perhaps influenced by the SEAL Team Attack Boat or STAB

PB MK III underway.

fabricated by SEAL Team TWO. In the late 70's and early 80's, the Special Boat Units used unarmed 22-foot Boston Whaler PBLs as utility boats.

The first combatant PBLs were fabricated by the Navy's Harbor Patrol Unit in the Panama Canal, which was taken over by NSW in 1987 and designated Special Boat Unit 26. The men of this command developed PBL's using two 18-foot Boston Whalers mounted with two M-60 light machine guns. The first production PBL's were two 22-foot Outrage Boston Whalers, purchased and sent to the Ramo Corporation for outfitting with weapons, communications, and navigation systems. The boat had two .50-caliber machine-gun mounts and a single M-60 mount, and was characterized by its speed and quick-strike/ interdiction capabilities.

The Naval Small Craft Instruction and Technical Training School at the Stennis Space Center, Mississippi is a component of NSW Group FOUR. The school provides partner nations withfocused riverine warfare training, including boat operation and maintenance using the PBLs, which are affordable options for a variety of military applications.

PBLs on operations.

Special Boat Squadrons and Units

In 1979, the Coastal River Squadrons and Divisions were reorganized as Special Boat Squadrons and Units. All remained at their current locations. Special Boat Unit 26 was later established at the Panama Canal Zone, but was disestablished when the canal was turned over to Panama. Special Boat Unit 13 was eventually disestablished. In August 2002, Special Boat Unit 22 was moved to its present home at Stennis Space Center, Mississippi.

NSW Groups

In October 2002, as the result of a force-structure review entitled *NSW 21*, Special Boat Squadron ONE became NSW Group THREE, and Special Boat Squadron TWO became NSW Group FOUR. All of the Special Boat Units became Special Boat Teams. Organizationally, every command in NSW was designated a NSW Group, NSW Unit, or SEAL and Special Boat Team. It was during this period that the Patrol Coastal

Ships were divested and turned over to the U.S. Coast Guard or the Navy. At the same time, SEAL Delivery Vehicle Teams ONE and TWO were moved under the administrative control of NSW Group THREE and FOUR respectively. Several years later, both SEAL Delivery Vehicle Teams were moved under NSW Group THREE and all Special Boat Teams were moved under NSW Group FOUR.

U.S. Special Operations Command

The U.S. Special Operations Command was established in Tampa, Florida in 1987. Since its formation, their Maritime Program Office has assisted in procuring the expanding inventory of NSW's Special Operations Craft. These include the Mark V Special Operations Craft (Mark V SOC), 11-meter NSW Rigid-Hull Inflatable Boat (NSW RIB), and Special Operations Craft, Riverine (SOC-R), and Combat Rubber Raiding Craft (CRRC). For several years, NSW operated and maintained Patrol Coastal ships (PCs), which were manned by regular Navy Sailors and officers.

NSW Rigid-Hull Inflatable Boat

The NSW Rigid-Hull Inflatable Boat (NSW RIB or simply "The RIB") has been the workhorse utility boat in NSW for over 20 years. It is now being phased out of service. The 36-foot boat was designed as a "high-speed, high-buoyancy, all-weather" craft with a primary mission of SEAL insertion and extraction. The boat's draft was two-feet and 11 inches, and it could achieve a top speed of 40 knots. It was propelled by water-jets powered by two 470-horsepower diesel engines. The boat was constructed with glass-reinforced plastic and incorporated an inflatable tube gunwale made out of neoprene-nylon reinforced fabric. The boat could operate in heavy sea state and wind speeds approaching 45 knots.

The RIB could accomplish a range of missions that included clandestine or non-clandestine ship-to-shore movement of SEALs and other Special Operation Forces, maritime interception operations,

The NSW 11-meter RIB.

An 11-meter NSW RIB being recovered by an MH-47G Chinook helicopter using MEATS.

limited coastal patrol and interdiction, and reconnaissance and information gathering. The RIB was manned by a crew of three Special Warfare Combatant-Craft Crewmen (SWCC) and could carry eight SEALs or other Special Operations Forces.

The RIB was very versatile and easy to transport; getting in and out of water and easily moved over highways and under bridges. It could also be moved over unimproved roads and taken into austere operating environments. Using the Maritime Craft Air-Delivery System (MCADS), the boat was deployable from the C-130 Hercules or C-17 Globemaster aircraft under parachutes with SWCCs and SEALs jumping behind. The MCADS capability extends NSW's reach globally. The NSW RIB was also air transportable by helicopter with the Maritime External Air Transportation System (MEATS) using Army, Navy, or Air Force heavy-lift helicopters. The system allowed the boat to be rigged to the underbelly of the helicopter with slings. The crew and passengers fast rope onto the boat during launch, and climb up a ladder during recovery.

Photo left: MCADS dragging parachute pulling an NSW 11-Meter RIB out of a C-17 Globemaster III aircraft. Photo right: RIB under canopy with jumpers following it into the water.

Special Operations Craft, Riverine

The Special Operations Craft, Riverine (SOC-R) replaced the Patrol Craft, Riverine (PBR) and the Mini-Armored Troop Carrier (Mini-ATC) in the Special Boat Teams. Prior to introduction of the SOC-R, however, Special Boat Team 22 acquired an experimental boat created by one of the SEAL Teams. It was called Coastal Assault Craft (CAC), and it became the forerunner of the SOC-R, which was a vastly improved production version.

The SOC-R is operated and maintained by Special Boat Team 22. Its mission is to perform short-range insertion and

Special Boat Team 22 CAC transporting SEALs.

128

extraction of SEALs and other Special Operations Forces in riverine and littoral environments. The boat is a high-performance, aluminum-hull craft that can be air-transported aboard a C-130 or larger aircraft. The boat is powered by twin diesel engines with water-jet propulsion, and can attain speeds in excess of 40 knot. Its speed and tight-turning radius are facilitated by the V-shaped hull design that allows the boat to, in effect, glide along the surface of the water with relatively little drag on the hull. Each SOC-R is manned by a crew of four Special Warfare Combatant-Craft Crewmen, trained to operate clandestinely under the cover of darkness. The boat has five weapon mounts that provide a 360-degree field of fire, and can carry eight SEALs or other SOF personnel. The SOC-R is air transportable by helicopter with the Maritime External Air Transportation System using Army, Navy, or Air Force heavy-lift helicopters.

The SOC-R in use during various training operations.

Patrol Boat Mark IV

In 1987, NSW inherited Mark IV PBs when it took over the Harbor Patrol Unit in Panama and established Special Boat Unit 26. It was located at Rodman Naval Station, and its mission included defense of the Canal Zone and providing Mobile Training Teams throughout Latin America. When reestablished as SBU-26, the command reported to Commander, Special Boat Squadron TWO, and was the only Special Boat Unit ever located outside the U.S. It was disestablished in 1999, when control of the Panama Canal was turned over to Panama.

PB MK IV was employed by SBU-26 in the Panama Canal Zone.

Mark V Special Operations Craft

The Mark V Special Operations Craft (SOC) was in service from 1995 through 2013. One of the boats was transferred for display at the UDT-SEAL Museum in Fort Pierce, Florida. The Mark V was a medium-range insertion and extraction platform for SEAL and other Special Operations Forces in a low-to-medium threat environment. Its secondary missions involved limited coastal patrol and interdiction, and capabilities to conduct reconnaissance and information gathering.

Mark V SOC could be transported by appropriately equipped surface ships to forward-base locations, where it would then tactically self- deploy on its own bottom and at speed and fuel consumption rates determined by overall design parameters. The boat was also sized for air deployment aboard U.S. Air Force C-5 Globemaster aircraft, while mated to an organic prime mover (truck and trailer), and in company with other support equipment. The Mark V was manned by a crew of five Special Warfare Combatant-Craft Crewmen, and could transport 16 SEALs and their Combat Rubber Raiding Craft.

The Mark V had specially designed seats for crew and passengers that were intended to mitigate pounding from the underway boat. The seats never really performed satisfactorily, and new ways of mitigating shock was and remains a constant task. Plans are to replace the Mark V SOC capabilities with a new and more capable vessel called the Combatant Craft, Attack (CCA).

A MK V SOC with a "razzle dazzle" camouflage pattern for operating in the near shore regions.

SEALs being cast aboard a MK V SOC. Note the stern ramp, which was designed to capture a SEAL Team CRRC while underway.

High-Speed Boat

The High-Speed Boat (HSB) was somewhat an anomaly, since Special Boat Unit 12 was the only unit that had them. The boats were 40-feet long and made by Fountain Boat Builders. The boats were acquired for combat operations in Operation DESERT SHIELD and DESERT STORM in 1990 and 1991.

The boats ran on two 580 HP gasoline engines and could attain a speed of 55 knots. Crew members that served on the boats during both operations observed: "Fountains are very loud but the news is that the new Halters have a very quiet exhaust system, but I have found that another boat can't really hear us while underway until we are right on top of them, which is then too late for them. We spent an enormous amount of hours prepping the boat and post-op, but the ride is worth it."

Although used in a combat role, the boats were still experimental and far too expensive to operate and maintain. They would eventually be replaced by the Mark V Special Operations Craft and 11-meter NSW RIB.

The HSB on operations during Operation DESERT STORM.

Combat Rubber Raiding Craft

Last, but certainly not least, is the ubiquitous inflatable Zodiac F-470 or Combat Rubber Raiding Craft (CRRC). These boats are in the SEAL Team inventories and not operated and maintained by Special Warfare Combatant-Craft Crewmen. They are the mainstay platform for getting SEALs ashore from host ships or submarines. They can also be transported aboard several kinds of helicopters.

CRRCs are generally controlled by two SEALs; one operating the outboard motor in the stern, and another maintaining visual or radio contact with companion CRRCs or other vessels or host ships. The remainder of on-board space is taken up by other SEALs, their weapons, and mission equipment. CRRCs are at the mercy of small-arms fire, but use silenced motors and low-profile positions to enhance stealth.

Members of SEAL Team Five from Golf Platoon conduct an exercise in a CRRC.

Cyclone Class Patrol Coastal

On behalf of Special Boat Unit 26 and Special Boat Squadron TWO, NSW outlined the need for a patrol boat that could transport SEALs and other Special Operations Forces to countries throughout Central and South America and the Caribbean. The new PBs were intended to replace the aging Mark III and Mark IV PBs. The new PB requirement specified an unrefueled range of 1,000 nautical miles. Concurrently, the U.S. Southern Command identified a requirement for a Patrol Craft Coastal with unrefueled range of 2,000 nautical miles. The Navy staff in the Pentagon studied both requirements, and assessed that both requirements could be accomplished in a single program—the Patrol Coastal boat.

When introduced, the Patrol Coastal (PC) became a class of ships that were unique and perhaps somewhat of an anomaly in NSW. They were funded as the result of a congressional plus-up (when a congressman inserts money into the federal budget to go to a specific contract or contractor), directed toward NSW and the Bollinger Shipyard in Lockport, Louisiana specifically. Largely based on the Southern Command and NSW requirements, the money was placed in the Special Operation Command's budget.

The NSW requirement was originally conceived to be for non-commissioned patrol boats, employed along the lines of other NSW combatant craft. Southern Command's 2,000 nautical mile range was an additive requirement for NSW that drove up the cost and physical features of the boat. Two attempts were made by NSW to change the Navy staff position, however, the two requirements remained combined, and thus the draft and beam of the ship became fixed in the requirements. Because of its size, the Navy had a reckoning that these were indeed miniature ships, and that they should be commissioned. And, so, they were.

The PC became a study in "be careful what you ask for." The Navy's decision had two significant impacts on the Special Operations Command-sponsored program. Foremost, specifications for a ship's construction are more rigorous than those required for small craft. Also, Surface Warfare-qualified Sailors were required to man commissioned Navy vessels. NSW had an established schoolhouse and training program for its Special Warfare Combatant-Craft Crewmen, but this provided no benefit to prospective PC crews.

USS Cyclone (PC-1), the first of 14 ships built in its class. In 2000 it was transferred to the U.S. Coast Guard..

The Navy staff and the Naval Sea Systems Command made no attempt to determine the cost impact of the commissioning recommendation before making the decision. It is unclear if the Special Operations Command was ever consulted or ever concurred in the decision. This was significant, because the money was in the Special Operations Command budget and not the Navy's. This decision also changed the acquisition strategy from what the Department of Defense calls a non-developmental to a full-blown acquisition program. As a result, in 1994, Bollinger submitted a "Request for Equitable Adjustment," which claimed $44 million in cost overruns that resulted from the Navy's decision.

Sixteen ships were planned, but only 14 were built. The lead ship was *USS Cyclone* (PC-1) in 1993, hence, Cyclone Class. The last ship built was *USS Tornado* (PC-14) in 2000. It was probably the best built design for NSW. Among other improvements, it had shaping features for signature management and a ramp on the stern, which could be used to launch and recover SEALs and their CRRCs. By the year 2002, the Special Operations Command determined it could not sustain the ships operation and maintenance costs, and divested itself of all PCs. They were subsequently turned over to the U.S. Coast Guard or Navy for decision making.

The NSW mission of the ship was to operate globally in low-intensity environments, conduct coastal patrol and interdiction, insertion and extraction of SEALs, and conduct operational deception and information gathering among others. The ship had a crew of four officers and 24 enlisted Sailors, and could (without berthing) support an embarked detachment of nine SEALs. The commanding officers were Navy lieutenants (O-3) that reported to commander, Special Boat Squadron ONE or TWO. Having command of a PC was a dream tour for Surface Line Navy lieutenants, and only the best and brightest officers were selected—to the benefit of NSW.

Four PCs serving duty in NSW were assigned to Special Boat Squadron ONE. They were: *USS Hurricane* (PC-3), *USS Monson* (PC-4), *USS Squall* (PC-7), and *USS Zephyr* (PC-8). Ten PCs were assigned to Special Boat Squadron TWO. They included: *USS Cyclone* (PC-1), *USS Tempest* (PC-2), *USS Typhoon* (PC-5), *USS Sirocco* (PC-6), *USS Chinook* (PC-9), *USS Firebolt* (PC-10), *USS Whirlwind* (PC-11), *USS Thunderbolt* (PC-12), *USS Shamal* (PC-13), and *USS Tornado* (PC-14).

Special Warfare Combatant-craft Crewmen (SWCC)

In large measure, the "Big Navy" responds to training, war plans, and contingencies in a variety of small craft transported by ships. For example, in Amphibious Warfare, small craft are used by the Navy and Marine Corps in complex amphibious assault operations. As a result, small craft operations accomplished by the Navy differ from small craft operations accomplished by NSW. Doctrinally, small boats in the Navy don't operate independently; they operate in orchestrated movements to get men and supplies ashore. On the contrary, in training for deployments and contingencies within NSW, SWCC and their boats are doctrinally trained to operate independently or in pairs—largely at night and perhaps without on-call air support.

Individually and collectively, SWCC are volunteers, who go through specialized training programs that emphasize the specialty skills needed for the men to conduct maritime special operations. The men are trained extensively in craft and weapons tactics, techniques, and procedures. They must be physically fit, highly motivated, and responsive in high-stress situations. The SWCC primary focus is on clandestine infiltration and exfiltration of SEALs, with dedicated and rapid mobility in littoral and shallow-water areas where larger vessels cannot operate.

On 1 October 2006, the Special Warfare Boat Operator (SB) rating was established by the Navy. The new rating replaced previous Navy specialty source ratings, which had been assigned Special Boat Team Sailors by job classifications e.g., Electronic Technician (ET), Boatswain Mate (BM), Gunners Mate (GM), etc. The Special Boat rating created a professional SWCC career path and established a military source-rating "A School" at the NSW Center in Coronado, California. Upon completion of basic and advanced training, all SWCCs are qualified in combatant craft operations, parachuting, craft weapons, and many maintenance skills. SWCC operational units are the Special Boat Teams, where they train and deploy to support theater-based day and night operations in all weather environments.

SWCCs have demonstrated the ability to operate across the spectrum of conflict and in operations other than war in a pro-active and professional manner. Their ability to provide SEAL support and other special operations in the high seas, littorals, and inland waterways provide operational commanders unlimited options in meeting crises globally. If this sounds like an advertisement, I hope so. To learn more about the SWCC program, please visit: https://www.navy.com/careers/special-operations/swcc.html

SWCC gunner at his battle station.

SWCC and SEALs underway at high speed in an 11-meter NSW RIB.

SWCC Helmsman and crew aboard the MK V Special Operations Craft.

SWCC MK 11 RIB operator.

Original U.S. Navy uniform breast insignia for SWCC approved in 2001.

New (l-r) Basic, Senior, and Master SWCC qualification insignias approved in August 2016.

CHAPTER 12

SUBMARINES 1940'S

Since the earliest days of World War II, submarines have become increasingly important host ships to our SEAL and SEAL Delivery Vehicle Teams. Except for one special mission, submarines were never considered worthy host ships for the UDTs during World War II. This was because the UDTs had to get so many men to the beach that submarines simply weren't practical. Surface ships and specifically Amphibious Personnel Destroyers (APDs) were ideal. The UDTs would not seriously consider the use of submarines until the post-war period.

Scouts and Raiders—Special Mission Group

The first recorded wartime use of a submarine by a U.S. maritime special unit was at Operation TORCH during the invasion of North Africa in November 1942. Amphibious Scout and Raiders were comprised of Army and Navy personnel. U.S. Army 1st Lieutenant Willard G. Duckworth was selected to lead a special mission team. He carefully selected five men, whom were sent to the Navy's Groton, Connecticut Submarine School for training. Their mission was to launch from the submarine *USS Barb* (SS-220), paddle an inflatable boat to a designated location off the Jette Principal at Safi, Morocco, then guide destroyers *USS Cole* (DD-155) and *USS Bernadou* (DD-153) around the jetty and into the harbor under cover of darkness.

While aboard the submarine preparing for the mission, Lieutenant Duckworth asked repeatedly to make periscope observations at frequent intervals to verify coastal landmarks, however, all requests were strangely denied; except for one brief periscope view just before his mission was launched. Nonetheless, the men departed from the surfaced submarine at 2200 on 7 November. *Barb's* commanding officer assured Lieutenant Duckworth that they were on station, which would have placed them three miles from Safi. In

USS Barb (SS-220).

fact, the men ended up paddling for over six hours, and still had not made their destination. Lieutenant Duckworth later estimated that they had actually been launched at least seven miles off shore. The men drifted south for the remainder of the night, and eventually made it ashore near an old fort built by the Portuguese. Their mission of guiding in the *Cole* and *Bernadou* was subsequently accomplished by Ensign John J. Bell and his Scout Boat crew.

USS Burrfish – UDT Special Mission Group

Bill Perkins, son of the late of Rear Admiral William B. Perkins, USN provided a priceless collection of documents to me, which were sent to the National UDT- SEAL Museum on behalf of the Perkins family. This collection of papers described the Third War Patrol of *USS Burrfish* (SS-312), which occurred between 29 July and 4 August 1944. This patrol included a special reconnaissance of Peleliu, Angau, and Gagil Tomil of the Yap Island Group in the Pacific Ocean about 500 miles southwest of Guam. At the time, Lieutenant Commander Perkins was commanding officer of *Burrfish*.

On this patrol, the submarine carried a special-mission detachment of UDT volunteers comprised of men from the Naval Combat Demolition Training and Experimental Base, Maui, Territory of Hawaii and new members of UDT-10, who had been trained by the Office of Strategic Services Maritime Unit (OSS-MU). Bill Perkins related to me that: "My father never referred to these men as UDT, but simply called them 'the swimmers.'"

This patrol has gained legendary significance in the history of Naval Special Warfare, since it was the first and only submarine-launched reconnaissance operation accomplished by the Pacific UDTs during World War II. It is also the only combat mission ever accomplished by Naval Special Warfare operators, where men were lost in action and their remains never recovered.

Admiral Perkins' *Burrfish* records provide a detailed accounting of the UDT mission, but nothing about the fate of the men after they went missing. The *Burrfish* records state: "After considering all possibilities it is believed that the three men joined up, saw something interesting near the shore line, decided to investigate and were captured. They must have been on, or very near the shore, as they were much too experienced swimmers for all of them to have been taken in the water. The men were covered with commando black paint, and were very difficult to see in the water."

On 9 July 1944, the UDT men embarked *Burrfish* for the planned mission. They remained

USS Burrfish (SS-312).

Aboard *USS Burrfish* (SS-312) 16 August 1944: (l-r) Leonard Barnhill, John MacMahon, LT M.R. Massey, Bill Moore, and Warren Christiansen. These UDT men were preparing to conduct a reconnaissance mission.

aboard for over one month before conducting any tasking. The UDT men were: LT M.R. Massey; CBM(AA) Howard "Red" Roeder; CBM(PA) John E. Ball; CM3c Emmet L. Carpenter; QM1c Robert A. Black, Jr.; SP(A)1c John MacMahon; SP(X)1c William Moore; S1c Leonard Barnhill; and QM3c Warren Christensen.

On the night of 16 August 1944, the submarine surfaced, and "swimmers" Lieutenant Massey, Warren Christensen, Leonard Barnhill, William Moore, and John MacMahon departed *Burrfish* and paddled to the near shore and anchored their rubber boat. Lieutenant Massey and three of the UDT men, having been grease-camouflaged, swam onto the reef and back. They discovered that discolored patches shown in air photos were only sea grass instead of reeds which might strand a landing craft.

Two nights later, *Burrfish* surfaced again two miles off the strongly guarded east shore of Yap. Chief Howard Roeder led this mission with Chief John Ball, Emmet Carpenter, Robert Black, and John MacMahon. They paddled within a quarter mile of shore and found a barrier reef just below the surface. Fearing the breakers might carry the boat ashore; they dropped an anchor and left Chief Ball aboard. The other four started for shore.

Fifteen minutes later, Black brought Carpenter back to the boat because of fatigue. Black rejoined MacMahon and Chief Roeder, and they began swimming toward the island. The three men never returned. Ball and Carpenter became worried, and finally decided to hoist anchor and search for their Teammates. They made a sweep along the reef, but there was no sign of the men. Time had run out, and they had to return to the *Burrfish*, hoping against hope that the others had swum straight out to the ship. But, there was no such luck.

The submarine searched close inshore until dawn. The coming daylight forced the ship to submerge and move farther to sea. Later the next morning *Burrfish* patrolled submerged off the reef in another vain attempt to spot the men. The surviving UDT men pleaded with Commander Perkins to let them go back to the barrier reef that night, being certain the lost men would try to make it after dark. The sea had grown rougher, however, and he made the hard decision that having alerted the Japanese and already losing three men, he didn't want to lose more. *Burrfish* gave up the search for the missing men and left for its next mission.

In concluding his report, Lieutenant Commander Perkins stated: "In this officer's experience, this group of men was outstanding—both professionally and as shipmates. They have had a long and difficult cruise in the submarine, but have acquitted themselves admirably. It is a tragedy that Roeder, MacMahon, and Black are not on board." Several days later, an intercepted Japanese document revealed the following:

UDT men launched from *USS Burrfish (*SS-312) at Peleliu on 18 August 1944: (l-r) Chief Howard "Red" Roeder (KIA), Emmet L. Carpenter, Bob Black (KIA), John MacMahon (KIA), and CPO John Ball. The men were captured and killed while in captivity.

```
ANNANSAKI 22 August 1944
Special Report GOTTO Unit
Intelligence Office (JOKOSHITSU)
```

On the 20th we seized three American prisoners at the TOBARU Battery on Yap. They belong to the FIFTH Demolition Unit. These men were transported by submarines. They jumped into the sea at points several miles distant from shore and by swimming reached the reefs off Tobaru Island, Leng and Lebinau. When they tried to return they lost sight of their submarine and swam back to the sea coast. They were captured while hiding. In view of this situation we must keep a strict watch especially in regard to infiltration of these various patrols and spies from submarines.

In view of the case, every lookout, whether it be night or day, shall carefully watch the nearby coast line, and if he observes any examples

139

of the above, shall report it immediately without fail. He should without hesitation emulate the above captures. We are confident there is safety in this manner.

The observation in this documentation indicated that the UDT men gave their Japanese captors a false story; one that they were briefed to provide if needed during pre-mission planning. Post-war research negated a story speculating that they were lost when a Japanese vessel was sunk by the U. S. Navy. According to Dr. Patrick J. Scannon, MD, PhD: "This 'sinking history' appears to have been used by the Japanese military in Palau on at least two other occasions as a decoy (documented from War Crimes Tribunal hearings), to hide the Kempeitai (the military police of the Japanese Army) execution of American U.S. Army Air Force airmen and civilian Catholic missionaries. No concrete evidence exists that any American POW ever left the Palau Islands alive, before or after the war."

Nothing was really known except that the UDT men gave their lives for their country. Each was posthumously awarded the Silver Star Medal. Their surviving teammates returned to Hawaii in December. Moore, Barnhill, and Christensen joined the Maui training staff, since their team, UDT-10, was already in Hollandia, New Guinea, preparing for its fourth beach mission. The three survivors were also awarded the Silver Star Medal and the right to wear the submarine insignia.

Men of *Burrfish* and the BentProp™ Project

Very few have seen the accounting provided by Dr. Patrick J. Scannon, MD, PhD. He is leader of the BentProp Project, which is dedicated to locating and assisting with identifying the remains of American prisoners of war and missing in action from World War II and other conflicts around the world—men who gave their lives in defense of America. Here is what I learned several years ago through correspondence with Dr. Scannon:

It is both right and timely to inform you [Tom Hawkins] that, based on multiple and independent sources from Palau, Japan, and the United States, we have now generally reconstructed what happened to Chief Gunners Mate Howard "Dynamite Joe" L. Roeder, QM1c Robert A. Black, and Sp(A)1c John C. MacMahon.

Briefly, on 21 August 1944 the Japanese 46th Naval Garrison reported by telegram to Palau command that three members of an American "Naval Combat Demolition Unit" had been captured by soldiers of the Imperial Japanese Army (IJA) on Yap. Two days later, these POWs were taken from Yap by Auxiliary Subchaser #27 to Koror, Palau. Thereafter Palauan eye witnesses saw two or three "frogmen" in bondage taken from Koror to Babeldaob – more specifically to the headquarters of the 30th Advanced Base Group Kempeitai (military police) on Babeldaob; under the overall command of LTGEN Sadae Inoue (IJA). Their presence at the Babeldaob headquarters was confirmed by a Japanese former intelligence officer in 1947. Sadly, evidence strongly supports that in late August 1944, the UDT men were executed by Japanese Army officers (most likely Kempeitai). One Palauan elder has taken us to where he believes the UDT men's execution/burial area is located. Our search is a work in progress and we are still far from discovering the exact burial site, given the size of the area described by the Palauan elder and other confounding factors.

Dr. Scannon also stated that: "Each of us remains haunted by their journey from the Yap shoreline to Koror, their march in bondage from Koror to Kempeitai headquarters, and finally their last ride in a Japanese staff car. Our searches are the least we can do to honor these brave Americans." As of this writing, the remains of the men have never been found.

Lieutenant Commander Perkins' *Burrfish* report stated that Chief Howard Roeder was not married; his next of kin was his mother Isa G. Roeder of Hollywood, California. Robert Black was married; his wife Ida lived in Glen Rock, New Jersey. John MacMahon was married; his wife's name was stated simply as Mrs. John C. MacMahon c/o Dr. A.S. Michalson, Minneapolis, Minnesota. If either had children, they would certainly be very proud for their father's service to their country. It will be a remarkable day if and when these men are ever returned to the land and flag they served, and for which they died so bravely.

Submarines Post-War Activities

The UDTs would not seriously consider submarines until after World War II, when, at the island of Vieques, Puerto Rico in early February 1947, UDT-2 and UDT-4 began experimental operations by launching and recovering rubber boats from *USS Grouper* (SS-214). Some days later, on 20 and 21 February, with *Grouper* sitting on the bottom of Lindberg Bay at St. Thomas, in the U.S. Virgin Islands, the UDT men, using the Lambertsen Amphibious Respiratory Unit (LARU), began for the first-time practicing lock-out and lock-in operations through the ship's escape trunk. The LARU was the same diving apparatus utilized by the OSS Maritime Unit during World War II.

UDT operators wearing the LARU at St. Thomas, USVI, 1947.

UDT men preparing to dive the LARU at St. Thomas in 1947.

On 22 February, with *USS Grouper* underway at a dead-slow speed (ideally one knot or less), Lieutenant Commander Doug Fane, the UDT commanding officer, and Dr. Chris Lambertsen, inventor of the LARU and trainer of the OSS MU swimmers during World War II, were the first to ever lock-out and lock-in to an underway submarine. Thus, they demonstrated the feasibility of launching and recovering UDT divers from a submerged and underway submarine.

These UDT men are wearing the LARU at St. Thomas.

On 14 October 1948 at St. Thomas, this time aboard *USS Quillback* (SS-424), the UDT men launched and recovered the British-made *Sleeping Beauty* submersible for the first time from the deck of a submerged submarine. This operation was accomplished with men from East and West Coast UDTs. When the men returned to their home bases at Little Creek, Virginia and Coronado, California, the concept for the "Submersible Operations" platoon had been established. The UDTs had expanded their operational capabilities beyond simply being combat swimmers performing hydrographic reconnaissance, to now include capabilities as combat divers with a host of new clandestine underwater infiltration, exfiltration, and sabotage capabilities.

From 1948 through the outbreak of the Korean War, UDT-1 and UDT-3 conducted training operations with a host of submarines that included *USS Redfish* (SS-395), *USS Seafox* (SS-402), *USS Ronquil* (SS-396), and *USS Perch* (SSP-313).

CHAPTER 13

KOREA AND POST-WAR SUBMARINE ACTIVITY

USS Perch

On 31 January 1950 *USS Perch* (SSP-313) was reclassified an Amphibious Personnel Transport Submarine (APSS), becoming the first submarine dedicated primarily for Marine Corps and UDT training. She operated up and down the West Coast. *Perch* saw distinguished service during the Korean War; conducting a host of combat patrols transporting British Royal Marines 41 Commandos, Korean Special Forces, and working with the UDTs and U.S. Marines. After the war, *Perch* continued to support UDT and USMC training along the coast of Southern California.

In October 1962, *Perch* was home ported to Subic Bay, Philippine Islands, the Western Pacific base of operations for West Coast UDTs. During January 1966, *Perch* launched UDT personnel for beach survey work in South Vietnam. She then provided services for training Filipino and American UDT personnel. *Perch* also worked with Nationalist Chinese Special Forces at Kaohsiung, Taiwan, and with Army Special Forces at Keelung, Taiwan. In July and August, *Perch* participated in Operation DECK HOUSE II, which involved several independent beach surveys with UDT personnel in South Vietnam. For Operation DECK HOUSE IV in September, *Perch* landed UDT personnel on five successive nights for pre-invasion beach reconnaissance.

USS Perch (APSS-313).

USS Tunny

In March 1953, *USS Tunny* (SSG-282) became the first Regulus-missile firing submarine in the U.S. Navy, serving in that capacity for nearly 12 years. In 1966, her missile hanger was converted into a troop

USS Tunny (APSS-282).

berthing compartment for operations involving Naval Special Warfare. She was re-designated a troop transport submarine.

Tunny was uniquely and specifically adapted to support waterborne unconventional warfare. One of many modifications was to the sea-suction piping (water inlet to cool the equipment), customized to allow either a bottom or top inlet depending on the tactical situation. Switching to upper inlet allowed the ship to be rested on the bottom before lock-out operations commenced, thus, allowing a stationary platform and safe haven for the UDT and SEAL combat swimmers.

Tunny relieved *Perch* in August 1966 at Subic Bay, and spent much of the next two years operating in the South China Sea and elsewhere, conducting unconventional warfare operations. *Tunny* carried UDT, SEALs, Army Special Forces, UK and Taiwan Special Forces, U.S. Marine Corps Force Recon, and others on a variety of special missions. The ship also conducted reconnaissance in preparation for amphibious assault operations off the coast of Vietnam, where she gathered navigational and oceanographic information.

UDT operators paddling their inflatable boat after an at-sea rendezvous with *USS Tunny* (APSS-282).

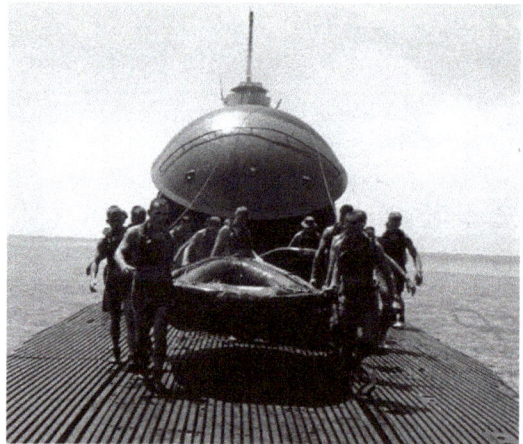

UDT operators preparing to launch an inflatable boat from the deck of the *USS Tunny* (APSS-282).

USS Sealion

The East Coast UDTs continued to refine their underwater skills with *Grouper* and *Quillback*, but most frequently with *USS Sealion* (APSS-315), which had been on service in the Pacific during World War II. Along with *Perch*, she had been designated for conversion as a troop carrier. During *Sealion's* conversion in April 1948, her torpedo tubes and forward engines were removed, and her forward engine room and forward and after torpedo rooms were converted to berth troops. The forward engine room and after torpedo room were designed for alternative use as cargo space. The wardroom was redesigned for use as an operating room as needed. The beam aft of the conning tower was extended. A large watertight cylindrical chamber was installed aft of the conning tower to store equipment.

In the spring of 1949 *Sealion* was ordered to the Atlantic and home ported at various times in New London, Connecticut and Norfolk, Virginia. Throughout the 1950's and 1960's she conducted numerous training operations with Marines, UDT, and Beach Jumper Units; and, on occasion, with Army Special Forces off the Virginia and Carolina coasts and in the Caribbean. In October 1962, *Sealion* embarked a detachment of frogmen from SEAL Team ONE for contingency operations during the Cuban Missile Crisis. On 15 September 1967, she was moved to Key West, Florida for her last two years of active service.

The MK VII SDV and cradle bolted to the super-structure deck of *USS Sealion* during training operations in February 1970.

USS Sealion (APSS-315).

The SDV in its cradle had no protection, restricting the sub's speed to under one knot during submerged and underway operations.

CHAPTER 14

SUBMARINES 1970'S - 2000'S

USS Grayback

During their many years of active service, *Perch, Tunny,* and *Sealion* represented an era when submarines could be somewhat dedicated for UDT and SEAL Team operations. These submarines were very old and always in line to be retired. Fortunately, the need for their replacements was considered by Naval Special Warfare's leadership.

Working with the Navy Staff in the Pentagon on a long-range development plan called the Swimmer (later SEAL) Support System, a program was established to accommodate conversion of two former missile carrying submarines, *USS Grayback* (SSG-574) and *USS Growler* (SSG-577), for UDT and SEAL Team use. Like *Tunny,* these submarines also had been purpose-built to launch sea-to-surface Regulus missiles. Two chambers had been constructed into the bow of these submarines to provide them this capability.

As more modern Polaris nuclear submarines entered service, *Grayback* and *Growler* became obsolete for missiles, but ideal candidates as troop transports. They could be used specifically to conduct mass-swimmer lock-outs and to transport, launch, and recover SDVs.

Grayback's conversion began in November 1967 at the Mare Island Naval Shipyard in Vallejo, California. The conversion was originally estimated at $15.2 million, but actually took $30 million, all the while absorbing funds intended for *Growler's* conversion. *Grayback* was re-classified from SSG (Submarine, Guided Missile) to ATS (Amphibious Transport Submarine) on 30 August 1968, and once again entered active service. During this period, she was deployed to the Western Pacific and considered for unconventional warfare operations against Viet Cong and North Vietnamese targets.

Hangers aboard *USS Grayback* (LPSS-574), taken from the sail in Mare Island Naval Shipyard, 31 July 1969.

Changes to *Grayback* during conversion included her sail being extended 10 feet, auxiliary tanks were added to the forward position of the engine room, her missile chambers were converted to carry SDVs, a diver's decompression chamber was constructed in the starboard hanger, and the ship was provided the capability to accommodate 67 embarked troops. By adding the auxiliary tanks to the engine room her length was extended 12 feet to an overall length of 334 feet.

Growler, which was intended for service in the Atlantic Fleet, was never converted. A construction accident involving *Grayback* at Mare Island resulted in severe damages. This caused substantial cost increases, and the money came from *Growler's* conversion funds. Many lessons were learned during operations with *Grayback*; however, because of age she was decommissioned in January 1984.

This is an early artist concept of *USS Grayback* and *USS Growler's* capabilities to support UDT, SEAL, and SDV operations.

Dry Deck Shelters

During the 1970's, as an extension of the SEAL Support System, and while the *Grayback* was still in service, plans were formulated for development of six air-transportable submarine Dry Deck Shelters (DDS) that would be attachable to seven ships in the 637 (Long Hull) Class of nine nuclear submarines. Each submarine

USS Grayback (LPSS-574) off Mare Island, CA on 24 July 1969, with a great view of the Regulus missile hangers that were converted for UDT, SEAL, and SEAL Delivery Vehicle Team use.

DDS safety crew seen in a flooded shelter. Above their heads are single-hose regulators mated to a hookah rig that will supply air to the SEALs.

would carry one shelter, and each shelter would carry one SDV. This program expansion resulted from a revision and increased funding for Technical Development Plan 38-02, which earlier had called for conversion of *Grayback* and *Growler*.

The DDS concept was to have a specially built external chamber that could be bolted on and bolted off a submarine and, when installed, could transport the SDV or be used for mass-swimmer lock-out operations. Six DDS were constructed, each measuring 11.6 meters (38 feet) long by 2.7 and meters (9 feet) diameters (external). They added about 30 tons to its host submarine's submerged displacement. The DDS was designed to be highway transported on specially built transporters, which could also be taken aboard a USAF C-5 or C-17 aircraft. Once at the port of embarkation, one to three days would be required to install and test the shipboard system.

Each DDS was built with three HY-80 steel sections covered with a glass-reinforced plastic fairing: a spherical hyperbaric chamber at the forward end to treat injured divers, a smaller spherical transfer trunk (entry point into the submarine), and a cylindrical hangar (i.e., "the Shelter") with elliptical ends to house one Mark VIII SDV or 20 SEALs with four Combat Rubber Raiding Craft.

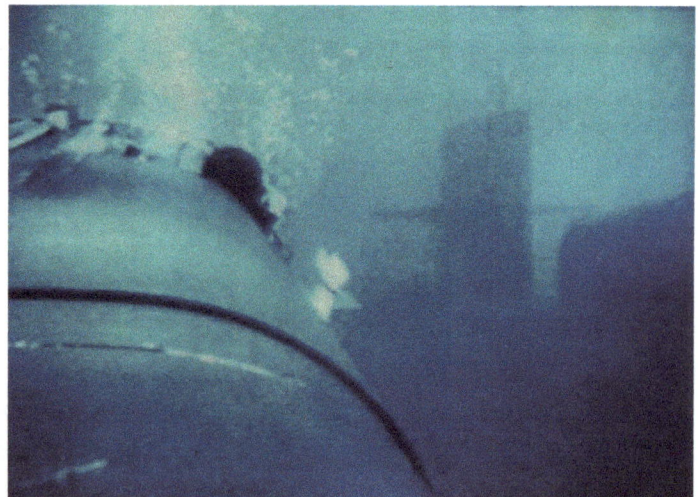

A MK VIII SDV crew doing a "fly-by" of the DDS-01S mated with *USS Cavalla* (SSN-684) during its first sea trials off Hawaii in the early 1980s.

The first DDS was built by the Electric Boat Division of the General Dynamics Corporation in Groton, Connecticut and designated DDS-01S. The "S" indicated Starboard, or the side to which the outer hangar outer door swings open. It was completed in 1982. The remaining five shelters: DDS-02P ("P" for Port), -03P, -04S, -05S, and -06P, were built between 1987 and 1991 by the Newport News Shipbuilding Company in Newport News, Virginia. The DDS needed port and starboard swinging doors, because it was known that future host submarines would have the capability to carry two DDS side-by-side, and this required the doors to swing in opposite directions. Each DDS was designed to have a useful life of about 40 year's time.

DDS seen without its protective fiberglass cowling.

637 Sturgeon-Class (Long Hull) Submarines

After a comprehensive study, the 637 Sturgeon-Class (Long Hull) submarines were considered the only fast attack submarines in the fleet that had the inherently designed ballast needed to carry a DDS. The first ship planned to be modified was *USS Silversides* (SSN-679) in the Atlantic Fleet, which was home ported close to the shipbuilder in Groton, Connecticut. Problems occurred with that plan, and trials were shifted to the Pacific Fleet and *USS Cavalla* (SSN-684). And, indeed, *Cavalla* was the first to successfully perform DDS sea trials in 1983. Five other ships in the class would eventually complete modifications to carry the DDS: *USS Archerfish* (SSN-678), *USS Silversides* (SSN-679), *USS William H. Bates* (SSN-680), *USS Tunny* (SSN-682), and *USS L. Mendel Rivers* (SSN-686).

These submarines were used extensively for training and often for long-duration patrols in the Mediterranean and Pacific oceans with DDS and SDV Team personnel embarked. While it was originally envisioned that every shelter would fit every 637 Class (Long Hull) submarine, such was not to be the case. The fact is that not all submarines in the same class are built to the same exact specifications. It was realized during testing that each submarine in the same class was slightly different, and required its own set of piping to accommodate a particular shelter. Differences included: appropriate mating hatch configuration, electrical connections, piping for ventilation, divers' air, and draining water. Consequently, any DDS in the Atlantic would only fit submarines assigned to the Atlantic, and vice-versa for those in the Pacific. During one contingency planning operation, a Pacific Fleet submarine with a DDS transited through the Panama Canal to begin rehearsals and remained on standby in Puerto Rico.

Ethan Allen Class Submarines

DDS crew assisting the launch of a MK VIII SDV.

Follow-on submarines designated for modification were two Ethan Allen Class ballistic missile submarines: *USS Sam Houston* (SSBN/SSN-609) and *USS John Marshall* (SSBN/SSN-611). These were the first former ballistic-missile submarines converted as attack submarines (SSNs) for SEAL and SDV Team use. These would become the first submarines to have the capability to carry two DDS simultaneously. They became available only because of the Strategic Arms Limitation Treaty (SALT) between the U.S. and the Soviet Union, when the U.S was required to eliminate numerous missile silos; including many on submarines.

On 15 December 1986, the *John Marshall,* in conjunction with SDV Team TWO, began transit for deployment with its DDS crew embarked as a part of ship's company to the Mediterranean Sea. When a DDS is not attached to a submarine, it is stored and maintained by SDV Team fleet-diver technicians, and can be used for shore-based training by flooding it with fresh water.

In an arrangement worked out with the Submarine Force, it was agreed that when the DDS Detachment was embarked aboard a host submarine, it would become a department of the ship and directly responsible to the ship's commanding officer. The SDV and SDV operators remained an embarked (supported) detachment.

On 1 May 1989, after conducting a variety of exercises with carrier battle groups and other submarines, the *John Marshall* departed again for a Mediterranean deployment. This was the first time a submarine had deployed anywhere in the world with two DDS on board, adding unique flexibility and endurance to the Theater Commanders for Naval Special Warfare operations.

On 26 January 1991, the ship again departed Norfolk for what would be its final deployment to the Mediterranean. Outfitted with two DDS, the ship operated in direct support of Operation DESERT STORM and provided significant capability options to the Central Command and Sixth Fleet Commander.

DDS seen operating at periscope depth. The hinges display that the hanger doors open in opposite directions.

Before her retirement in 1991, the *John Marshall* served as flagship in the Caribbean Ocean for the largest submarine special operations exercise since World War II. Over 191 personnel, including three flag officers, SEALs, and Army Special Operations Forces, embarked to conduct operations during a training exercise called PHANTOM SHADOW. The *USS Sam Houston,* sister ship to *USS John Marshall*, performed the same deployment capability with SEALs in the Pacific, supporting many SDV and dual-DDS operations and deployments.

USS John Marshall on deployment with the Dry Deck Shelter in the Mediterranean.

Benjamin Franklin Class Submarines

The next ships to be modified came from the Benjamin Franklin Class of submarines. They were *USS James K. Polk* (SSBN/SSN-645) for service in the Atlantic and *USS Kamehameha* (SSBN/SSN-642) for the Pacific. Both of these former ballistic-missile submarines had the capability to carry the DDS in a single or dual side-by-side configuration. Decommissioning of these ships in 2002 was offset by modification of the improved Los Angeles Class submarines, which were the first host ships to have the capability to carry the DDS and the new Advance SEAL Delivery System (ASDS).

USS Kamehameha (SSN-642) in a dual Dry Deck Shelter (DDS) configuration.

Los Angeles Class Submarines

Los Angeles Class ships supporting SDV-DDS operations included: *USS Los Angeles* (SSN-688), *USS Charlotte* (SSN-766) and *USS La Jolla* (SSN-701) in the Pacific and *USS Dallas* (SSN-700), *USS Philadelphia* (SSN-690), and *USS Buffalo* (SSN-715) in the Atlantic. These submarines were modified to transport the DDS and ASDS, and had the capability to carry one or both simultaneously.

Seawolf Class Submarines

The *USS Jimmy Carter* (SSN-23) is the third and last Seawolf Class submarine to be built, and one of the few ships in the U.S. Navy to have been named for a person still living at the time of the ship's naming. The *Jimmy Carter* is roughly 100 feet longer than the other two ships of her class. This is

USS Jimmy Carter (SSGN-23) with a Dry Deck Shelter installed.

USS Greeneville (SSN-772) completing sea trials with the ASDS off the coast of Pearl Harbor, Hawaii, July 1, 2003.

due to the insertion of a section known as the multi-mission platform, a modification that was necessary to allow installation of the DDS and ASDS and to permit the ship to perform other classified missions. Despite these modifications the ship retains all war fighting capabilities, and now supports the fleet commander as an attack submarine conducting undersea missions and clandestine special operations. The ship also incorporates a specially designed combat-swimmer silo or internal lock-out chamber that can support up to eight combat swimmers and their equipment.

Ohio Class Submarines

With the end of the Cold War, the Navy realized that it no longer needed all 18 of its Ohio-class SSBN submarines to fulfill the nation's strategic deterrence. Rather than scrapping submarines with decades additional service remaining, the U.S. Navy began converting them to guided-missile submarines (SSGNs), and working with the SDV Teams to begin transforming four of the submarines into multi-mission ships equipped to conduct maritime special operations.

In December 2006, the Electric Boat Division of the General Dynamics Corporation completed conversion of the *USS Ohio* (SSGN-726) from a ballistic-missile platform to a guided-missile submarine capable of carrying 154 Tomahawk cruise missiles and more than 66 SEALs or other Special Operations

USS Ohio (SSGN-726) submarine with two DDS embarked.

Forces for extended periods. Additional berthing was installed in the missile compartment to accommodate the added personnel, and other measures were taken to extend the amount of time that SEALs can spend deployed aboard the SSGNs. The two forward-most missile tubes were permanently converted as lock-out chambers that allow clandestine insertion and retrieval of SEALs. Each lock-out chamber can also accommodate a DDS, enhancing the SSGNs' SEAL capabilities. Also converted were the *USS Michigan* (SSGN-727) at Puget Sound

Naval Shipyard, and *USS Florida* (SSGN-728) and *USS Georgia* (SSGN-729) at the Norfolk Naval Shipyard in Virginia.

Virginia Class Submarines

The Navy is now building the next-generation attack submarine, the Virginia Class. This submarine has several innovations that significantly enhance its war-fighting capabilities with an emphasis on littoral operations. They have a fly-by-wire ship control system that provides improved shallow-water ship handling; this and other special features to support SDV-DDS, SEALs and other Special Operations Forces; including a reconfigurable torpedo room that can accommodate a large number of embarked troops and all their equipment for prolonged deployments. In August 2015, the *USS John Warner* (SSN-785) was commissioned. It was first in the Virginia class to be named after a person; the previous 11 were named after states - all other Virginia class submarines will be named after states.

ASDS embarked and underway on *USS Jimmy Carter* (SSGN-23).

USS Virginia (SSN-774)

CHAPTER 15

COMBATANT SUBMERSIBLES

SEAL Delivery Vehicles

The term Swimmer Delivery Vehicle and acronym SDV became SEAL Delivery Vehicle (SDV) in 1983; at the same time Underwater Demolition Teams 12 and 22 were reestablished as SEAL Delivery Vehicle Teams ONE and TWO. Before the subject of SDVs is outlined, it would be appropriate to review the requirement for combatant submersibles, ergo, why are they needed? A concise answer to this was provided in a CONFIDENTIAL report entitled *Underwater Swimmers* prepared for the Office of Naval Research by the Panel on Underwater Swimmers, Committee on Amphibious Operations of the National Research Council, dated November 1952. Although written in 1952, these now unclassified words are just as descriptive today.

Whenever it is necessary to operate near an enemy held shore in as complete secrecy as possible, the approach to the objective must be made under water. The first part of the approach can be made in a fleet-type submarine, but these 1500-ton vessels cannot operate submerged in water shallower than 60 ft. and depths less than 150 ft. are considered hazardous. The final submerged approach must be made by swimming or in a small submersible. On many coasts throughout the world, depths less than 60 ft. extend out several miles from shore. In these areas [that] even men equipped with SCUBA would not have enough breathing gas to swim the distance and return. Moreover, they would be seriously fatigued when they reached their objective after their swim of several hours. To supplement their swimming, they must have a small, powered submersible…

1939 to 1945 Italian Activities

During World War II, the Italians and the British pioneered the use of small submersibles for stealthy attacks on shipping. Throughout the war, the Italians used so-called two-man human torpedoes. The British used this type of vehicle for only a short period preceding the launching of their small submarines called X-Craft. Swimmer transport submersibles were first employed at the beginning of World War II by the Italians against the British in the Mediterranean.

Lacking a large navy, Italy pioneered the use of underwater swimmers as military weapons. They concurrently developed underwater vehicles and operating procedures to transport swimmers and their explosive payloads to target areas. The targets were enemy warships and merchantmen in their own harbors. The first Italian vehicle for swimmer use was the famous two-man human torpedo designated the SLC (*Siluro a Lenta Corsa*); nicknamed "*Maiale*" or "Pig." Torpedo-like in general configuration, the Pig carried its explosive pay-load as one or two detachable nose sections.

Two crew members wearing closed-circuit underwater breathing apparatus sat astride the vehicle. The forward diver operated the vehicle and maintained longitudinal trim; the buddy diver controlled the vehicle buoyancy and placed the explosive payload beneath the hull of the target ship. The Pig's operator was provided with basic navigation and control instruments that included a magnetic compass, clock, and depth gauge.

Prototype human torpedoes were first designed and operated by two Italian naval engineering officers in 1936, both submariners. That same year, interest in these vehicles faded and the few that had been built were placed in storage. With the deteriorating world situation in 1938, however, the vehicles were resurrected, improved, and in 1939 the 1st Light Flotilla began training with the Pigs. In March 1941, the Assault Craft Department of the 1st Light Flotilla became the 10th Light Flotilla, a cover name for the command responsible for all Italian naval special assault craft; surface and subsurface. Pigs and their operators became part of the 10th Light Flotilla.

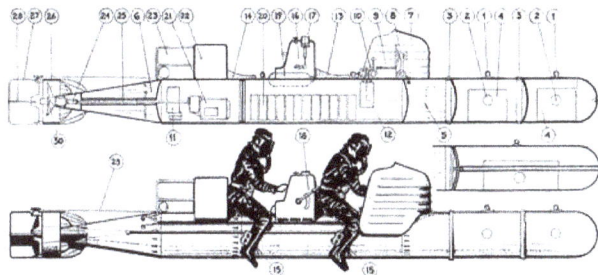

Italian Mark I *Siluro Lenta Corsa* (SLC) slow-speed torpedo nicknamed *'Maiale'* (Pig).

Decima Flottiglia Motoscafi Armati Siluranti, was an Italian commando frogman unit of the Regia Marina. The acronym MAS translates to "speedboats armed torpedo," which were active during World War I and World War II. The frogmen were called "Gamma" operators after the name of the Pirelli-made dry suits they wore.

Italian "Maiale" *or "Pig." SLC Mark II*

Decima Flottiglia MAS "Gamma" Italian frogman.

The first Italian operation using Pigs was planned for August 1940 against shipping in the harbor at Alexandria, Egypt. To accomplish this task, the submarine *Iride* was to moved from La Spezia in northern Italy to the Gulf of Bomba in Libya and rendezvoused with the torpedo boat *Calipso,* which was transporting four Pigs and their operators. The Pigs were lashed to the submarine with chocks on her deck. On 22 August *Iride* was conducting operations in the Bay of Bomba, when British aircraft attacked and sunk the submarine and, of course, the Pigs.

After *Iride,* the submarines *Gondar* and the *Scire* were converted as assault-craft transporters. Three steel cylinders were installed on the submarine decks (two aft and one forward) to transport the Pigs. With these watertight cylinders installed, no limit was placed on the operating depth of the transport submarine other than the limits of the submarine itself.

Waterproof and pressure proof containers on *Scire.*

In September 1940, *Gondar* was underway to attack Alexandria, but the mission was aborted when the submarine received a radio message that her targets had left the harbor. During the return transit, she was attacked and sunk by Allied aircraft. *Scire* aborted a duplicate task to attack the harbor at Gibraltar for the same reason. The next month, *Scire* carried out the first Pig attack at Gibraltar. It was a complete failure. Three Pigs were launched from the bottomed submarine in the Bay of Algeciras. Each Pig developed various malfunctions. None could make a successful attack and all of the Pig operators were captured. In May 1941, *Scire* again launched three Pigs for another attack at Gibraltar; and, again the mission was a failure. One of the Pigs was badly damaged immediately after launching from the bottomed submarine. The other two were lost during some phase of the attack. Despite these failures, the Italians persisted and were learning many lessons.

It was not until September 1941 that the Italians had their first success during another attack on Gibraltar Harbor. This attack resulted in the sinking of two tankers and a motor vessel. Within two years, using underwater swimmers, motor torpedo boats, and Pigs, the 10th Light Flotilla sank or damaged 31

Battleship *HMS Valiant.*

Battleship *HMS Queen Elizabeth.*

ships representing 265,352 tons of shipping. Their most spectacular attacks were against the battleships *HMS Queen Elizabeth* and *HMS Valiant* in the harbor at Alexandria in December 1941. Both were seriously damaged, but were later repaired and returned to service.

British Activities

The British Navy was not blind to what the Italians were doing, and was already in the process of producing a midget submarine—the X-Craft. Construction of a midget submarine presented special problems that increase rapidly and in severity as the size of the submarine is reduced. A typical submarine is designed so that all available space is used in the most economical manner. The problem becomes more severe in the design of a midget submarine. Safety margins are necessarily reduced, accessibility is restricted, accommodations are more confined, and only limited maintenance is possible; hence, a drastic reduction in equipment provided in a fleet submarine. The X-Craft was a complete submarine in miniature with internal "dry" living space for its small crew.

Artist renderings of the British "Chariot" combatant submersible.

British "Chariot" operator with thermal-protective dress.

British "Charioteers" maneuver their Chariot on the surface wearing underwater breathing apparatus.

The British human torpedoes, called "Chariots," were developed as an interim capability; awaiting completion of their first X-Craft. An Italian Pig had been salvaged by British divers after one of the unsuccessful Italian attacks on Gibraltar. The British copied, improved, and added new equipment in their design. That's why in a casual glance, the submersibles look like twins. It was manned by a crew of two wearing self-contained underwater breathing apparatus and diving suits for thermal protection. Like the Italians, they sat astride their "wet" submersible, exposed directly to the ambient ocean environment. British newspapers were the first to coin the term "frogman."

In early June 1942, the first Chariot was assembled and tested. The following October, the British undertook an operation using two Chariots to attack the German battleship *Tirpitz* lying in Asensjord, Norway. A Norwegian coastal vessel, manned by a Norwegian underground crew with properly forged papers, departed for Norway with Chariots and operators (called Charioteers) aboard. The Chariots were mounted for transport underneath the vessel. After the attack, the plan was to scuttle the Chariots, abandon the transport vessel, and escape and evade through Norway to safety in Sweden via the Norwegian underground.

After passing numerous barriers, including inspection by German military authorities, the Norwegian vessel arrived within 10 miles of the *Tirpitz* only to run into a sudden, severe storm. The pitching and rolling of the vessel caused the Chariots to shake loose; striking the bottom of the hull. The attachment bolts sheared and both Chariots were lost. All members of the party escaped as planned; except for one man, who was captured and later executed by the Germans as a saboteur.

British "Chariots" shown with the cradle and rail system used for extraction, launch, and recovery.

Chariots could also be transported by submarines in waterproof and pressure-proof steel cylinders. This method didn't restrict the operating depth of the host submarine. The cylinders were flooded at the time of launch. The submersibles, being neutralized, were extracted using a cradle and rail system.

British operations with Chariots were not as successful as the Italians. Indeed, the only completely successful operation occurred on 28–29 October 1944, when two Chariots were launched from the submarine *HMS Trenchant* and sank two ships in the Japanese-occupied harbor at Phuket, Thiland.

On 15 March 1943, the British launched the first X-Craft, which had been under construction for the better part of three years. A total of 14 X-Craft were built; they were the first dry swimmer delivery submersibles built. These craft had a wet and dry section, commonly called the "W&D" compartment, which was used by the combat divers to lock-in and lock-out of the submersible.

Divers could be used to cut through anti-submarine nets blocking an enemy harbor or place explosive charges on or underneath target ships. The X-Craft also had the capability to drop side-loaded explosives—one load carried on each side of the pressure hull; each containing 4,000 pounds of high explosives. Timers to explode the charges were set from within the X-Craft before release.

Out-of-water view of the British X-Craft.

On 22 September 1943, two of six X-Craft successfully placed four of the two-ton explosive charges beneath the *Tirpitz* as she was anchored in a Norwegian fjord. When the charges detonated, they resulted in severe damage to the large battleship. The success of this and other operations in European and the Mediterranean waters resulted in a modified design of an X-Craft for operations in the Far East.

British command pilot at the controls in the "dry" space in the X-Craft.

The result was the XE Craft (presumably the "E" was for East). The XEs were slightly increased in size to accommodate a Freon™ air-conditioning system, additional fresh-water capacity, air-purification equipment, and certain other features. Six XEs were deployed to the Pacific in the later stages of the war, and a total of 12 had been built or were being built at the end of the war. Their capabilities were amply demonstrated in Pacific operations.

In July 1945, the XE-3 transited the Johore Strait to attack the Japanese cruiser *Takao* in the harbor at Singapore. Under

British XE-Craft on trials in Scotland.

extremely difficult conditions beneath the cruiser, the combat divers attached six limpet charges to the bottom of *Takao's* hull using an improvised piece of rope–the hull was covered with a thick layer of seaweed, and the magnets of the limpet mines could not hold them on the hull. When the mines exploded, they blew a hole 20 by 10 meters (66 by 33 feet). The blast disabled some gun turrets, destroyed *Takao's* rangefinders, and flooded a number of compartments, but didn't sink the ship. It was discovered after the end of the war that *Takao* was manned by a skeleton crew and had no ammunition aboard.

American Activities

In the United States, the OSS attempted to duplicate the combat-swimmer capability exploited by the British. The OSS MU was formed for the purpose of maritime sabotage, and adopted many of the British training and tactics. In the autumn of 1942 the OSS MU tried to exploit a submersible they called the "Toy." It was not a successful project; however, the significance of the Toy was that the OSS MU divers recognized the limitations of their breathing apparatus and the need for assisted propulsion.

The "Toy" was a failed OSS MU experimental submersible constructed entirely with wood.

During this same period, OSS MU acquired the British submersible "Sleeping Beauty." It was deployed to the Southeast Asia Theater of Operations, where they trained extensively with it in Ceylon, India for the anticipated invasion of the Japanese homeland. As far as can be determined "Sleeping Beauty" was never used in combat by the British or Americans.

American X-1

The British employed X-Craft submarines extensively during World War II. The U.S. had nothing comparable until 1953, when plans were drawn up for a miniature U.S. submarine. Its keel was laid on 8 June 1954 and the ship was accepted into the U.S. Navy on 7 September 1955 as the USS X-1. It was a

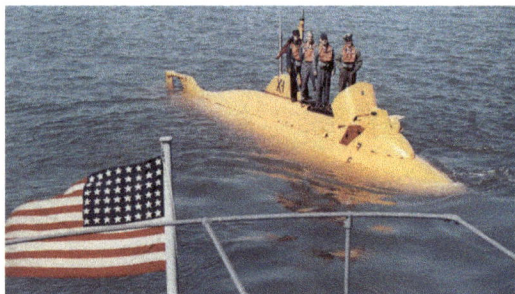

dry submersible, originally conceived for tactically transporting combat swimmers. It was diesel powered on the surface and used hydrogen-peroxide in the diesel engine for submerged operation. Batteries and a D-C motor provided emergency submerged propulsion. It always retained its "X" designation, which indicated that it was experimental. While UDT men did accomplish limited training with the X-1, it was never accepted for operational use, and never completed any kind of combat patrol.

USS X-1 on maneuvers in the Chesapeake Bay, circa 1955.

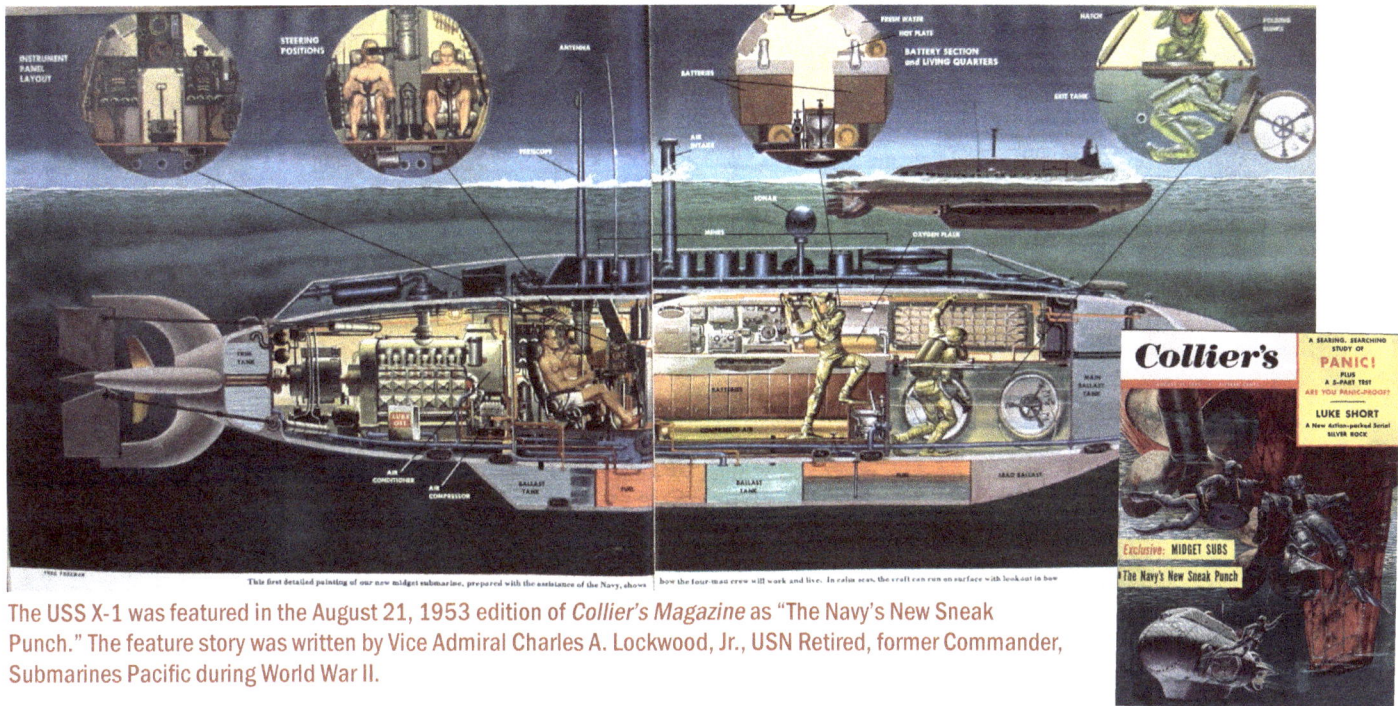

The USS X-1 was featured in the August 21, 1953 edition of *Collier's Magazine* as "The Navy's New Sneak Punch." The feature story was written by Vice Admiral Charles A. Lockwood, Jr., USN Retired, former Commander, Submarines Pacific during World War II.

The Fairchild Engine and Airplane Corporation began construction of the X-1 in 1954 under the oversight of the Office of Naval Research for ultimate assignment to the Amphibious Forces. Early in the construction phase, however, the Navy transferred the project to the Bureau of Ships, and the craft was delivered to the Submarine Force instead. With this change the X-1 became more of a Submarine Force submarine and less an amphibious force swimmer transport submarine. As observed by the British author Haden I. Sutton in his book *Covert Shores: The Story of Naval Special Forces Missions and Mini-Subs*: "The UDT wanted four X-1s to support [COMUDU-2], but the Submarine Force was unconvinced about providing the UDTs with dedicated midget submarines. Submarines were their territory and under no circumstances were submarines belonging to UDT to be tolerated." Haden Sutton's book was published in 2015. It is a well-researched compilation, and likely the most definitive history on world-wide small submarines and combatant submersibles published in recent years and perhaps ever.

The USS X-1 had a maximum range of 1,800 miles at 4 knots on the surface under diesel power. On its hydrogen-peroxide system, its submerged range varied from 180 miles at two knots to 140 miles at 10 knots. On battery power (emergency only), it had a submerged range varying from 12 miles at two knots to six miles at five knots. When the hydrogen-peroxide system was removed and replaced by increased battery capacity, the submerged range was reduced considerably to 11.5 miles, at two knots, or seven miles at six knots. The submersible was designed to carry two submarine crew members and six UDT divers with equipment. Additionally, 14 limpet charges could be carried in the forward section of the

USS X-1 miniature submarine at St. Thomas, USVI circa 1964. Notice the two SPUs mounted in port and starboard racks next to the man standing.

USS X-1 on display at the U.S. Naval Academy; providing a good out-of-water view.

free-flooding superstructure that ran the length of the hull topside.

As late as February and March of 1964, the X-1 operated for four weeks with UDT personnel at St. Thomas. As a result of these operations, the UDTs reaffirmed their requirement for a dry combatant submersible.

The X-1 was on display at the U.S. Naval Academy from 1974 through the year 2000. It was then transferred to the Submarine Force Museum in Groton, Connecticut, where it remains today.

The French PR-77

In 1964, the U.S. Navy's Mine Defense Laboratory (MDL) in Panama City, Florida was contracted by the Naval Ships Systems Command to exploit the technology of a French-built two-man submersible called the PR-77. This submersible incorporated a tear-drop design, where two operators rode sitting upright side-by-side. In 1965 the MDL redesigned and rebuilt the two-man submersible; basically, gutting the PR-77 and installing new test subsystems. Although this vehicle experienced significant operational problems, it was always intended to be the test bed for development of a contract specification for the Class I and Class II SDVs outlined in the Swimmer (later SEAL) Support System, the Navy's Technical Development Plan 38-02. The modified PR-77 was called the "EXP" for Experimental Platform. It was later designated the Mark VI SDV, but was never deployed operationally.

The Convair Model 14

In December 1966, the Convair Division of the General Dynamics Corporation in San Diego delivered five, newly-designed, four-man SDVs built under contract to the Naval Ship Systems Command (formerly Bureau of Ships). Operational and technical guidance were provided by Commander, Naval Operations Support Group, Pacific (today's Naval Special Warfare Group ONE).

It was designated the Convair Model 14 upon delivery. It was capable of a sustained five-knot cruising speed for eight hours' time. The four-diver crew sat upright in a free-flooding hull, which was constructed of 0.08-inch thick fiberglass. Two crew compartments fore and

Convair Model 14 / MK VII SDV underway.

aft were separated by a main ballast tank. These compartments were enclosed by sliding clear-plastic canopies intended to reduce drag. Men in the forward compartment faced forward; men in the aft compartment faced aft.

The Convair Model 14 represented the latest thinking in the design and construction of SDVs in the United States at the time. It was considered an interim capability as the Class I and Class II SDVs, to be acquired under the Technical Development Plan 38-02 program, were being prepared for design and construction by industry. The Convair Model 14 was a very basic design and had none of the sophisticated sub systems considered necessary for a truly advanced SDV design, i.e., mapping sonar, ahead-looking sonar, total-depth recording equipment, and other features that would be incorporated in the advanced-technology Class I and Class II vehicles. The Convair Model 14 was controlled by a stick and had bow planes and rudders to control depth and direction. The men called this "flying the boat," since the controls were like those of an aircraft.

In the early 1970's, the Convair Model 14 was designated the Mark VII SDV; and, because of substantial delays in building the 38-02 vehicles, this SDV would be substantially improved through progressive alteration and modification with advanced sonar and other capabilities. The Mark VII SDV was the first "production" SDV accepted by the U.S. Navy, and the first truly reliable submersible designated for combat operations by the UDT and SEAL Teams.

163

Swimmer Support System

The Swimmer Support System would revolutionize the underwater combat capabilities of the UDT and SEAL Teams. Originally conceived in the early 1960's, the plan called for development of Class I and Class II underwater breathing apparatus, Class I and Class II SDVs, and conversion of *USS Grayback* and sister ship *USS Growler,* former Regulus-missile submarines, as host platforms for transport, launch, and recovery of SDVs and crews.

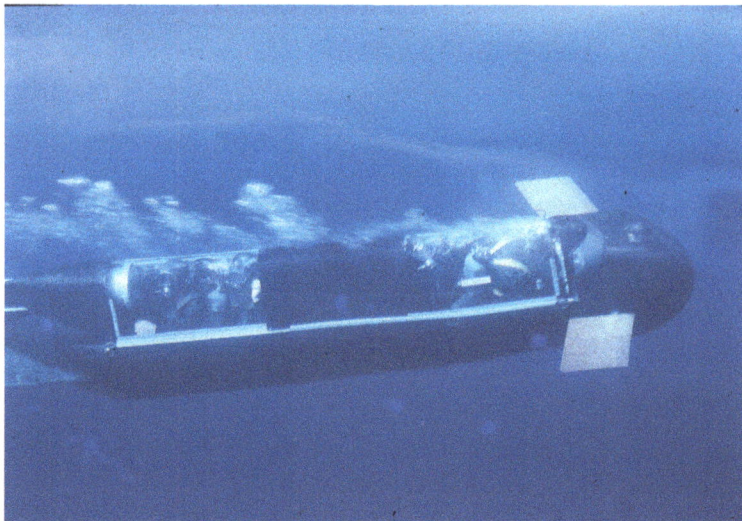

The Convair SDV seen from a surface safety boat off the coast of San Clemente Island, California in November 1967. With four men embarked, it is a tight fit.

MK VII, Mod 3 SDV underway. Note the improved hull design and black canopies.

Specifications for the new Underwater Breathing Apparatus (UBA) and SDVs were completed in 1968-69 period. A contract was awarded to the Scott Aviation Corporation in Buffalo, New York for development of the closed-circuit, pure-oxygen rebreather (Class I), and closed-circuit, mixed-gas rebreather (Class II) to replace the Emerson and Mark VI UBAs respectively. The closed-circuit, mixed-gas Class II UBA was intended to sustain a combat swimmer for six-hours at a depth of 33 feet. This was to complement the capabilities of the Class I SDV, which would have extended range, depth controls, and advanced technology navigational capabilities.

AeroJet General Corporation in Azusa, California was awarded the contract for development of the six-man Class I SDV and two-man Class II SDV. The Class I SDV's primary mission was infiltration and exfiltration of UDT and SEAL operators and delivery of special weapons. The primary mission of the Class II SDV was amphibious reconnaissance and weapons delivery.

The AeroJet SDV development program was technically complex, and after several years' time eventually ran into extreme performance difficulty. The single vehicle delivered was of the Class II design. The submersible was very heavy; making it next to impossible to attain the neutral buoyancy necessary to trim out the vehicle for speed, range, and safety. The AeroJet program was eventually terminated and placed under government control at a special project office set up for this purpose at the Naval Weapons Center, China Lake, California.

Because of the AeroJet contract delays, a separate and robust program was established to improve the Mark VII design and outfit it with advanced capabilities. Correcting the Mark VII SDV deficiencies became a matter of priority, and an aggressive program was directed from the highest levels of the Navy staff to modernize and improve this SDV. This was vitally important, since the Class I and Class II SDV development had been essentially stalled. New features included ahead and bottom looking navigation sonar's, internal and external communications systems, and improved control and propulsion systems among other capabilities. Some of the Mark VII's accelerated modernization was also driven by the fact that the *USS Grayback* had completed its hanger modifications and was returning to fleet service, thus, a more reliable SDV was needed.

A recruiting poster dated 1965 reads: "Project SURAC (Swimmer Underwater Reconnaissance and Clearance) and the "Seeing Eye," the newest addition in underwater detection, add increased capabilities to one of the most challenging and demanding missions in the world—the UDT and SEAL Teams."

165

CHAPTER 16

SUBMERSIBLE BASTARDS

This is a highly condensed and edited version of Submersible Bastards, *a memoir completed by retired UDT Frogman and Navy Captain Bruce Dunning in May 2003. The original manuscript contained 20,671 words, which I've abridged to approximately 3,000 words. The complete story is rich in detail about many events surrounding the life and times in UDT in the late 1940s. I've tried to focus on its main theme, which was development of UDTs first underwater operational capabilities. I've also included his story surrounding first use of open-circuit SCUBA. Significant in his memoir are the names of individuals involved. I've retained all segments where names of the men were used, because, at the end of the day, the story is about them. All, including Captain Dunning, are now deceased. He died on 10 June 2008. Captain Dunning's story is a tribute to all of the UDT men that served during a magnificent period in the history of Naval Special Warfare. Because of Navy promotion policies throughout the remainder of his career, Captain Dunning was never provided the opportunity to return to duty with UDT. Stories like his are treasures to behold.*

--Tom Hawkins

I make no claim that this is a history of Underwater Demolition. It is a personal memoir; my recall of events as I experienced them while assigned to Underwater Demolition Team TWO at Little Creek, Virginia from April 1947 until June 1950. Under the best of circumstances, memory becomes unreliable as we twist events, circumstances, and participants to fit what we want to believe. Add to that the porosity of time -- more than 50 years in this case -- and I am not sure of what is left of reliability. In the end, my criteria of reliability more often than not are: this is the way I remember it; it seems logical; it feels right.

So, why bother? I believe that the period between the end of World War II and the beginning of the Korean War was crucial to the development of what is now known as Naval Special Warfare, because it was a period in which that development might well have halted. It was a period when the very life of UDT was threatened, when there were only some 200-300 UDT-officers and men in the entire Navy, when many in the Navy questioned the need, when service in UDT-imposed limits on career advancement, and when material support was paltry at best.

There was no career path in Special Warfare then. The Bureau of Naval Personnel strictly limited regular Navy officers to three years in UDT, and enlisted men were handicapped in their advancement efforts by chances to gain shipboard experience in their rates. UDT officers and men from both the East and West Coast teams hung on.

The period is also important because it marked the submergence of UDT, the development of a capability to remain underwater for more than the span of a man's breath, and the capability to operate from submerged submarines. Lieutenant Commander Francis Douglas Fane, commanding the UDTs at Little Creek, recognized that the "Underwater" in Underwater Demolition Teams was a misnomer, since virtually all operations were conducted on or very near the surface. In the latter case, only for the duration of a man's held breath. If UDT was to survive and progress, a true underwater capability had to be developed. At Little Creek, what became known as the Submersible Operations Platoon (SUBOPS) came into being to pursue new underwater techniques and tactics.

I was fortunate enough to be assigned to SUBOPS from its inception until I was ordered out of UDT. Consequently, the focus of this memoir is on SUBOPS and my experiences with the men of that unit. This focus, however, is not intended in any way to downgrade or detract from the accomplishments of all the other UDT officers and men, both on the East and West Coasts. While we "Submersible Bastards" were playing our games, the rest of the officers and men of UDT were working under the same difficult circumstances to keep alive in an unbroken tradition in what has come to be known as Naval Special Warfare; exemplified today by the U.S. Navy SEALs.

In the spring of 1947, I volunteered for Underwater Demolition, and in April of that year, I reported for duty to UDT-2 at Little Creek, Virginia. Lieutenant Junior Grade "Ski" Wryczinski, a former Yeoman, was Executive Officer of UDT-2. Lieutenant "Hal" Iverson commanded UDT-4. Among the other wartime officers in the two teams were Lieutenants Junior Grade Carson R. "Rip" Tallent, Bill Mason, and H.L. "Gary" Garren, Jr. Gary Garren was deployed to the Antarctic with Team 4 at the time. It was Garren, as Commanding Officer, who had brought the newly designated UDT-2 from Coronado, California to Little Creek.

LCDR Fane exiting the *USS Grouper's* escape trunk wearing the LARU during trials at St. Thomas, February 1948.

In January 1948, Fane brought Dr. Chris Lambertsen to Little Creek, where he spent several days indoctrinating selected personnel in the use and maintenance of the LARU (Lambertsen Amphibious Respiratory Unit). This indoctrination was essential if UDT men were to start using the LARU since, without such training, use of a breathing apparatus would be extremely dangerous.

Fane had also recognized that most of the advantage of a true underwater capability would be lost if swimmers had to be transported to their target areas on surface ships or in submarines required to surface to launch their swimmers. Ideally, an underwater mission would be conducted entirely submerged. With this in mind, he contacted Commander, Submarine Squadron TWO to propose launching swimmers utilizing the submarines' escape trunks.

With such future operations in mind, Fane led a detachment of UDT officers and men to the U.S. Navy Submarine Base at new London, Connecticut, where personnel instructed and qualified the UDT men in locking out of a submarine escape trunk as well as in free ascent (i.e., surfacing without a breathing apparatus) from 100 feet. Additionally, all the UDT-men underwent oxygen toxicity susceptibility testing; breathing pure oxygen in a recompression chamber pressurized to the 60-foot level for up to 30 minutes. (This was a test for oxygen tolerance under pressure. Actual dives do not exceed 30 feet). A solid relationship between UDT and the Submarine Force was [quickly] established. Vice Admiral James Fife, Commander, Submarine Force, U.S. Atlantic Fleet was enthusiastic in his support.

Interior view of a submarine escape trunk seen through the top hatch outside the submarine.

In February 1948, men rendezvoused at St. Thomas, U.S. Virgin Islands with the submarine *USS Grouper* commanded by Commander Charles F. Putnam. The UDT detachment included: Dr. Lambertsen, Fane, Garren, Jones, Foster, Devine, Bailey, Kappesser, Piotrowski, Petway and I, among others. Operations were conducted in Pillsbury Sound between St. Thomas and St. Johns. The objective was to test the feasibility of launching and recovering UDT-swimmers from a submerged submarine.

On February 20, 1948, *Grouper* bottomed in 54 feet of water to attempt to launch and recover swimmers via the ship's escape trunk. (Note: with the submarine on the bottom in 54 feet of water, it's deck, from which the swimmers would work, would be at about 30 feet, thus, safe for breathing pure oxygen.) Because of the bulkiness of the LARUs and the necessary presence of an escape-trunk operator, only two swimmers at a time could occupy the cramped, cylindrical escape trunk. Fane and Lambertsen were the first to exit the submarine and swim to and from the surface; after which they reentered the submarine. Other UDT-men followed in pairs, each making two exits and recoveries that day.

The next step was to test the capability of leaving and reentering a submerged, underway submarine. On February 22, 1948, Fane and Lambertsen again led the way, locking out of the underway *Grouper* and then returning. Again, the other swimmers followed. These exercises proved the feasibility of delivering and retrieving combat swimmers by submerged submarines and gave the UDT swimmers a high degree of confidence in their ability to operate successfully from submarines.

Upon completion of the St. Thomas exercises with *Grouper*, COMUDTLANT formally established the Submersible Operations Platoon, or SUBOPS as it came to be known. I was fortunate to be assigned as Platoon Officer, with Lieutenant Junior Grade Al Jones as Assistant Platoon Officer. The enlisted personnel who made up the initial complement of SUBOPS included: MRC Al Foster, GMC Andy Devine, GM1 Sam Bailey, GM1 H.L. Piotrowski, DC1 Wilson Bane, BM3 Frank E. Kappesser, Frank Hale, GM3 J.J. Petway, BM2 Roy O Rollins, QM3 Ronald LeMay, GM2 Henry Spiegel, TM3 John P. O'Brien, GM2 Chester C. Stevens, BM3 Glen Baker, BM2 Joseph DiMartino, GM3 Benny Sulinski, QM3 James Cook, Thomas McAllister, BM3 George Phipps, BM2 William C. Hollingsworth, DC3 Harold L. Crowell, and "Robbie" Robinson.

There seemed to be a danger that SUBOPS identity could easily be lost in daily routine activities of the Teams. There was also a need for work space as well as for separate and secure storage for the LARUs and supporting equipment such as bulk oxygen bottles, a compressor, a variety of tools, and so on. Another consideration was classification security. By the very nature of their work, combat swimmers require secrecy. While there was a need to advertise UDTs accomplishments in going underwater to gain higher level support, it seemed advisable that the general population, Navy and civilian, not be afforded free access to what we were doing. SUBOPS clearly needed a "home" of its own, separate from the regular UDT warehouses and offices at Little Creek. UDT was granted permission for SUBOPS to occupy an abandoned brig behind their headquarters.

Even back in the early days of SUBOPS, UDT-men were thinking about expanded missions. Fane, of course, had already established the viability of UDT submarine operations. In early 1947, Fane proposed development of a ship assault capability.

UDT men seen entering the escape trunk of a submerged submarine.

At "The Brig," we talked about what missions beyond conventional beach reconnaissance and obstacle clearance we might perform; such missions as ship assault, hinterland penetration for reconnaissance and intelligence collection, sabotage, and commando-style raids. We also discussed the potential of air delivery to supplement submarine transport. Despite the valuable contributions of NCDUs, Scouts and Raiders, and UDTs during World War II, or the feats of British and Italian underwater operators, few in the U.S. Navy seemed to consider unconventional operations appropriate in the nuclear age.

Fane, however, was persistent. He located two crated British submersible boats in a West Coast warehouse and had them shipped to Little Creek. Dubbed "Sleeping Beauties" by the British, these were capable of a maximum surface speed of five knots and maximum depth of 50 feet. The operator, sitting in an open cockpit had, of course, to wear a breathing apparatus.

SUBOPS personnel promptly shortened "Sleeping Beauty" to "SB" - from which other UDT-personnel derived SUBOPS' alternate sobriquet: "Submersible Bastards." We tried to figure out how to use them, with little success. Dr. Lambertsen again came to the rescue, and quickly taught the SUBOPS men how to operate the boats.

In October 1948, Fane, with a detachment from SUBOPS and a heavy load of equipment, including one SB, were flown to St. Thomas to rendezvous with *USS Quillback* commanded by Lieutenant Commander C.R. Clark. The detachment included Dr. Lambertsen; Lieutenant Commander E.R.F. Johnson, USNR (as underwater photographer); A.C. "Al" Dyer (Johnson's assistant and technician); a lieutenant colonel from U.S. Army Engineers (name unrecalled,) William Fields (a civilian engineer from the Bureau of Ships); and, a Navy Chief Photographer's Mate (name unrecalled). The SUBOPS detachment consisted of Ensign

Sleeping Beauty in its transport and shop cradle.

Sleeping Beauty being maintained in preparation for pool training.

George Atcheson (from the West Coast Teams,) Chiefs Devine and Foster, Sam Bailey, Henry Piotrowski, Frank Kappesser, George Kudravitz, A.B. Henderson, J.J. Petway, and myself.

A major objective with *Quillback* was to develop techniques for operating small submersibles from a mother submarine. At the outset, Lambertsen had the opportunity for the first time to

Rare color photograph of Sleeping Beauty.

train and qualify SUBOPS SB operators in water of more than a few feet in depth. The next step was to experiment with taking the SB off the deck of the bottomed submarine and landing it again. This, too, was accomplished rather quickly.

The logical extension of these operations, and of infinitely greater tactical significance, was developing the capability to take off and land on the deck of a submerged and underway submarine. Once again, Dr. Lambertsen made the first try, and proved that such a launch and recovery was entirely feasible. Soon, I and a number of the men became quite adept at the maneuvers.

The limited capacity of a submarine's escape trunk became a source of concern. It took a number of minutes to put each pair of swimmers out and recycle the trunk for the next pair. Launching even the number of men required to handle the SB on deck could easily consume half an hour. In an attempt to find a faster way of getting swimmers in and out of a submarine, Fane and Kappeser made a daring and almost fatal attempt to test the feasibility of exiting and reentering through the submarine's forward torpedo tubes. As it turned out the tubes' controls caused sharp fluctuations of the pressure inside the tube causing swimmer's face masks to be lifted off their faces. Fane did succeed in reentering the submarine through a torpedo tube and, fortunately, both emerged from this experiment without serious damage, if somewhat shaken.

SUBOPS returned to Little Creek with a clear sense of accomplishment. We were stunned when a letter was transmitted through the chain of command several weeks later directing COMUDTLANT to confine future operations to conventional reconnaissance and beach clearance missions. Fane was, however, not to be deterred. We would place greater reliance on activities at New London and cooperation with COMSUBLANT, but SUBOPS would have to maintain a low profile while at Little Creek.

SUBOPS itself remained fairly stable. Army Warrant Officer Williams, a reconnaissance expert and skilled photographer, was detailed to six months' temporary duty with UDT and assigned to SUBOPS as Assistant Platoon Officer. Fane was able to bring in Count Roberto Frassetto, a former Italian Navy officer who had participated in swimmer and small submersible assaults on British warships in the Mediterranean Sea during World War II. Frassetto spent several weeks with SUBOPS, giving us the benefit of his experience. He returned to Little Creek several times during the next few years.

While SUBOPS was doing its work at Little Creek, New London, and in the Caribbean, a French Navy officer, Commandant Jacques Yves Cousteau (not as famous then as he came to be in later years), had been pursuing vigorously the development of underwater swimmer capabilities for the French Navy. Cousteau was concentrating his effort on use of an open-system, non-recirculating breathing apparatus in which compressed air was fed to the diver through a three-stage pressure valve, then exhausted to the sea as the diver exhaled. Such an apparatus had the advantage of virtually eliminating the danger of oxygen toxicity, although the diver did remain vulnerable to other common diving hazards.

Fane had heard about Cousteau's work and made contact when Cousteau visited New York. As a result, in the spring of 1949, Emile Gagnon arrived at Little Creek with a one-bottle Cousteau unit. Gagnon was an engineer employed by Cousteau and the key designer of the air pressure regulator, which was the heart of the Cousteau lung. Gagnon spent several days with the SUBOPS men, teaching them how to use and maintain the Cousteau equipment.

Shortly after Gagnon's visit, SUBOPS again deployed to New London. There, Fane made the first dive ever in the United States with the Cousteau-designed breathing apparatus, and the SUBOPS men followed. Not long after that, Cousteau licensed the manufacture of his equipment in the United States under the trade name, Aqualung. SUBOPS quickly acquired a number of two-bottle Aqualungs.

Although the Cousteau open system offered obvious advantages, particularly the ability to dive deeper without worrying about oxygen toxicity, we weren't ready to give up on closed, recirculating oxygen systems. I, for one, was concerned with the loss of concealment caused by the stream of bubbles emitted by an open-system apparatus. Others objected to the mouthpiece, which replaced the face-covering mask of the LARU, and the loss of voice communication between swimmers.

Although the two bottle Aqualungs obtained by UDT provided ample dive time, they were much bulkier than the LARU, making exits from submarine escape trunks even more problematical. The Aqualungs also created a pesky logistics problem for SUBOPS. Pure oxygen of breathing quality for the LARUs had been readily available from the Navy supply system, the same oxygen used by aviators. We needed much larger volumes of compressed air for the Aqualungs. Ironically, compressed air wasn't available, not in breathing quality. When it was available in large tanks, it was often contaminated with oil and other impurities. Eventually a compressor designed to provide breathable compressed air was obtained.

About a week after the North Koreans invaded South Korea (25 June 1950), I received orders to report to *USS Newport News* (CA-148) for duty. Lieutenant Junior Grade Philip Clark relieved me as SUBOPS Platoon Officer. Subsequently, after Phil Clark left for duty in Washington, Lieutenants William Huckenpoehler, A.A. Moore, and Robert Fay (killed in action in Vietnam in 1966), among others, served as SUBOPS officers.

The one thing that I do know beyond any doubt is that being associated with the men of UDT during those years, most especially being associated with the superb men of SUBOPS that took UDT underwater and laid the groundwork for the future development of Navy Special Warfare, was one of the greatest privileges of my life. (May 29, 2003, Fairfax, Virginia)

CHAPTER 17

SDV TEAMS, TRAINING, AND OPERATIONS

SEAL Delivery Vehicles

In a Navy Training Plan for the 38-02 development program, it was envisioned that each UDT and SEAL Team would be outfitted with SDV capabilities. In practice, however, it was quickly learned that SDVs were very maintenance intensive, and that the skills necessary to pilot and navigate these sophisticated platforms were not just unique, but extraordinary. For several years, the Mark VII SDV had been distributed to all of the UDT and SEAL Teams. Some simply let them sit idle, because they didn't have the training time or personnel to establish or maintain their capabilities. (Note: Swimmer Delivery Vehicle was renamed SEAL Delivery Vehicle in 1983.)

With the planned reestablishment of UDT-22 at Naval Amphibious Base, Little Creek, Virginia in 1979, however, it was decided to organize this command as the first team dedicated solely to the operation and maintenance of the SDVs. Over the ensuing years, this was accomplished very effectively. This closely coincided with the pending introduction of the Mark VIII and Mark IX SDVs, which at long last represented materialization of the Class I and Class II SDVs envisioned under Technical Development Plan 38-02.

The SDV program was managed out of the Naval Special Warfare Program Office at the Naval Sea Systems Command in Washington, DC by a SEAL program manager. It would take several years for the Mark VIII and Mark IXs SDVs to phase-replace the Mark VIIs. This was because the new SDVs were assembled one at a time at the Navy Laboratory in Panama City, Florida, and were not mass produced. The focused SDV "build" program at Panama City was unique, and a full-blown SDV support organization was established without which the SDV Teams might have floundered. The organization in Panama City resulted from a relocation of a previous organization established at the Naval Weapons Center at China Lake, California in the early 1970's. A dedicated Panama City staff also created the opportunity to continually upgrade the SDV's operating capabilities through a continuous experimentation and modernization program. In addition to Panama City, many of the electronic subsystems designed and built for the SDVs were accomplished at the Navy's Applied Research Laboratory at the University of Texas in Austin.

When the UDTs were reorganized as SEAL Teams in 1983, UDT-12 and UDT-22 were officially established as SDV Teams ONE and TWO respectively. Within 12-18 months, the teams began deploying SDVs operationally. SDV Team ONE had the advantage of *USS Grayback* to provide tactical mobility. During this period, *USS Cavalla*, the first of seven Sturgeon-Class, long-haul submarines was being modified to accept a bolt-on, bolt-off Dry Deck Shelter, which could transport SDVs.

SDV Towing Sled

The East Coast had considerable difficulty finding operational mobility platforms for the SDVs, and was largely relegated to deployments on amphibious ships. This created the opportunity for creativity and innovation. SDV towing sleds had been fabricated. They could also be used to assist launching and recovering SDVs from the high freeboard of amphibious ships. These sleds were quite ingenious, since at idle speed they would sink on pontoon floats that would allow them to remain just below the surface of the water. The SDV could easily maneuver in and out of the sled on the surface; and, when secured to the sled, could be towed by a high-speed support craft. The forward speed of the boat would cause the sled and the SDV to drain residual

The MK VIII SDV on the towing sled.

water and allow the sled to get upon plane for high-speed transits. The sled could actually increase the tactical range of the SDV mission by getting the men closer to the shoreline before they had to use their own life support and battery power.

SDV Wet-Deck Shelter

Because *USS Growler* had not been converted for use on the East Coast, the men fashioned the concept of a "wet" deck shelter to be used on conventional submarines in the Atlantic. One shelter was fabricated and delivered. It was designed to accommodate either a Mark VII or Mark VIII SDV (with bow planes removed). The shelter and its cradle and track system were bolted to the superstructure of the host submarine. This shelter was used several times for training, but was never deployed operationally.

Submarine Wet Deck Shelter aboard *USS Cutlass (*SS-478) at Key West, Florida.

I know of only one use of the Wet Deck Shelter (we didn't call it the WDS, simply "The SDV Shelter"), and that was aboard *USS Cutlass* (SS-478) at Key West, Florida. I was the senior UDT-SEAL officer embarked, and doctrinally called the Officer Coordinating the Exercise. UDT Lieutenant Jim Harper and his men were the embarked detachment. I took the pictures seen here, and these may be the few existing. Complex scheduling of submarines prevented routine use of the shelter, and it was not something that could be used to deploy overseas. To do so restricted the submarine's capability to deep dive with the SDV embarked, and the SDV would have been harmfully exposed to salt water during prolonged submerged operational periods. Also, the SDV would have been difficult to maintain; battery charging, for example.

A funny story happened during this embarkation, but it wasn't really funny at the time. We had got to Key West and installed the shelter and SDV on the submarine, and headed out to stay ashore overnight. When we got back to the ship the next morning, it was populated with a full crew of Sailors from the Republic of China (Taiwan). This was very concerning, since our training operations were classified confidential. After a hasty meeting with the commanding officer, who had already phoned his submarine command, we were told there had been a scheduling snafu, which anyone could have figured out. The submarine was being turned over to the Taiwan navy, and the Taiwanese submarine crew had showed up early for training and turn over. We determined that our operations would continue, so long as the Taiwan sailors were kept away from the shelter and SDV, and that they would not be permitted in spaces around the escape trunk, while we were doing lock-out/lock-in operations. There was an extreme language barrier, so we'll never know what they thought about our operations.

Submarine Training Platform

Because submarine services in general were difficult to obtain for underway training, a submersible training platform or SUBTRAP was fabricated. With a variable ballast system, SUBTRAP was towed by a surface vessel and designed to characterize the deck of an underway submarine. The training device was operated and maintained by the SDV Teams. Although quite innovative, they were very maintenance intensive and not often used. Moreover, they took SDV operators and technicians away from their primary jobs, and the SDV Teams were already undermanned.

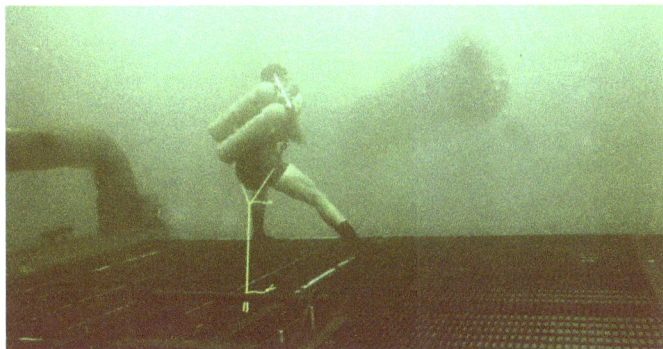

An SDV launching from the SUBTRAP. The deck crewman was secured to the deck for safety, since the SUBTRAP is being towed at a speed of one knot or greater.

A MK VIII SDV aboard the SUBTRAP in Puerto Rico.

Pre-dive maintenance on a MK IX SDV aboard SUBTRAP before training operations.

Standoff Weapons Assembly

The Mark VIII SDV was designed for personnel and weapons delivery. It could carry six fully equipped divers or two or three divers and weapons. These weapons included the complete inventory of limpet mines and a family of demolition charges. The Mark IX SDV had a low-profile design intended primarily for reconnaissance missions and had a cargo compartment that could carry these weapons. The pilot and navigator lay in the Mark IX SDV in a prone position. Under Technical Development Plan 38-01, the Swimmer Weapons System, (later SEAL Weapons System) a special weapon was designed exclusively for the Mark IX SDV. It was called the Standoff Weapons Assembly or SWA.

The SWA on the surface, periscope up in the firing position.

The SWA was a modified U.S. Navy Mark 37 torpedo, which had electric propulsion and didn't need to be ejected out of a torpedo with compressed air like older torpedos. This made it ideal for SDV use. For a long time, the Mark 37 was the primary U.S. submarine-launched torpedo. It was replaced by the Mark 48 torpedo starting in 1972. As a result, many remained in the Navy inventory and were available for use. Among the largest technical challenge in modifying the Mark 37 torpedo for the Mark IX SDV was its unique swing-arm assembly, a launcher-rail system for integration with the submarine Dry Deck Shelter (DDS). The SDV and weapons were required to fit inside the DDS. The only way to do this was to hard mount the SWAs inside the DDS to accommodate submarine-safety requirements. Once the DDS was flooded, the SWAs became near neutrally buoyant, and could be taken from their mounts and placed on the on the swing-arms. Once outside the DDS, the torpedoes would be swung down and locked into position for SDV transit and launch.

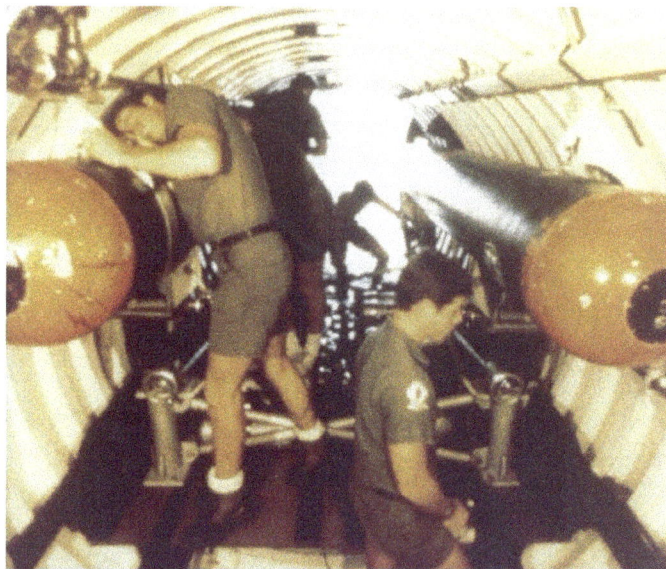

Men from UDT-12 are seen hard-mount installing the SWA inside the DDS. The MK IX SDV was cradled underneath the SWAs.

Another major technical problem involved the actual launch-firing system. The SWA was aimed using a periscope encompassing a stadimeter (cross hairs in the lens). Once prepared for launch, it could be fired only after its gyro-compass had stabilized, which didn't take a long time. The aiming and firing took some skill, since the SDV on the surface was prone to rocking motions created by the environmental conditions. The weapon was fired when range and bearing of the target was determined. The weapon would be fired when the target was centered in the cross hairs of the stadimeter. Targets were assumed to be stationary in anchorages or at pier side. Safety was built into the SWA, since it could not arm itself until it travelled a distance of 750 yards. The SWA capability completed successful operational evaluation and was being prepared for fleet service. Because of cost

A MK IX SDV being launched from the deck of a submarine with the SWA. The SDV is still tethered to the submarine to adjust balance and trim before release and departure.

considerations, however, the Mark IX SDVs were instead removed from the SDV Team inventory, and the SWA capability went with it. The SWAs were not compatible with the Mark VIII SDV.

Little Bo Peep

Before the Mark IX SDVs were eliminated from the active inventory, the men at SDV Team TWO developed a concept that they called the "Little Bo Peep" weapons-delivery configuration. This involved carrying a limpet-mine on the SWA swing arms. This would have allowed the Mark IX to carry an even heavier payload of weapons than could nominally be employed on a single SDV combat sortie. The concept was never taken beyond the SDV Team, since the Mark IX was being phased out. Moreover, it would have involved a lengthy and expensive weapons-safety review and approval process. This concept demonstrated the traditional and never-ending innovative thinking of the men.

The name "Little Bo Peep" derives from the title of a children's poem of the same name by Mother Goose. The first line of the poem goes: "Little Bo-Peep has lost her sheep." The weapon to be carried on the swing arms was called the

MK IX SDV in "Little Bo Peep" configuration.

Limpet, Modular, Assembly or LAM, thus, sheep translated to lamb, and the nickname Little Bo-Peep for the capability.

The Mark VIII SDV remained the workhorse submersible throughout the 1980's and into the early 1990's, when a complete modernization program was initiated. This was called the "Mod 1" program, and resulted in a new SDV with substantially more capable and efficient propulsion, navigation, sonar, and electronic subsystems.

Operation THUNDERHEAD

Early in 1972, *Grayback* and the Mark VII SDVs got their first call to combat duty. Their highly-classified operation surrounded the escape and recovery of two U.S. airmen being held as prisoners of war at the infamous "Hanoi Hilton" prison in North Vietnam. Fresh intelligence indicated that the prisoners were planning to steal a boat and travel down the Red River to the Gulf of Tonkin. Admiral Thomas H. Moorer, chairman of the Joint Chiefs of Staff, authorized the U.S. Pacific Command to execute Operation THUNDERHEAD, which involved a rescue plan. Full details of the operation were known to only a handful of officers individually cleared by Admiral John S. McCain Jr., the Pacific Command commander.

The rescue plan was set in motion and involved two Mark VII SDVs and operators from SEAL Team ONE and UDT-11, led by SEAL Lieutenant Melvin Spence Dry (known as "Spence" to his Teammates). An SDV was to be launched at night from the submerged submarine in an SDV crewed by two UDT-11 operators, who would deliver two SEALs to a small island off the mouth of the Red River. There, SEALs would establish a hide-site to watch for any sign of the escapees. Should they be sighted, the SEALs would intercept them and coordinate their rescue with waiting ships and aircraft of the Seventh Fleet.

This 1971 photo shows a MK VII SDV being maintained in the starboard chamber aboard *USS Grayback* (LPSS-574).

Grayback arrived on station on 3 June 1972. The SEALs decided to conduct their first clandestine SDV reconnaissance mission that night. One of the two SDVs aboard was launched shortly after midnight, but a combination of navigational errors and strong currents took them off course. After searching for more than an hour without sighting the island, the crew aborted the mission. They were unable to locate the *Grayback*, and a decision was made to abandon the SDV after its battery power was exhausted.

Back aboard *Grayback,* the second SDV got underway for near-ship rehearsals that involved practice launch-and-recovery operations—what Navy pilots would call "touch and go" training for landing aboard aircraft carriers. The SDV was to remain within the range of the ship's acoustic homing beacon so that it could easily return to the *Grayback's* hanger on-call or when planned. Upon launch, however, the SDV foundered in approximately 60 feet of water. Its four-man crew abandoned the boat and came to the surface, where they were subsequently recovered.

The first SDV crew was rescued early the next morning by a Navy HH-3A combat search-and-rescue helicopter, and *Grayback* was informed. To preserve operational security, the helicopter's door gunner sank the SDV, which was too heavy to be retrieved. The four SDV crew members were flown to the nuclear-powered guided-missile cruiser *USS Long Beach* (CGN-9), where they were debriefed and then made plans for their return to *Grayback*.

The SEALs were eager to get back to *Grayback*, and a decision was made to transport the four men by helicopter from the *Long Beach* for a water cast (free-fall jump) adjacent to the submarine on 5 June. Unfortunately, it became a night-time water drop, and Lieutenant Spence Dry was killed after impacting the water. He became the last SEAL lost during the Vietnam War. The authoritative book surrounding this mission is *Hope for Freedom: Operation THUNDERHEAD: A True Story,* self-published by Edwin L. Towers, the helicopter commander on this mission. A more recent accounting, is *Operation THUNDERHEAD: The True Story of Vietnam's Final POW Rescue Mission--and the last Navy SEAL Killed in Country* by Kevin Dockery.

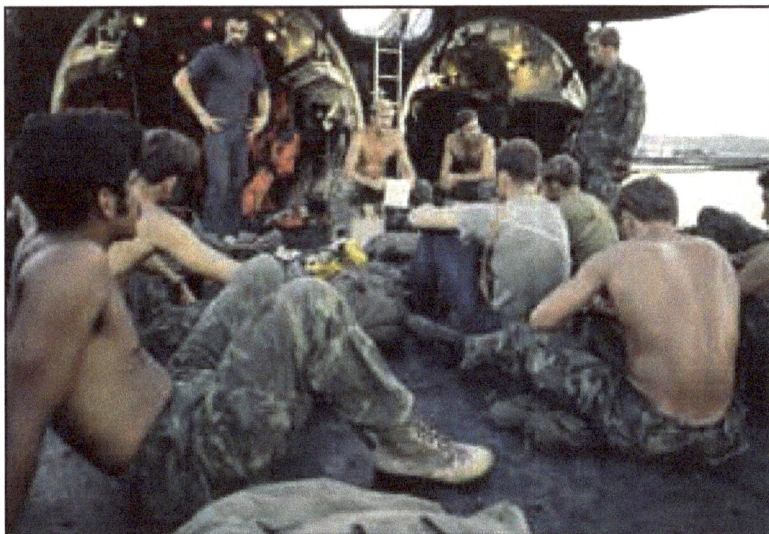

SEAL LT Spence Dry, holding a white tablet in the middle of this photo is briefing his men aboard *USS Grayback*.

The Mark VII SDV was vastly improved after this failed mission; a mission which remained highly classified for many years. The improved Mark VII became the workhorse of the 1970's through several capability upgrades. The last SDV in this class was the Mark VII, Mod 6. The increasing sophistication of the SDVs was largely responsible for establishing dedicated SDV Teams on both coasts. When the teams were organized, they included a mix of SEAL operators and fleet-resourced divers and technical rating to maintain the SDVs and support the DDSs.

Advanced SEAL Delivery System

After the establishment of SEAL Delivery Vehicle Teams (SDV Teams) in April 1983, the relationships between the Naval Special Warfare SEALs and the submarine community became solidified. The Navy began long-range planning to convert additional submarines for conducting maritime special operations. This included preparation for the new Advanced SEAL Delivery System (ASDS), which was becoming a reality that needed an operational-host platform.

Early on, it was decided that the ASDS would be a one-atmosphere environment miniature submarine. (One atmosphere means that when the hatches are closed, the submarine is pressurized to a one-atmosphere (33.8 feet) environment to assist water tightness.) It was also conceived that the ASDS would be operationally and tactically transported by the Navy's Submarine Force.

In 2003, the ASDS and its host submarine became a reality. The single ASDS was assigned to SDV Team ONE at its homeport location at Pearl Harbor, Hawaii. The ASDS completed a successful operational evaluation (OPEVAL) and certification process aboard *USS Greeneville* (SSN-772). After OPEVAL and deep-dive certification, the vessel was designated ASDS-1. The submersible completed its first deployment aboard *Greeneville* to the Indian Ocean and Arabian Gulf, where it was remarked that, "It [ASDS] has been used operationally to great advantage and has proven successful…The capability is greater than we ever expected…There is no substitute for this capability, it is both covert and persistent."

The ASDS-1 seen mated with the *USS Jimmy Carter* (SSN-23) during operations off the coast of Hawaii.

Even with glowing remarks operationally, the ASDS was not without difficulties. It experienced significant growth problems, and the cost of the capability was ever increasing. In a Congressional Budget Office study issued in 2003, two major technical problems were cited: a noisy propeller and silver-zinc batteries that depleted more quickly than anticipated. A new propeller made of composite material was developed to rectify noise problems, and development of lithium-ion batteries was undertaken to replace the silver-zinc batteries. Unfortunately, the cost of the ASDS continued to spiral, and Congress withdrew funding for additional platforms until the technical difficulties could be overcome. ASDS-1, however, is no longer in service. It was destroyed by fire pierside during battery charging by contractors in November 2008. The development program was stopped after that incident.

As a 65-foot miniature submarine, ASDS provided increased range, speed, and capacity over the in-service Mark VIII, Mod 1 SDV. ASDS was operated by a crew of two, and could carry eight SEAL operators. The ASDS pilot was a qualified submarine officer, a lieutenant, while the co-pilot was a SEAL officer, also a lieutenant. ASDS was connected to its host ship via a watertight hatch, and was equipped with sophisticated electronic subsystems. It had a diver lock-out, lock-in capability that could also serve as a hyperbaric recompression chamber.

USS Greenville (SSN-772) with ASDS-1 embarked and SEALs fast roping aboard from an HH-60 helicopter.

SEALs That Operate SDVs

The operating characteristics of the SDVs and ASDS and their tactics, techniques, and procedures remain classified. All of the men that operate these submersibles are Navy SEALs. They go through a comprehensive SDV training and qualification course of instruction. The men who choose to become SDV pilots and navigators represent

A rare outside view of the ASDS.

a special breed, even among SEALs. The complexity of the SDV electronic communication, navigation, and submarine-support systems require extensive basic, qualification, and requalification training to acquire and maintain demanding operational skills and capabilities. The need is to master the efficiency to undertake multi-faceted operations that occur entirely underwater, often in obscure environmental conditions in hostile or non-permissive waters. These operations are compounded substantially in complexity when conducted from an underway submarine at night.

SDV missions may extend for several hours' time with the men all-the-while exposed to the ecological extremes of water depth, temperature, and sea conditions. The men are clad in thermal-protective dress, the Mark 16 UBA with full-face mask, life preserver, compass, depth gauge, and other electronic devices with which to perform their mission. This makes the SDV very "tight" when six operators or two or three operators and weapons systems are onboard. Moreover, for the duration of the SDV mission, the men conduct essentially "non-working" dives as they simply sit in the SDV during transit. This makes the prolonged-dive hours physically and psychologically monotonous and, thus, offers plenty of time for the men to think about how cold they are.

While never considered by the United States in World War II, the SDV has evolved as a fully developed capability of vital importance within our country's National Command structure. As current SDV capabilities continue to evolve, the next-generation combatant submersibles are already being considered; and, together with the Navy's Submarine Force, will continue to insure a fully clandestine capability that separates U.S. Navy SEALs from all others.

CHAPTER 18

MENTORS

When young officers come in to the SEAL Teams, none will admit it, but they are generally a bit lost and confused and need time to establish themselves, while trying to understand their new environment. Especially in the SEAL Teams, young officers must demonstrate their leadership, competence, and decision-making capabilities with the men. Most likely that will be done under the tutelage of a chief, senior chief, or master chief petty officer. This is largely understood by the chief petty officers, who develop the knack of educating young SEAL officers without being demeaning or disrespectful, while still assisting them to lead in a very demanding environment—especially in the current environment, where actual combat comes very quickly. SEAL chief petty officers don't just hope for a good platoon commander or department head; he makes them good. Of course, that takes demanding patience, since, in the life of a chief petty officer, the flow of young officers just keeps coming.

The officers that influenced me the most are those that led by example, and took the time to teach, directly or indirectly, the ways of the Navy, the Teams, and Naval Special Warfare; especially with ensigns and lieutenant junior grade officers. Not all senior officers are given that gift. I was lucky enough to have served with and learned from two of the best and brightest, and hopefully their influence guided me substantially once I became a senior officer. All of the men described below were not only great mentors, but all became valued life-long friends.

Boatswain Mate Master Chief James L. "Gator" Parks, Jr.

As a new ensign, my first deployment in UDT in charge of anything was to the West Coast to participate in an experimental test program. Upon reporting to UDT-21 in early 1967, I was assigned as an assistant platoon commander for a forthcoming cruise with the Mediterranean Amphibious Ready Group. Within several weeks, however, I was abruptly pulled from that assignment, and told I was instead going to head up a special detachment deploying to San Diego to work on a program involving SDVs. I was assigned two men each from UDT-21, UDT-22, and SEAL Team TWO. We arrived at the Naval Amphibious

Jim "Gator" Parks overseeing the SDV training, build, and management program at the Navy Laboratory in Panama City, FL.

Base, Coronado, California in April 1967. The length of our deployment was uncertain, because of the experimental nature of our assignment.

Our project was to serve as experimental-test subjects in a study sponsored by the Officer of Naval Research involving SDVs. The aim was to determine the effects of diver performance in cold water with exposures up to six-hour durations. No one knew if we could even attain six hours; especially since the average water temperature in San Diego was 55 - 65 degrees. The test protocol had us accomplishing SDV dive profiles that were incrementally increased through a range of one-to-six hour exposures. The Officer of Naval Research investigator was Dr. Bill Vaughan.

We reported to the Research, Development, Test, and Evaluation Department of the Naval Operations Support Group, Pacific for duty. The waterfront facility, which supported the SDVs, was run by Master Chief Petty Officer Jim "Gator" Parks. Gator would go on to become one of the most influential men in the history of the Naval Special Warfare SDV program. We had daily contact with Gator, and he had responsibility for the entire function and coordination of all ongoing projects.

Gator knew SDVs. I'm not sure his exact role in acquiring the Convair Model 14—the SDV of our test project. It had been designed and built by the Convair Division of the General Dynamics Corporation, which was based in San Diego, and I'm sure Gator had a large hand it its design. When I left San Diego in December 1967, I left some good friends and memories behind. I wouldn't encounter Gator again until several years later.

I detached from SEAL Team TWO in the summer of 1972, and was assigned duty at the Navy Experimental Diving Unit in Washington, DC. During that assignment, I also worked as an assistant for special units at the Naval Sea Systems Command under Lieutenant Commander Caythal "Irish" Flynn and later Lieutenant Commander Irve Charles "Chuck" Le Moyne. A collateral duty involved working with the SDV development program. At this juncture, the Mark VIII and Mark IX SDV design and build programs had been moved from industry to a program set up at the Naval Weapons Center China Lake in Ridgecrest, California. It was just like being in Coronado in 1967, since the retired Gator Parks supervised the program. Other retired frogmen working on the program were Frank Gorlic, Frank Flynn, and Lonnie Price. They were a good bunch of men, and the SDV program thrived at China Lake.

We were having an SDV design review at China Lake, and because of flight delays coming into Los Angeles I got to the meeting late. When I arrived, the meeting had already started, and my seat was empty. I sat down with Gator sitting next to me. As I was trying to figure out what was going on, my attention was on my briefcase notes, and I wasn't paying much attention to the proceedings. As only Gator could, he leaned over and whispered into my ear, "You better watch out, that's your money they're spending!" It was government money of course, but he was right. They were making design changes as fast as you could count them, and any change to a project means more money. Gator got my attention, and we slowed things down until I could figure things out.

That was Gator. He was a civil servant, working in a Navy lab, when the grab for money from the NAVSEA program managers was always job number one. Gator's loyalty however, was always to the Teams and their best interests. He was driven to make the best and most capable and reliable SDV possible. I learned much from Gator, and he was a great counselor and advisor to a long string of senior SEAL officers.

The SDV program was eventually moved from China Lake to the Navy Laboratory in Panama City, Florida, and Gator was one of the few former frogmen that moved with it. He and his wife Cathy were a true Navy family, and his dedication to the SDV program was everlasting.

I could write endlessly about Gator, but suffice to say his impact on the SDV programs was monumental, and an often awe-inspiring endeavor. When Gator spoke about SDVs, everyone listened. His word was trusted. He was a great mentor to me as a young ensign, during my time in Washington, and especially when I became commanding officer of UDT-22/SDV Team TWO.

Gator died unexpectedly of cancer after a very short illness. The measure of his influence on the SDV program was such that the Mark VIII, Mod 1 SDV was name in his honor. It was formally designated the "Gator Class" SDV in 1996 at a formal ceremony at the Naval Coastal Systems Station, Panama City with Gator's wife Cathy in attendance. Gator was beloved by all, and naming the SDV in his honor was a great tribute to a great man.

GATOR CLASS SDV

Ship Fitter Senior Chief Donald R. "Blackie" Blackwell

I deployed with six men to the Naval Operations Support Group, Pacific in Coronado, California to work on a focused SDV experimental project for the Office of Naval Research. Upon reporting, I was told that Chief Petty Officer Don "Blackie" Blackwell would be assigned as my detachment chief. Blackie would coordinate everything needed for Dr. Vaughn and me and the men, and he would be with us for duration of the project. This turned out to be an almost nine-month deployment, and having Blackie assigned to our group couldn't have been a better choice. We were immediately compatible. Blackie knew his way around, and served always as a superb diving supervisor. Blackie had a bit of the "old-school" UDT countenance—mission focused, no BS, get the job done, and do it well.

Don Blackwell with me in April 1981 when I was in command of UDT-22 / SDV Team TWO. Nancy Blackwell crafted the framed rendering of Freddy Frog.

More than our detachment chief petty officer, Blackie and his wife Nancy and their two daughters became really good friends with our group. Nancy became our "mom." The men and I spent countless hours at their home eating, drinking, and partying. Nancy never seemed to get tired of us. Blackie had a great sense of humor, and took us all in stride. Nancy and Blackie are now deceased. Blackie died fairly young from complications from dementia. Nancy died several years ago. I was fortunately able to see her in her final months at an annual UDT-SEAL West Coast Reunion. Having a leader and mentor like Blackie in my formative years as a young UDT-SEAL officer was more than a blessing.

Boatswains Mate Master Chief Edward C. "Ed" Schmidt

Ed Schmidt is hard to define, yet he was one of the most capable leaders that I ever observed and worked with. Nothing ruffled him. He could handle problems and men with the greatest of ease. When I returned from the West Coast SDV project, I was officially designated UDT-21's Submersible Operations. Department Head. Senior Chief Ed Schmidt was the department chief petty officer officially in charge, and he ran the show. Other than attending the Navy's Underwater Swim School in Key West, I'd had very little experience in submersible operations not involving an SDV.

I'm pretty sure that when I reported to Submersible Operations Department, Ed Schmidt probably thought "here comes another one." Back in those days, UDT officers were largely "one-tour wonders." All were reserve officers, coming into the Navy for their own various reasons. Once they got in UDT, they considered it the "fun and sun" club, and generally completed only one tour of duty in UDT. Then, they got out of the Navy, because they either had to go to sea if they wanted to advance their Navy careers, or get out and pursue a civilian career path. Most got out. I was one of those reserve officers, but I still had several years on my enlistment to complete.

I never really thought about the reserve status of officers at the time, because I was too young and naive to know if you wanted to stay in the Navy, you had to request "augmentation" into the "Regular Navy." Most officers coming into the Navy are reserves. If you had a good record, and wanted to stay in the Navy, you had to be augmented through a formal review process. This couldn't be attempted until you were a Lieutenant (0-3), and had a performance record. I was still a Lieutenant Junior Grade (0-2).

On 7 July 2000, (l-r) Tom Hawkins, Ed Schmidt, Jim Allgeier, and Dennis Richardson were the first men inducted into the SDV Hall of Fame.

I sat down with Chief Schmidt and asked him what we need to do to make Submersible Operations successful. He had a laundry list about a mile long. As good as Chief Schmidt was at just about everything, he was no administrator. Except for filling out supply chits, he didn't know which end of the pencil was up.

It ended up that I was a pretty good writer and administrator, so we quickly became a great team, and set out to get Submersible Operations rules, regulations, and a host of Navy and command instructions up to par. This enhanced my knowledge of diving rules and regulations, and gave me the opportunity to watch Chief Schmidt in action. He was quite adept at handling seniors and juniors alike. Ed had a really dry sense of humor, the kind where he was often really funny and didn't know it. He

actually complemented me about my ability to focus on Submersible Operations and get things done. He was not known for complementing anyone, so I apparently passed his muster.

Ed rode a motor scooter from home to work, and it was funny to see him motoring on it, because not many did that at the time. Ed's wife was Hilda and she ruled the roost at home. I think he was always hiding from her. In my experience she was a stern lady, but also charming at the same time. They were not social, so I only knew Hilda from the rare occasions that she would show up at the office to see Ed.

My stay at Submersible Operations was short lived, because within several months, I was sent to our senior staff, Naval Operations Support Group, Atlantic, to serve as the interim Research, Development, Test and Evaluation Officer. It was a one-man show, and was nothing like the large department they had in Coronado. Chief Schmidt and I would part ways, and I would not see him again until I took over as commanding officer of UDT-22 in April 1981. By then, a master chief petty officer, Ed was the most senior enlisted man in the command. He was running the command's SDV maintenance program.

The first thing I found regarding my old chief, was that he wanted to hide out with the SDV maintenance group, where he felt comfortable with few command-level administrative duties, or, he wanted go on cruise to the Mediterranean with the men. He liked going on cruises. Regardless, he didn't fill the designated senior enlisted position in the command, and didn't want it, yet he was still my senior enlisted advisor. He would come and tell me things I needed to know. I would go to him when I had a problem; especially in the chief petty officer ranks, where I did have a fair share of problems. Ed Schmidt was essentially a Gator Parks on the East Coast. He knew diving, he knew SDVs, and he knew people and was a natural leader. He was a great influence on me.

Boatswain's Mate Master Chief Cornelius J. "Corny" or "C.J." Leyden

When I was a budding mid-grade officer, Cornelius J. Leyden, a.k.a. "Corny" or "C.J." was perhaps my greatest mentor and friend. Corny was smart, and he knew his way around the "system" of the Navy diving and acquisition community. I first knew Corny after I got back from California in late 1968. He was running the Submersible Operations Department at UDT-22, which was next door to us at UDT-21. He had a robust SDV program, which he had built from the ground up.

Corny was an anomaly in UDT. He had been a qualified Navy diver assigned to the Navy Experimental Diving Unit in Washington, DC. He came to UDT-22 on a temporary assignment to teach the men to operate, maintain, and dive the then new Mark VI semi-closed circuit underwater breathing apparatus. At some point in time, he became essential to having and maintaining this capability, and was issued a set of orders formally assigning him to UDT-22. He then set out to build a diving and SDV capability second to none in UDT.

Corny's assignment to UDT-22 became problematic later on, since the needs of the Navy diving community dictated that he be transferred to a fleet diving activity. Unlike UDT men, who were "closed looped" detailed, meaning they could stay in UDT for an entire career, Corny was subject to "the needs of the Navy," which dictated that he be transferred. A series of back-door deals were made, however, and Corny was permitted to remain with UDT for another tour. The Navy came calling again several times, and eventually there were no arguments to retain him in UDT. The solution was to make Corny a qualified UDT operator. Back then, the Team commanding officer could award the Naval Enlisted Code to men that had completed a requisite level of training. This Naval Enlisted Code was 5326, which identified to the detailers in Washington that the individual was a qualified UDT-SEAL operator. Thus, Corny was granted a Naval Enlisted Code 5326, although he never went through a UDT qualification-training program. He remained in UDT until his retirement.

Master Chief Leyden and Tom Hawkins on assignment at the NAS Roosevelt Roads, PR, cira 1972.

When I became the Research, Development, Test and Evaluation Officer at the staff, the first person to grace my door was Master Chief Leyden. It was all about "who you know," and Corny wanted to get to know me, since he always had an alternative motive—which I didn't figure out until later. He pumped me for information, and I did the same to him. Corny was savvy and connected. Once I figured out that he knew just about every important diving person in Washington and at the Navy Lab in Panama City, we became cohorts in getting things done.

I really didn't get to know the real Corny Leyden until I was assigned duty at the Navy Experimental Diving Unit in 1972, where I was the resident UDT-SEAL project engineer. If we ran a test project; we depended on getting men from the UDT and SEAL Teams in Little Creek and Coronado. Any time I ran a project, I wanted Corny Leyden at my side, and he wanted that too. We completed several complex evaluations with the German Draeger LAR III and advanced-technology U.S.-made Westinghouse BioMarine, and General Electric experimental diving apparatus. Most operations were accomplished at the Explosive Ordnance Disposal Technical Facility at Indian Head, Maryland or at the Naval Air Station, Roosevelt Roads, Puerto Rico.

We were also social friends; drinking buddies actually. I spent endless hours in the chief petty officers' club "solving the world's problems" with Corny and others. I was especially close to his wife Barbara, and spent a lot of time at their apartment visiting. She died an early death. As with many in the military, once I began getting transferred to various places and he got out of the Navy, we eventually lost contact. I actually wouldn't have any association with him until his funeral. I spoke an impromptu eulogy to his current wife and children and friends, who knew nothing of his extraordinary accomplishments in the UDT-SEAL Teams. To this day, I thank my lucky stars for Cornelius J. Leyden.

Captain Norman H. Olson

In the springtime of 1968, I was serving as the Submersible Operations Officer at UDT-21. I arrived for work one morning, the Chief Master at Arms, Sam Bailey, greeted me loudly by asking me: "Why are you here," which of course seemed obvious to me. Thus, I replied, "Because I work here!" To which he replied, "No, you're now working at Nose Group." "Nose Group" was the pseudonym used by the men to describe the Naval Operations Support Group Atlantic staff; UDT-21's superior in the chain of command. This staff was generally perceived by the men as a military version of the Keystone Cops, i.e., generally ineffective and not a good place to be assigned. I was to temporarily fulfill the job as Research, Development, Test, and Evaluation Department Head. Sounds robust, except that I was the only one in the department and only a lieutenant junior grade to boot. The lieutenant to fill the permanent position was in Vietnam and wouldn't return for some time.

The commodore was a Navy captain and the world of what would become Naval Special Warfare was fundamentally beyond his grasp. His chief of staff wasn't far behind. The staff responded to things; never taking leadership of a particular issue. As a result, I got little direction on how to perform my tasks, and I knew nothing about the formality of the Navy's acquisition process.

This was an important time in the progression of the UDT and SEAL Teams. The Pentagon had funded two major Technical Development Plans: 38-01, the Swimmer Weapons System, and 38-02, The Swimmer Support System. These robust programs called for development of numerous demolition devices, advanced technology combatant submersibles and diving apparatus, and conversion of submarines to accommodate UDT, SEALs, and submersibles. To say that I was out of my league would be an understatement, however, I was a quick study and, fortunately, I was strongly mentored by Charlie Young, a great civil servant, and leader of the Swimmer Weapons Program at the Naval Ordnance Laboratory at White Oak, Maryland. Charlie made me smart enough to hold my own, while I continued becoming educated.

My job required that I attend all design reviews surrounding the new development programs. It was often pretty complex stuff. The front office was not inquisitive and mostly disinterested in getting briefings, leaving the details to me. "Sleepy Hollow" would be a good characterization of my early days on that staff. Alas, that was all soon to change in a very dramatic fashion.

Enter "Storm'n Norman," a.k.a. "The Skull," (skin tight hair cut), a.k.a. the new Chief of Staff Commander Norman H. Olson. If any single person could put the fear of God in a lethargic staff, Norm was born to do it; smart, focused, interested, determined, and brutally, yes, brutally intimidating. You did not want to get on the bad side of Norm. Upon arrival, he definitely did not come across as Mr. Nice Guy. He expected you to do your job, and do it more than well. Great expectations for a staff that was pretty adept at running itself on cruise control. To say the least, there was a definite and immediate change in the culture at Naval Operations Support Group Atlantic.

It took awhile, but once you figured out that Chief Staff Officer Olson wanted perfection, you gave him perfection or something close to it. He was, however, the man with a poison green pen that he would use to brutalize documents sent to him for review. He would tear correspondence apart until he got you to put it in language that was concise and to the point. It was definitely a learning experience. A part of the intimidation process was his avoidance of the telephone intercom system. You knew exactly when he was reviewing your "polished" work. He would yell very loudly from his office: "Hawkins get your ass down here now!" Of course, the others on the staff got the same treatment. Eventually, most of the staff were able to adapt to his style, which at the end of the day was terrific learning and leadership. We became better writers and better officers; well educated on where the direction of the budding Naval Special Warfare community was going. If you could not adapt or figure out the Olson way, life could be very miserable.

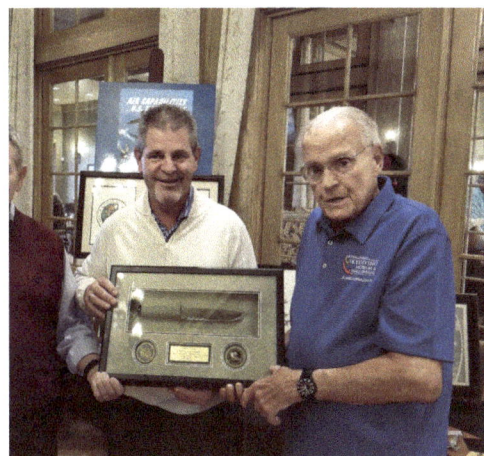

CAPT Norman Olson during ctive duty, being inducted into the U.S. Special Operations Command "Commando Hall of Honor," and at the launch of *Air Capabilities of the U.S. Navy SEALs,* the first book in the Phoca Press SEAL capabilities trilogy.

Needless to say, my time on the staff under Norm Olson was life changing, and it extended beyond that assignment. I left the staff and went to SEAL Team TWO and picked up a platoon for a tour in Vietnam. After SEAL TWO, I was transferred to the Navy Experimental Diving Unit in Washington, DC. I cannot remember the issue now, but there was something of grave concern to me, and I sent a somewhat long hand-written letter to Norm, who as the operations officer at the Naval Inshore Warfare Command in Norfolk. I waited and waited for a response, and got nothing, and this concerned me. I had to make a visit to Norfolk, and went to see Norm. He was not in a good mood that day. In fact, when I went to the quarterdeck to ask to see him, the administrative officer came out and told me that it really wasn't a good time to visit. You could hear a pin drop in that place. I pressed on, and told them he wouldn't mind. He was in his office behind a closed door, so I just knocked and went in. When I entered, I think he was about to throw something at me, but when he saw it was me, he just smiled. Still, Mr. Intimidation.

I got up the courage to ask him about my letter. He opened the top draw of his desk, picked up the letter, and threw it across his desk to me. All I could see was his familiar green ink scribbled over every page. After one big gulp, I asked him what he thought. His reply was not what I expected. He said only one thing: "You need to start acting like a senior officer!" A real lesson in reality. Message received. Norm Olson probably had more impact on me that any other individual in the Teams.

We maintained contact throughout the years as great family friends, post-Navy business associates and, recently, co-authors. Were it not for Norm Olson, I probably would not have remained in the Navy. It was he and the new commodore that convinced me that the new Naval Special Warfare officer career program was coming, and that I should augment into the Regular Navy.

Captain Wendel "Wendy" Webber

Captain "Wendy" Webber came to the East Coast in 1969 to become the Commodore at NSWGLANT. This was several months after the arrival of Norm Olson, and if anyone was more terrifying than Norm, it was Captain Webber, or at least the build up to his arrival by Norm Olson, who had the staff shaking in our tracks. He and Norm had a background; both coming from the West Coast. At the time, Wendy undoubtably was the most distinguished figure in the UDT-SEAL community, and Norm Olson, knowing his reputation, was not going to have an unprepared staff upon the new commodore's arrival.

Wendy Webber was already acclaimed as a dynamic, resourceful, and visionary leader. He led a UDT platoon during the Korean War, planned and executed SEAL Team activities during the early days of Vietnam, and fought many administrative battles from the waters of the Pacific to the depths of the Pentagon. He remained a reserve naval officer, and this allowed him to take assignments outside of UDT, and return for subsequent tours of duty. He understood the value of new and emerging technologies and their potential application by the UDT and SEAL Teams, and the need for established programs and procedures for the acquisition of new and enhanced operational capabilities.

Webber was a senior UDT officer in the early 1960s, and as commanding officer UDT-11 and commander, Underwater Demolition Unit ONE, he had responsibility for the establishment and organization of SEAL Team ONE. During his tenure as commander of Underwater Demolition Unite ONE, the Navy formally established the Naval Operations Support Group staffs in the Atlantic and Pacific. The UDT community had few officers above the rank of lieutenant commander (0-4), and this became problematic as the new staffs began forming. Webber became the Naval Operations Support Group Pacific chief staff officer under Captain Phil Bucklew; a Scout and Raider during World War II. He was not UDT-qualified, but brought a wealth of operational prowess, large staff experience, and substantial Navy influences. Webber, always a stand out individual in the UDT community, contributed operational savvy, UDT-SEAL community credentials (never to be underestimated), and perhaps most important, great vision and understanding about the issues, needs, potential, and direction necessary to make the embryo command a significant operational influence in the Navy. The combination of Bucklew and Webber was a warrior's dream team. Both were known to be dynamic, demanding, aggressive, and forward-thinking leaders.

Before his arrival at NSWGLANT, Norm Olson had the staff construct numerous formatted position papers on every conceivable topic. I was assigned 19 topics, and each paper was to be not more than two pages. Short, concise, and to the point; all reviewed and approved by Olson before presentation to Commodore Webber. The officer writing the paper had to brief the Commodore personally. I don't remember my topics, but I will never forget the drill. Of course, like others on the staff, and thanks to Norm Olson, I was struck with anxiety, since I thought Webber would have fangs. Instead, with Norm Olson in the room, he listened patiently, ask a lot of questions, then informed if he agreed or disagreed with a position. I got turned around on several conclusions and recommendations. Importantly, Commodore Webber explained the rational surrounding his thinking on each topic, and why we needed to adapt our position. Most of these issues were later moved into the

CAPT Webber through the years.

mainstream of staff actions and activity. Wendy Webber was and remains an significant architect of the Naval Special Warfare community. His visions and insights, while known only by a select few at the time, resulted in often profound contributions of enduring importance to the direction of the budding Naval Special Warfare community. He was an exceptional leader and teacher, and I learned many career and life-changing lessons during my time on the staff with Captain Webber and Commander Olson.

ABOUT THE AUTHOR

Tom Hawkins retired from the U.S. Navy after 24-years active service as a career SEAL and Naval Special Warfare (NSW) officer. Upon college graduation, he entered the Navy in February 1966, and was commissioned in May. He completed Basic Underwater Demolition/SEAL Training with Class 38 in Little Creek, Virginia, and was assigned to UDT-21, where he served as a Platoon Commander and Department Head. He later served as the Research, Development, Test, and Evaluation Department Head at Naval Operations Support Group, Atlantic (later Naval Special Warfare Group TWO), and was subsequently assigned to SEAL Team TWO, where he deployed to South Vietnam as a SEAL Platoon Commander.

Tom's SEAL career continued with assignments that included: Assistant for Special Units at the Naval Sea Systems Command, Project Engineer at the Navy Experimental Diving Unit; Executive Officer, UDT-21; and, Operational Test Director at the Navy's Operational Test and Evaluation Force. He commanded UDT-22 for 33 months during its reorganization as SEAL Delivery Vehicle Team TWO. After assignment as Deputy Commander and Chief Staff Officer, Naval Special Warfare Group TWO, he served in the Naval Special Warfare Directorate (OP-31) in the Pentagon, and retired as Director, Naval Special Warfare Programs and Program Manager at the Naval Sea Systems Command.

After leaving the Navy, Tom served in various defense contractor positions related to Naval Special Warfare, including assignment as staff requirements analyst and science and technical advisor to the Commander, Naval Special Warfare Group FOUR. He finished his career as an acquisition and requirements

analyst within the Combat Development Directorate at the Naval Special Warfare Development Group until his retirement on May 20, 2014.

Tom is past president of the UDT-SEAL Association, where he also served as editor and publisher of their quarterly publication *The BLAST – The Journal of Naval Special Warfare*. He also served as president of the UDT-SEAL Memorial Park Association and on the Board of Directors at the UDT-SEAL Museum Association. Tom conceived the Naval Special Warfare Foundation (now Navy SEAL Foundation), serving as founding President, Chairman of the Board, and Director, History and Heritage.

Tom was featured in and served as an advisor the PBS documentary, *Untold Story of the U.S. Navy SEALs* and on the History Channel's *Navy SEALs: America's Secret Warriors*. He contributed five chapters and numerous photographs to the book *United States Naval Special Warfare U.S. Navy SEALs* by Greg Mathieson and David Gatley. He is the author of *The History and Heritage of U.S. Navy SEALs* published by the Pritzker Military Museum and Library in Chicago. Tom founded Phoca Press to serve as an outlet for the wealth of material of educational and historical importance especially surrounding maritime special operations. Tom's second book, *America's Hidden Heroes: The History and Evolution of U.S. Navy Frogmen and SEALs*, was published in February 2014. With Captain (SEAL) Norman H. Olson, he co-authored the *Air Capabilities of the U.S. Navy SEALs*, which was published in December 2017, and is available through PhocaPress.com.

SOURCES

More Than Scuttlebutt: The U.S. Navy Demolition Men in World War II, by Sue Ann Dunford and James Douglas O'Dell, self-published, 2009.

The Men from Fort Pierce: A Chronological Survey of the Underwater Demolition Team of World War II, by Marvin Cooper, self-published, undated.

Hidden Heroes: The Story of Special Services Unit #1, by Theresa Staudt and Henry Staudt, self-published and undated.

Scouts and Raiders: The Navy's First Special Warfare Commandos, by John B. Dwyer, New York: Praeger Publishers, 1993.

Commandos from the Sea: The History of Amphibious Special Warfare in World War II and the Korean War, by John B. Dwyer, New York: Paladin Press, 1998.

The Naked Warriors, by Commander Francis Douglas Fane, USNR and Don Moore, New York: Appleton-Century-Crofts, Inc., 1956.

Reminiscences of Rear Admiral Draper Laurence Kauffman, U.S. Navy Retired, Volume 1, interviewed by John T. Mason, Jr., Annapolis, Maryland: Naval Institute Press, May, 1982.

Reminiscences of Captain Francis R. Kaine, U.S. Naval Reserve (Retired), Interviewed by Etta-Belle Kitchen, U.S. Navy Retired, Annapolis, Maryland: Naval Institute Press, November 1981.

OSS: The Secret History of America's First Central Intelligence Agency, by R. Harris Smith, Berkeley, California: University of California Press, Ltd., 1972.

OSS Weapons, by John W. Brunner, Ph.D., Williamstown, New Jersey: Phillips Publications, 1994.

History of the OSS Maritime Unit, compiled by the OSS, Washington, DC: National Archives, undated.

A Handbook of Amphibious Scout and Raider Training, U.S. Amphibious Training Command, Fort Pierce, Florida, Washington, DC: U.S. Government Office, 1944.

Secret Flotillas: Clandestine Sea Operations to Brittany 1940-44, Volume: 1, by Brooks Richards. Republished by Pen and Sword Books, Ltd, Barnsley, South Yorkshire, England, 2004, 2012.

Utah Beach to Cherbourg (6 June - 27 June 1944, United States of America War Office; American Forces in Action Series, Nashville, Tennessee: The Battery Press, undated.

Spearheading D-Day: American Special Units of the Normandy Invasion, by Jonathan Gawne, Havertown, Pennsylvania: Casemate Press, 1998.

Maritime Unit Field Manual – Strategic Services (Provisional) No. 7, SECRET, Office of Strategic Services, Washington, DC, 18 July 1944. Declassified 12/03/13.

Amphibious Operations: Employment of Underwater Demolition Teams, PHIB-24, Marine Corps Schools, Quantico, Virginia, January 1946.

Underwater Demolition Teams in Amphibious Operations (U), Naval Warfare Publication (NWP) 22-4 (Rev. B), September 1989.

"Navy Swimmer/Diver Equipment: Past, Present, and Future," by Commander W.E. Webber, USNR, American Society of Naval Engineers, *Naval Engineers Journal,* June 1965.

Covert Shores: The Story of Naval Special Forces Missions and Mini-Subs, by H.I. Sutton, self-published, 2015.

Interview with Master Chief Petty Officer Don Rose; A Career in Diving in the Underwater Demolition Teams," Interviewed by Captain (SEAL) Richard Vann, USNR, 25 July 2006.

Naval Forces Under the Sea; A Look Back, A Look Ahead, March 2001 Symposium at the U.S. Naval Academy, Supported by the Office of Naval Research, Flagstaff, AZ: Best Publishing Company, 2002.

"Problems of Shallow Water Diving: Report Based on Experiences of Operational Swimmers of the Office of Strategic Services," by Christian J. Lambertsen, MD, *Occupational Medicine*, March 1947, Vol. 3, pp. 230-245.

Office of Strategic Services – Maritime Unit – A History, by U.S. Navy LTjg Theodore A. Morde, USNR, November 1944.

War Report of the O.S.S. (Office of Strategic Services), by Kermit Roosevelt, New York: Walker Publishing Company, Inc., 1979.

Submersible Operations Training Manual [for] Underwater Demolition Teams U.S. Atlantic Fleet, distributed by Commander Amphibious Force, U.S. Atlantic Fleet Cover Letter Serial 0825 dated 8 December 1954.

A History of Self-Contained Diving and Underwater Swimming, Publication 469, by Howard E. Larson, Committee on Undersea Warfare, Washington, DC: National Academy of Sciences—National Research Council, 1959.

SEALs: UDT-SEAL Operations in Vietnam, by T.L. Bosiljevac, Boulder, Colorado: Paladin Press, 1990.

Joint Publication 1-02, Department of Defense Dictionary of Military and Associated Terms, November 2009.

Air Capabilities of the U.S. Navy SEALs: A History of Innovation, by Norman H. Olson and Tom Hawkins, New York: Phoca Press, 2017.

"Underwater Breathing Apparatus Compared," by Lieutenant Thomas Hawkins, *Faceplate Magazine,* Volume 3, Number 3, Fall 1972.

Open Sea Evaluation of the Bio Marine CCR-1000, General Electric MK 10 MOD 5, and Westinghouse CCM-1 Closed-Circuit, Mixed Gas, Underwater Breathing Apparatus, U.S. Navy Experimental Diving Unit Report NEDU-9-72, by Lieutenant Thomas L. Hawkins, Lieutenant Commander Alfred B. Quist, and EMCS (DV) Thomas C. King, dated August 1972.

Evaluation of the Prototype General Electric Model 1500 Sensor Controlled, Closed-Circuit, Mixed Gas, Underwater Breathing Apparatus, U.S. Navy Experimental Diving Unit Report NEDU 11-73, by Lieutenant Commander Thomas L. Hawkins and EMCM Thomas C. King, dated November 1973.

Evaluation of the Draeger LAR III Pure Oxygen Scuba," Navy Experimental Diving Unit Report 11-74*, by Lieutenant Commander Thomas L. Hawkins, USN and EMCS (DV) Thomas C. King, USN, dated 5 May 1974.

United States Naval Special Warfare; U.S. Navy SEALs, by Greg E. Mathieson, Sr. and David Gatley, Centreville, Virginia: NSW Publications, LLC, 2012. Narrative by Rear Admiral (SEAL) George Worthington, USN (Retired) and Commander (SEAL) Tom Hawkins (USN, Retired).

www.ingramcontent.com/pod-product-compliance
Lightning Source LLC
Chambersburg PA
CBHW040246100426
42811CB00011B/1173